# Taras
## ITS HISTORY AND COINAGE

Frontispiece: Terracotta figure of actor, third century B.C.
*Reproduced with the kind permission of André Emmerich Gallery, New York
Photographed by Bettina Sulzer*

# Acknowledgments

Special thanks are due to Mr. R. Darby Erd of the Institute of Archeology and Anthropology, University of South Carolina, for the map, and to Mr. Milton Butterworth of the Instructional Services Center, University of South Carolina, for the photographs of coins in my collection. Photographs kindly supplied by the British Museum and the American Numismatic Society are acknowledged in the captions to the plates.

# Introduction

Commercially, artistically, intellectually, and politically, the Spartan foundation of Taras in southern Italy ranks among the more important Greek cities of the Mediterranean area, yet it is probably less familiar than places such as Ephesus, Syracuse, even Croton or Sybaris. Students of ancient history hear of it in its late stages as Tarentum, partner of Pyrrhus and friend of Hannibal. Students of ancient philosophy associate it with Archytas, rescuer of Plato. Students of numismatics identify it with one of the most varied and beautiful of Greek coinages. A few scholars—most notably the brilliant Pierre Wuilleumier—have been fascinated by its fortunes and achievements. On the whole, however, it has not received the recognition or appreciation that it deserves.

One reason for this comparative obscurity may be the fact that a great deal of archaeological investigation remains to be carried out at Taras (modern Taranto). The ancient city does not lie before us to the extent that Athens does or Ephesus. Another reason may be that its later history—its involvement with the growing power of Rome—has attracted most of the attention, to the neglect of its earlier history as an influential Greek state. Even that later history has been treated from the Roman point of view rather than from the point of view of Taras itself—naturally enough, since Rome was the significant, rising nation and Taras by this time a city in decline. There are, besides, few highly dramatic events or incidents to associate with Taras: no Battle of Marathon, no Syracusan expedition, no Milo caught in the cleft of a tree while wolves ate him alive. Ancient myth and legend do not, of course, acquaint us with Taras during our childhood, when we are introduced to Athens, Thebes, Sparta, and Corinth through the acts of gods and heroes.

Whatever the causes of Taras's obscurity may be, major aspects of the city's history—its successes, its failures, its cultural life and daily concerns—are traceable in ancient sources, in artistic products, and in a prolific coinage. What I have tried to do is to bring together a number of those aspects, treating them chronologically on the whole, making use of the invaluable work of Wuilleumier and scholars who came after him, and paying particular attention to the coinage, an interesting topic in its own right. The result will not lift Taras out of disregard but may at any rate constitute a minor tribute to a great place.

A few words on the vexing matter of names are, I suppose, necessary. Since I am considering the city largely as a Greek colony, I have called it Taras rather than Tarentum until toward the end. Other proper names follow the spellings in the *Oxford Classical Dictionary*.

# 1

# The Foundation

During the great period of Greek colonization of the known world—in 706 B.C., according to the traditional dating—a group of colonists set out from Sparta. On a bay of southeastern Italy, just about where the high heel of the peninsula meets the arch of the foot, these people established the city of Taras, later called Tarentum by the Romans. In the succeeding five centuries it was to develop remarkably, to flourish proudly, and to fade.

The circumstances of the founding, veiled in legend, hearsay, and invention, come down to us mainly through Strabo, writing seven centuries afterward under Augustus. Strabo reports the accounts of a Syracusan historian named Antiochus, who lived in the fifth century B.C., and a geographer and generally learned man, Ephorus of Cyme, who lived in the fourth.[1] Their stories differ in several respects, but both make it clear that the founders, whatever they may have been, were not in a complete sense Spartans.

In the second half of the eighth century B.C. Sparta fought the first of several wars against its neighbors, the Messenians. According to Antiochus, there were Spartans who did not take part in the Messenian war. They were judged to be slaves, and their children by Spartan women were called Parthenians, or children of unmarried mothers, and were denied the rights of citizens. Ephorus gives the Parthenians a different origin. The Spartans fighting the war, he says, swore an oath—apparently early during the conflict—not to return to Sparta until the enemy was defeated. They did not break their oath; and after ten years of neglect the Spartan women felt that something should be done. The ladies sent a complaint to their men, to the effect that the population of the state must not be allowed to decline. The army, realizing that many of the most virile soldiers were too young to have taken the vow a decade before, ordered these soldiers to visit the city and do what they could to increase the population. But the products of these slapdash unions were called Parthenians and, as bastards, were refused citizens' rights, which, when the war was over, included shares in the recently conquered and very rich fields of Messenia.

Whatever their origin may have been, the Parthenians were clearly disgruntled, and their discontent constituted a serious problem for the state.[2] Antiochus says that they plotted against the government; Ephorus, that they joined with the helots, the body of state slaves, chronically unhappy with their lot. According to Ephorus, the raising of a Spartan cap in the marketplace was to be a signal for a helot/Parthenian revolt. In Antiochus's version—the earlier of the two and therefore perhaps the more trustworthy—a man called Phalanthus, whom the Parthenians seem to have regarded as their leader, was to signalize the rebellion by putting on a leather cap during a festival to the god Hyacinthus at the temple of Apollo at Amyclae, close to Sparta.[3]

But somehow, perhaps through Phalanthus himself, the incipient insurrection was revealed to the authorities, who sent the Parthenians off to start a new life—under Phalanthus's leadership, according to Antiochus. The authorities must have congratulated themselves on getting rid of so troublesome an element of the population.[4]

First, however, the oracle of Apollo at Delphi had to be consulted—by Phalanthus in Antiochus's version, by envoys from the Parthenians according to Diodorus Siculus, whose *World History* was written in the middle of the first century B.C. or slightly later.[5] Diodorus says that the Parthenians had some idea of settling in the territory of Sicyon, close to Corinth and not far from Sparta. But Apollo, perhaps prompted by the Spartan government, had other plans for them. The priestess at Delphi uttered two injunctions, which Diodorus has kindly preserved for the student of history. The first, which dealt with a spot where a goat dipped its gray beard in the water, was not very clear. The second, omitting the goat, said more plainly that the Parthenians were to go to a place called Satyrion, where the Taras River enriched the land.

We know nothing of the departure from Greece or the crossing of the Ionian Sea, except for an incident mentioned by Pausanias in his *Description of Greece*, which dates from the middle of the second century A.D. Pausanias remarks that Phalanthus was shipwrecked in the Gulf of Crisa before getting clear of Greece but was saved by a dolphin which carried him ashore.[6] The helpful dolphin was to appear in later centuries on Tarentine coins.

Pausanias has another story, more charming than credible, concerning Phalanthus's early days in Italy. The hero was discouraged. He had already won some battles against the barbarian inhabitants of the land, but these victories were minor. The Delphic oracle had informed him that he would gain a territory and a city only when rain fell from a cloudless sky. This, he reasoned, must mean that he would never gain a territory and a city. His wife Aethra, trying to console him, put his head between her knees and affectionately started picking out the lice. In her sympathetic grief she showered his head with her tears. It occurred to Phalanthus that her name meant Clear Sky. He jumped up, gathered his men, and that same night took from the barbarians their greatest city, which was to become the Greek Taras.[7]

The goat in the oracle cited by Diodorus and others turned out to be a wild fig tree in the area, with a vine clinging to it that dipped like a goat's beard into the water. But the oracle had named Satyrion, not the barbarian predecessor of Greek Taras, as the place where the Spartans should settle. Satyrion was in classical times a town immediately southeast of Taras. It appears that the Parthenians did settle there first, but moved within a short time to the site of their future home.[8]

That site was well chosen. On a bay giving on what is now the Gulf of Taranto (the body of water lying between the heel and the toe of Italy), Taras was to control the only fine port on Italy's southeast coast, with, of course, the exception of Brundisium in later times. The original Greek settlement, like the barbarian settlement that Phalanthus overcame, occupied the elevated, rocky tip of a peninsula jutting out northwestward into the bay. The present Mare Grande, or greater part of the bay, lay on its southern and western sides, protected from the open gulf by islands and suitable for an outer harbor, while the present Mare Piccolo, a sizable lagoon, occupied the northeastern or landward side, offering superb potential for an inner harbor. From Taras, sailors in later centuries would set out via the Gulf of Taranto to Epirus on the Ionian Sea, to Illyria on the Adriatic, or farther on to the ports of central Greece, or south to Sicily and across the Mediterranean to Carthaginian Africa.[9]

But to these first Spartan settlers in a strange land, the fact that their new home was easily defensible—at the high point of a peninsula washed by water on all sides except for its juncture with the mainland— no doubt weighed much more heavily than future possibilities for trade. So, perhaps, did the lovely climate, not too harsh in the winter and mild in the summer, with the golden warmth moderated by a breeze from the southwest by day, from the northeast by night. On the mainland the rich soil of southern Italy put the valleys of Greece to shame; and the translated Hellenes found that fruit trees thrived and grain could be sown, and that herds were easy to graze.

Although indigenous peoples probably accounted for most of the population of southern Italy during these early years, Phalanthus's followers were by no means the only Greeks. Southwestward across the gulf, and a distance inland, lay Sybaris. Past the gulf, on the Ionian Sea, Croton had been established. At the point of the Italian boot Rhegium watched the strait between Italy and Sicily. In Sicily itself, Syracuse and Naxos had already been in existence for almost three decades. These Greek towns were still in large degree outposts, connected by tenuous sea routes with the main Greek world. Some of them, like Taras, would in time become famous, but they were only beginning to develop when the colonists from Sparta arrived. The sense of isolation and the fear of attack by the native peoples must have been strong.

The Tarentine area was old in cultures if not civilizations. Even as long ago as the fifth and fourth millennia B.C., people in the locality were making pottery, scratched and notched with crude designs. Neolithic families lived in huts on the shores of the Mare Piccolo, the inner bay or lagoon. They practiced agriculture, tended herds, and no doubt fished as well; and they buried one another in stone-lined graves, probably in contracted positions. Around 1800 B.C. new peoples arrived. They settled at Satyrion among other places, and imported products from the Helladic folk living in the part of Greece where Sparta was to flourish. About four centuries later they were making pottery decorated with painted bands and with spiral and meander patterns, and were trading with Mycenaean Greeks as far away as Rhodes and Cyprus. There may have been a Mycenaean emporium in the vicinity of what became Taras. At any event, the Greeks who fought the Trojans must have cast some influence over the inhabitants of the area—that is, until perhaps the late twelfth century B.C., when commerce between Italy and the east faded with the fading of the Mycenaean world.[10]

Around 1100 B.C. at the latest, another ethnic group entered the scene. From Illyria on the eastern side of the Adriatic came the Iapygians—probably following the shoreline through the region where Venice now stands and continuing down the Italian coast as far as they could go, in other words into the heel, and some of them possibly traveling by water instead, across the Strait of Otranto. Strabo wrongly believed that the Iapygians had come from Crete and had arrived in Italy by way of Sicily (*Geography*, 6.3.2; 7.170). Actually far different from the sophisticated Cretans, they must have been close to savagery when they entered Italy, and whether they came with the intention of staying or only as traders or pirates and other raiders, they probably brought considerable distress to the long-established agricultural communities which they visited. Some of the folk living in these communities abandoned their homes and fled to Sicily.

These Iapygians were followed by their relatives the Peucetians, who took over the land immediately to the north of the Italian heel, and the Daunians, who occupied the territory north of the Peucetians. By the time the colonizers from Sparta appeared on the peninsula, therefore, there had long been three groups of people of Illyrian provenance stacked on top of one another in southern Italy. The Greeks sometimes lumped them all together under the name "Iapygians" and sometimes referred to the Iapygians of the heel as Messapians. They all spoke the Messapic tongue.

The distinction between the Greeks and these "barbarians" was perhaps not as sharp in the early years as is sometimes assumed. The Hellenes of 700 B.C. were, after all, still members of an Archaic culture, not yet wholly free from the protracted gloom of the so-called Greek Dark Age; the intellectual and artistic achievements of classical civilization were a long way off. In the centuries since their arrival, besides, the three branches of the Illyrian stock had advanced in various respects. They had settled down and practiced agriculture in contrast to their former life of wandering; and they had become urban to the extent of living in towns such as the one which the Greeks appropriated under Phalanthus and turned into Taras.[11]

In spite of Pausanias's story, it is not at all certain that the takeover of the Iapygian town was a military conquest or that the Iapygians and the Greeks were on particularly unfriendly terms in the early stages of the Greek colonization. We know nothing really definite about the founding of Taras—or even, in fact, about the supposed founder, Phalanthus. He may possibly have been an actual human being, with that name or some other name, around whom legends later accumulated.[12] Surely some actual man must have functioned as leader of the band of Parthenians and therefore as founder of the new city. In Greece the ancient cities, whose origins were lost in the past, sometimes claimed as founders mythical men such as Cadmus at Thebes. In historical times, however, it was normal practice for a Greek city sending out a colonizing expedition to appoint a man as founder, with complete control over the other members; or if the colonizing force was a group of exiles, it chose the founder on its own.

But the Phalanthus whose name has come down to us may have been in origin not a man but a god—perhaps a version of the vegetation god Hyacinthus who had been worshiped by the ancient population of Arcadia before the Dorians came. The cult of Hyacinthus was preserved in some form at Amyclae close to Sparta, where the Phalanthus of Antiochus's story was to start a rebellion by putting on a leather cap during a festival to Hyacinthus.[13] There is no way, at this late date, of ascertaining the relationship between the site and the hero.

If Phalanthus was a man and nothing more, there may eventually have been a reaction against him in the city he had fathered. At least, according to both Strabo and the epitomizer Justin (active in about the third century A.D.), he was expelled from Taras and ended his days in the Iapygian city of Brundisium, where, says Strabo, the inhabitants rewarded him with a magnificent funeral. In Justin's version, Phalanthus fared well after death. The Tarantines brought his ashes back to Taras, in the belief that the oracle of Apollo at Delphi had so ordered. They mistakenly thought that this act would help them regain their Greek patrimony—a suggestion (which is perhaps pure invention) that these Parthenians in Iapygian country were homesick for Sparta. At any rate a cult of Phalanthus was established at Taras; and once he came to be worshiped there, his position as hero founder was secure.[14]

# Notes to Chapter 1

1. See Strabo, *Geography,* 6.3.2-3.

2. H. Michell, *Sparta* (Cambridge, England, 1964), pp. 85-88, rejects both Antiochus's and Ephorus's accounts of the Parthenians' origin, as well as Aristotle's statement (*Politics,* 5.6.1) that the fathers of the Parthenians were equal to other Spartans and Theopompus's statement (*apud* Athenaeus, VI, 271C) that they were state slaves (helots) who were granted a certain class of citizenship as a reward for service to the state. Arnold Toynbee in *Some Problems of Greek History* (Oxford University Press, 1969) finds Ephorus's story incredible, pointing out the economic inadvisability of keeping men under arms for a long and uninterrupted stretch of time in the eighth century B.C. (pp. 217-18), G. L. Huxley in *Early Sparta* (Cambridge, Mass., 1962), p. 37, implies that the claim that the Parthenians were not true Spartans was in large degree trumped up by the authorities so that this element of the population need not be included in the land distribution. In any case, in the period of economic distress that apparently followed the First Messenian War, the denial of rights to shares in the land would have been a sufficient reason for strong discontent. See A. H. M. Jones, *Sparta* (Cambridge, Mass., 1967), p. 12.

3. For a discussion of the religious significance of the caps and and the question of whether or not they bear some relationship to the "liberty cap" assumed by Roman slaves on manumission, see Giovanni Pugliese Carratelli, "Per la Storia dei Culti di Taranto," in *Taranto nella Civiltà della Magna Grecia: Atti dei Decimo Convegno di Studi sulla Magna Grecia* (Naples, 1971), pp. 143-44. (This volume will be cited hereafter as Convegno 10.) Carratelli feels that Ephorus misinterpreted the cap as a symbol of liberty. Pierre Wuilleumier uses the association with the pre-Dorian city of Amyclae and with the pre-Dorian god Hyacinthus to suggest that the Parthenians were not by ancestry Spartans but derived from a pre-Dorian population which had been annexed by Sparta but still remembered its non-Spartan past; see his *Tarante des Origines à la Conquête Romaine* (Paris, 1939; reimpression Paris, 1968), pp. 40-42. (Unless another title follows his name, all subsequent references to Wuilleumier will be to *Tarante*.) See also the rejection of Wuilleumier's suggestion by Jean Bérard, *La Colonisation Grecque de l'Italie Mériodonale et de la Sicile dans l'Antiquité* (2nd ed., Paris, 1957), pp. 168-69. But the notion persists; see, for example, Huxley, *Early Sparta,* p. 37.

4. Paul Cartledge prefers to think that the Parthenians—resentful of Spartan policies toward them and perhaps motivated by "Amyklaian 'nationalism' "as well—set off entirely on their own accord and not as the result of any decision by the Spartan authorities; see his *Sparta and Lakonia: A Regional History 1300-362 B.C.* (London, 1979), pp. 123-24. This view, though no more than a conjecture, should not be dismissed.

5. See Diodorus Siculus, 8.21.3. See also Dionysius of Halicarnassus, *Roman Antiquities,* 19.1.3-4.

6. Pausanias, 10.13.10. Pausanias tells this story with reference to a statuary group at Delphi. Léon Lacroix, with much plausibility, suggests that the story was actually invented to satisfy the curiosity of visitors. See his *Monnaies et Colonisation dans l'Occident Grec* (Brussels, 1965), p. 90.

7. Pausanias, 10.10.6-8. Essentially the same incident is told of Myscellus, founder of Croton. On Eusebius's date of 706 B.C. as about right for the establishment of the Greek city, see especially Bérard, *Colonisation Grecque*, pp. 169-70, and F. G. Lo Porto "Topografia Antica di Taranto," Convegno 10, pp. 357-58.

8. On this long-discussed point see especially F. G. Lo Porto, "Satyrion," in *Notizie degli Scavi di Antichità* (1964), pp. 177 ff., and his "Topografia Antica di Taranto," p. 357.

9. See Florus, *Epitome*, 1.13.2-3.

10. On the archaeology concerning these early periods see especially Lo Porto, "Topografia," pp. 350-55, and his "L'Attività Archeologica in Puglia," in *Letteratura e Arte Figurate nella Magna Grecia: Atti del Sesto Convegno di Studi sulla Magna Grecia* (Naples, 1967), pp. 279-90. This volume will be cited hereafter as Convegno 6.

11. For the Iapygian invasion and culture see especially Wuilleumier, pp.9-27; Lo Porto, "Topografia," pp. 355-56; Luigi Moretti, "Problemi di Storia Tarantina," Convegno 10, pp. 23-30; and Aleksandar Stipčević, *The Illyrians: History and Culture*, Stojana Čulić Burton, trans. (Park Ridge, N.J., 1977), pp. 27-30. Stipčević prefers to call the new arrivals "proto-Illyrians" since they had not achieved an ethnic entity. He also observes that it is not at all certain that Messapian is an Illyrian tongue.

12. Bérard admits this as a possibility (*Colonisation Grecque*, p. 171).

13. See Wuilleumier, pp. 34-36. Michel P. Vlasto, ΤΑΡΑΣ ΟΙΚΙΣΤΕΣ: *A Contribution to Tarentine Numismatics* (New York, 1922), pp. 106-07, calls Phalanthus "a modification of the Delphinian Apollo of Cretan descent," considering the cicada which appears with Phalanthus on a Tarentine stater dated by Vlasto ca. 473-460 B.C. as a symbol of Apollo. Arnold Toynbee (*Some Problems*, pp. 280-81) supposes that the men governing Sparta after the First Messenian War deliberately transformed the god Phalanthus into a "fictitious human being" in order to give their controversial settlement of the Parthenian matter a semi-divine authority, just as, after the Second Messenian War, Spartan lawmakers transformed the god Lycurgus into a fictitious lawgiver in order to strengthen their own controversial revision of the Spartan constitution. But it is not easy to ascribe such contrived and sophisticated uses to Archaic Sparta.

14. See Strabo, 6.3.6, and Justin, *Epitome*, 3.4. Justin may have derived his account from Antiochus.

# 2

# The First Two Centuries

The early years of the young city are for the most part lost to us. We know, however, that the settlers established themselves on the somewhat elevated tip of the peninsula, which became the acropolis, with the Mare Grande to the south and west and the inner bay or Mare Piccolo to the northeast; and we can assume that they built a protective wall. As has been remarked earlier, they were in many ways no more advanced in civilization than their neighbors the Iapygians. But they were beginning to write, and perhaps they had brought with them from Sparta a greater capacity for civil and military organization than the native peoples possessed.[1]

The Parthenians, naturally enough, had carried to their new home various cults observed in the Peloponnesus, most notably, perhaps, those of Poseidon, Apollo, the Dioscuri, and the pre-Hellenic god Hyacinthus.[2] The extent to which they had also brought over Spartan social and political institutions is largely undeterminable. With regard to social institutions, they did not at any rate follow the path that Sparta was later to follow. When Phalanthus and his colonists came to Italy, Sparta had not yet developed the militaristic system which would be attributed to Lycurgus—highly concentrated, rather austere. This, plus the fact that the settlers were not in a whole sense Spartiates anyway, left Taras free to develop artistically and commercially as Sparta, after the so-called Lycurgan freeze, did not do.[3] With regard to politics, in Sparta royal power was for centuries divided between two kings, but the evidence suggests that Taras, if it had regal government at all, never had more than one king at a time, although we do not even know the name of any Tarentine monarch from Phalanthus himself until a certain Aristophilides of the early fifth century B.C. Because Sparta had a body of magistrates called ephors, and because there would be ephors at the city of Heraclea when it was founded, partly by Taras, in 433, it is generally assumed that Taras also had ephors. The Spartan ephorate had been in existence for half a century at most by the time Taras was established; it would acquire considerable executive and judicial powers, even a degree of control over the kings. We cannot tell whether Taras adopted an ephorate originally or later, and we do not know the powers and duties of the Tarentine ephors if there were ephors at all. There was apparently no gerousia, a body of elder citizens that also had great influence at Sparta.[4]

Practicing agriculture in the bountiful South Italian countryside, and no doubt fishing the waters of the bay as well, the early Tarentines must have constituted a largely self-sufficient state. But although they could not yet anticipate their later commercial activity, they imported a few amenities from other places. From seventh-century Crete, it appears, came terracotta plaques illustrating myths in painted narrative reliefs.[5] From the Peloponnesus, also still in the seventh century, came Protocorinthian vases pointing toward the highly decorative animal style, graced with lions, goats, and sphinxes, that Corinth would produce in such quantities in the late seventh and sixth centuries.[6] Taras did some trading with Sparta; and in the sixth century it imported vases not only from Sparta but from Corinth, Athens, and the island of Chios on the coast of Asia Minor.[7] A large hoard of coins discovered in 1911 at the modern Taranto, and apparently buried toward the end of the sixth century, suggests the breadth of Tarentine commerce at that period. The hoard included coins of Athens, Corinth, Chalcis in Euboea, Metapontum and Sybaris in southern Italy.[8]

The Tarentines of the seventh century could not have done much trading with the indigenous populations.[9] For their pottery, for instance, they turned mainly to the great pottery-producing centers in mainland Greece and farther east. This was in spite of the fact that the native peoples were developing distinctive traditions in ceramics. About 650, for instance, the Peucetians, the group living immediately north of Taras, began making bowls and jugs with geometric designs painted in black on a white slip—comb-shaped figures, swastikas, less frequently festoons, lozenges filled with cross-hatching or figures resembling chessboards. The Peucetians also produced vessels with designs painted in red and black on a white ground—combs again, circles and triangles, wide bands, meanders, once in a while geometric birds looking a little like turkeys. This red-and-black ware was no doubt influenced by early Corinthian ceramics but was even less sophisticated, though it indicates the comparatively advanced state of these people. To the north of the Peucetians the Daunians, perhaps not before 600, started making large bowls, high cups, and other vessels which they decorated with designs in dark violet and red, sometimes on a white slip. They painted wide and narrow horizontal bands and vertical lines dividing the field into panels in which they put figures such as, again, triangles and lozenges. As for the Messapians living south of Taras in the Italian heel, they did not have a distinctive pottery until the fifth century.[10]

During the first century of its existence and probably during much of the second, Taras must have ranked among the less powerful Greek cities in the Western world. It could not equal Sybaris to the south for instance, or Croton south of that, or Rhegium on the toe of the boot overlooking Sicily, or Syracuse in Sicily itself. Sybaris became opulent through trade; and although the term "Sybarite" has come to designate a person devoted to luxurious leisure, its citizens must have worked hard to establish and increase their state's far-flung commerce. The large number of Greek cities that sprang up in southern Italy, most of them in the seventh and early sixth centuries B.C., suggests the prosperity of this progressively Greek-dominated part of the world and meant, perhaps, more rivals than friends for Taras. Because Rhegium on the Italian toe and Zancle (Messana) across the strait in Sicily interfered with shipping between the waters west of Italy and regions to the east, Sybaris founded on the west coast the colonies of Scidrus, Laus, and Posidonia (Paestum); and it established a land route across the foot of the peninsula so that the strait controlled by Rhegium and Zancle could be avoided. From Miletus in Asia Minor, with which Sybaris was on close commercial terms, it imported products, which it then sent overland to the west coast along with its own manufactures in metal and clay. The Etruscans, flourishing north of young Rome, provided a lucrative market for the Sybarites.

Croton, founded from the Achaean part of Greece only a few years before Taras, was also a mother of colonies—Pandosia in the interior, Terina on the west coast of the toe, and possibly Caulonia on the eastern side of the toe, although Caulonia, like Croton itself, had probably been settled from Achaea. In any case, that city, like Pandosia and Terina, had a sentimental connection with Croton, which manifested itself through trade and made both cities richer.

On the western littoral Cumae, which had been founded from Chalcis in mainland Greece as early as the middle of the eighth century, recolonized the originally Rhodian colony of Parthenope in the second half of the seventh century—the city which from the mid-fifth century would be known as Neapolis, our Naples. Locri Epizephyrii was established about 680 B.C. on the east side of the toe, south of where Caulonia would soon stand, and it in turn established the cities of Medma in the western part of the toe and Hipponium, north of Medma and also on the toe, both probably before the end of the seventh century. In the early seventh century people from Colophon in Asia Minor settled Siris, about halfway between Sybaris and Taras. On the western coast, almost directly across the peninsula from Siris, Elea (Velia) was built by Phocaeans from Asia Minor around 540. According to Antiochus as reported by Strabo, Metapontum owed its foundation (in the late eighth or seventh century) to Sybarite hatred for the Dorian Tarentines and to a desire to prevent Taras from extending its control southward in the direction of Sybaris itself.[11] Metapontum, which would soon become one of the wealthiest Greek colonies of the West, was Taras's nearest Hellenic neighbor of any size and probably its most consistent enemy. The Metapontines farmed their fertile countryside, growing rich on grain especially. Unlike the Tarentines, they had no natural harbor, but they built a harbor from which they exported wheat.

Not much is known about the interrelationships of the various city-states until the second half of the sixth century, but their economic struggles and small wars must at times have been fierce. Not long after the mid-sixth century the three great Achaean powers— Sybaris, Croton, and Metapontum—united against Colophonian Siris, unhappily located between Sybaris and Metapontum, and destroyed it. Croton then attacked Locri Epizephyrii. The fact that Croton later turned on its ally Sybaris, and that Sybaris too was annihilated, is familiar from Herodotus.[12] They were like spiders trapped in a bottle and eating one another.

Taras seems to have been only indirectly involved in these affairs. We can, however, assume that in the latter part of the sixth century the city was developing its resources and growing into a state strong enough to threaten the security of others. It was not yet a great commercial city, but it was on the way. Its position was fortunate, as vessels sailing west from Greece itself would have reached it before reaching any other Hellenic colony in Italy. Taras's splendid harbor was its greatest advantage. Merchant ships from Greece and the East unloaded their wares here. Not only could Taras accommodate these commercial vessels, but it sent out ships carrying its own products, such as ceramic and metal work, to other ports, no doubt Carthage as well as Greek cities; and it also traded the products of an extensive agricultural area for the manufactured goods of the older Greek world. Cnidus in Asia Minor functioned as one of its chief trading partners, as Miletus did for Sybaris. Before the end of the sixth century Taras had founded two colonies, Callipolis and Hydrus, whose reason for being was to protect its trade. Callipolis, located in Iapygian territory near the tip of the heel and facing on the Gulf of Taranto itself, would prove especially useful in this regard.

Although the Tarentines probably did not start making their famous red-purple dye until the fifth century, they prospered from fishing the nearby waters. The land controlled by the state may have been less suited to the growing of grain than the lands of Metapontum or Hipponium, but the Tarentines cultivated the olive and in the open fields they bred horses and sheep. If they happened to be on friendly terms with their neighbors the Iapygians—and that could not have been often—they carried on trade with them.

The second half of the sixth century was in some degree a period of intellectual flowering for the Greeks of southern Italy. Pythagoras came to Croton from the East Greek world about 535/530, and it was at Croton that he talked with his devoted followers on numbers and acoustics, harmony and proportion, metempsychosis and the benefits of aristocratic government. Toward the end of the century, apparently, Croton earned a distinguished reputation for medicine. On the west coast the free-thinking and outspoken Xenophanes, driven from Asia Minor by Persian interference with the Greek cities there, settled around 540 with other Asiatic Greeks in the new colony of Elea, where he called the legends of the gods and goddesses lies, ridiculed the anthropomorphic conception of deities, and taught his own conception of a sole supreme god, not human in form or feeling, who ruled the world through thought. In the next century, of course, under the leadership of Parmenides and Zeno, this city would be the center for the so-called Eleatic School of philosophy.

But this earliest outburst of Western Greek speculation on the world and the divine was confined mainly to Croton and Elea. Taras, like most of the other Hellenic foundations, seems not to have participated very actively in it. The city's intellectual distinction, like its unquestioned commercial supremacy, would come later. Perhaps toward the end of the century, however, Tarentines did perform some intellectual service in teaching the alphabet to the Messapians.

And in the plastic arts and crafts Taras already showed signs of the creativity for which it would later be famous, although it is often impossible for us to determine which of the sixth-century objects found at modern Taranto had been made there and which had been imported. On a limited scale, workshops in Taras apparently produced archaic bronze vases and bronze mirrors whose handles were decorated with figures. With the bronze objects particularly, however, it is not easy to distinguish local products from imports.[13] Some limestone figures—of maidens, for instance—may have been made in Taras, though, again, they may have been imported; the city seems not to have exploited nearby limestone deposits on any scale very early. Southern Italy had no marble quarries, and presumably marble statues were brought from other parts of the Greek world. Some of these, though already cut from the block, may have been imported in an uncompleted form, to be finished at Taras. Even so, however, they were quite possibly finished by itinerant sculptors rather than by Tarentines themselves.[14]

Taras, which undoubtedly brought in most of its pottery from the older Greek world, may have made more clay vessels on its own than is sometimes assumed, however—imitating, for instance, the black-figure ware which Athens was now turning out in quantity.[15] Yet even if this is true, the potters and vase painters themselves may have been immigrants from Greece, just as similar craftsmen would come from Greece to Italy at the close of the next century, after the Peloponnesian War.

Roughly 40,000 terra-cotta figures have been found at Taranto. Most of these must be local products, and although many are as late as the third century B.C., they start as early as the seventh. Some of them, especially the earliest, were modeled by hand; but the more common mode of manufacture, which came into use in the Greek world in the seventh century, involved a mold. Only an archetypal figure was, in this case, made by hand. Usually of clay, it was fired hard. Around this figure the craftsman pressed a coating of wet clay, taking care that it fitted firmly into all the crannies and crevices of the archetype so that the details would be sharp. When the coating was dry, the craftsman removed it from the archetype, which of course entailed cutting it in half if it had covered the entire archetype (necessary only if the figure to be created was to be a fully rounded one rather than one intended for viewing solely from the front, for which only a partial mold was needed). The removed coating was fired at a high temperature to harden it. This was the mold, which could be used for a number of figures.

To make a figure the craftsman pressed wet clay into the mold, filling the mold completely to produce a solid figure or, as was generally done in periods later than the Archaic, simply lining the mold to produce a hollow figure. In drying, the figure shrank perhaps as much as 10 percent, so that the craftsman could easily take it out of the mold. If he had employed a mold for the back as well as the front of the figure, he now joined the two halves together with clay as unobtrusively as possible. He fired the figure, perhaps in the same kind of kiln used for pottery. Very likely he had to touch up details or even add protruding elements, such as wreaths, extended arms, or wings, which it would have been difficult to include in the original mold without breakage. Finally the terra-cotta piece was, like sculptures in stone, painted in more or less realistic colors. This process continued in use, not only at Taras but in the Greek world in general, through Hellenistic times.[16]

Most of the terra-cottas produced at Taras through the sixth century B.C., like a great many of those produced later, had a religious import; some of the earliest, dating from the late seventh century and the early sixth, come from a sanctuary of Persephone located outside the Archaic city. In an area devoid of marble quarries, decorations and figurines of fired clay were attached as antefixes to the exteriors of temples, evidently from the late sixth century on. The terrific Gorgon heads, with bulging eyes, great teeth, and lolling tongues, were favorites, probably because of their apotropaic powers. Other antefixes were in the form of silenus heads, with the same bulging almond eyes, moustache over thick sensual lips, long hair and beards. Typical Archaic figures—perhaps stiffly standing naked youths, hair in careful strands and arms at their sides, and standing maidens draped in garments that fell in graceful folds—

were placed in temples by worshipers as votive offerings: gifts to the goddess or god in gratitude or supplication. In Taras, possibly even more than in most Greek cities, religion paid attention to the dead. Before the end of the sixth century the Tarentines had already begun to bury terra-cotta figures with their dead—for instance, woman-headed sirens with their wings folded close to their bird bodies.[17]

We know very little about the appearance of the early city. Even later features of Taras were obscured by destruction of the ruins in the nineteenth century to make way for modern Taranto, and by unscientific, fanciful restoration in the years preceding responsible archaeology. Presumably the settlement, impregnable on the acropolis at the point of the peninsula, remained small during its first two centuries. One of the buildings erected there, probably around 575 B.C., was a Doric temple, dedicated perhaps to Poseidon, more likely to a goddess.[18] We know of a second temple, and others may lie under churches still surviving.

By the end of the sixth century, if not before, the layout of the city seems to have been orthogonal, the streets and alleys intersecting at right angles. The inhabited area could not have been more than sixteen hectares—in other words, 160,000 square meters or not quite forty acres. As the population grew, the acropolis, roomy enough to begin with, must have become uncomfortably crowded, and at some time— possibly before the end of the sixth century, although we are not sure— the Tarentines expanded southeastward to the area below the acropolis.[19]

About 530 B.C. the great Hellenic cities of Italy—Sybaris, Croton, Metapontum, Caulonia, and the Sybarite colony of Posidonia—adopted coinage, which was already being produced by states in mainland Greece and had come into existence before the close of the seventh century in Asia Minor. The silver was probably obtained from mines in Italy, either in land under the dominion of Sybaris or through trade with the Etruscans, who may have mined the metal themselves. The Etruscans, however, may have gotten the silver from their Carthaginian friends. Cities of mainland Greece may have been another source of supply, either directly or via intermediary ports in Sicily, such as Syracuse. Some silver was obtained in the forms of ingots and of actual coins from other states and then melted down or restruck for conversion into local currency. As was true with regard to other early coinages, these earliest Italiot Greek issues were not intended for the everyday purchases of the ordinary citizen. The coins—staters, weighing roughly eight grams—were worth too much for that. They facilitated significant commercial transactions, perhaps between states, more often within a state.[20] The normal business of the market was still a matter of barter.

For its money each of the city-states, like city-states in other parts of the Greek world when they started striking coins, chose an identifying device or symbol: Sybaris, a bull (associated with sexual force and the force of rivers); Caulonia, Apollo holding a laurel branch, bearing a small running figure on his outstretched arm, and accompanied by a stag; Posidonia, a standing Poseidon wielding a trident; Croton, the lion-footed tripod of Apollo; grain-growing Metapontum, perhaps for advertisement as much as anything, an ear of grain. These first Italiot Greek coins were different from coins produced anywhere else. They were broad and thin and flat—disklike—in a period when other coins tended to be thick and dumpy. Although most contemporary coins had a design (type) in relief on the obverse and punch marks or, gradually, another design in intaglio (incuse) on the reverse, the South Italiot coins had essentially the same design on both sides, in relief on the obverse and what appears as intaglio on the reverse. The obverse usually carried a cable border and the reverse a border of radiating lines. We have no idea what, or who, influenced the Greeks of South Italy to adopt this distinctive coinage. There used to be a theory that Pythagoras, who had been a gem engraver on Samos before coming to Croton and who could therefore have engraved coin dies as well as gems, invented it; but that idea is more attractive than plausible.[21]

Taras struck a few coins, and their correspondence in style and fabric to the issues of these other cities indicates that they were intended for trade. But in comparison with Sybaris, Croton, Metapontum, Posidonia, and Caulonia, Taras's output was minimal. The rarity of its earliest coins has been attributed to interstate politics. According to that theory, when the Italiot Greeks started striking money, they adopted a similar fabric and weight standard to facilitate trade with one another, but Taras withdrew from this informal economic "league" and consequently stopped issuing this coinage. A reason for withdrawal could have been the animosity of the other cities, Achaean-oriented, toward the only Dorian colony in Italy.[22] More recent theory, however, places the beginning of coinage at Taras later than its adoption by the other Greek colonies—perhaps around 520, perhaps at the earliest 510, the year of the destruction of Sybaris. The fact that Taras's earliest coins are a little lighter in weight than the earliest coins of the other cities, and are struck on flans that are less broad, points to a later date.[23] It is likely that Taras, not yet so important a city as the others, did not feel the need for coinage quite so soon as they.

Even though we do not always understand why a Greek city in Archaic times chose a particular type for its coins, we can assume that the city had a good reason—that the type was especially appropriate and that its significance would be clear to the population. Metapontum's ear of grain and Posidonia's standing figure of Poseidon are

Plate 1.   Silver stater, 520 B.C. or later. Obv. Kneeling figure 1. Ethnic retrograde. 23 mm. *BMC Italy*: Tarentum No. 33. *Courtesy of the Brittish Museum.*

obvious examples. Taras chose as its type a naked young male figure, down on one knee, holding a flower in the right hand and a lyre in the left (Plates 1-2). This figure, in relief on the obverse of the coin, in incuse on the reverse, has been identified as Apollo on the basis of the lyre but, on the basis of the flower, as one particular aspect of Apollo, namely Apollo Hyacinthus.[24] But the identification is far from definite. In 1873, for example, the British Museum considered the figure a representation of Taras, son of Poseidon and deity after whom the city was named.[25] More recent scholarship has discarded that identification but has also questioned an identification with Apollo in any form.

The people who lived in the Peloponnesus before the Dorians came there had worshiped a god of vegetation named Hyacinthus, a fertility deity associated with the renewal of life and quite distinct from Apollo. Amyclae in the Peloponnesus—the place where Phalanthus was to set off a revolt against the Spartan authorities, according to Antiochus's story—had been the center of the cult of Hyacinthus in Mycenaean times. Later legend treated this god of pre-Greek origin as a beautiful youth, prince of Amyclae and rival of Zephyr the West Wind for Apollo's affections. The sentimental tale is well known. One day, when Apollo was giving Hyacinthus a lesson in how to throw the discus, either Apollo threw it too carelessly or else the jealous Zephyr caught it and redirected it. In any case it hit Hyacinthus so hard that it killed him; and the disconsolate Apollo caused the hyacinth to rise from the dead youth's blood. When the Dorians came to the Peloponnesus with their own Hellenic gods, Hyacinthus was not forgotten. Even in classical times his tomb lay under a statue of the enthroned Apollo.[26]

The implication of Phalanthus's role as leader of an incipient revolt against the governing forces of Sparta, for which the rallying point was Amyclae, is that the founders of Taras—the Parthenians—were not Dorians at all but descendants of the pre-Greek population.[27] Whether

Plate 2.    Silver stater. Rev. of No. 1.
Kneeling figure r., intaglio.
*Courtesy of the British Mu-
seum.*

or not this implication is valid, it is clear that the colonists brought the cult of Amyclaean Hyacinthus with them to Italy. That they should picture him on their earliest coins would therefore be very appropriate, and the identification has received wide acceptance. [28] It has, however, been pointed out that we know too little about the iconography of Amyclaean Hyacinthus to be sure that the lyre and the flower are his attributes, and that in any case the Amyclaean god, unlike the boy lover of Apollo, would have been shown with a beard, which the god on the coins seems not to have. The figure on the coins, in this view, was not Hyacinthus but Eros the god of love, who, though usually winged, was not always given wings by the ancients, and who was associated with flowers and even with the lyre. Eros was adored by the Spartans; if his cult was carried by the colonists to Italy, as it apparently was, he would have been as fitting a deity as Hyacinthus for the Tarentines to place on their coins. [29]

At any event Taras did not keep the kneeling god on its money very long. In approximately these same years—certainly not much later— the city began issuing staters which had as a type a nude male figure riding a dolphin. From its meager origin Tarentine coinage was to become one of the most prolific and artistic coinages of the Greek world, and for its duration, down to the late third century B.C., the dolphin rider would persist as a type. [30] Whoever the young kneeling male may have been for the Tarentines, he proved unsatisfactory as a badge of the burgeoning state.

# Notes to Chapter 2

1. For early relations with the Iapygians, see especially Lo Porto, "Topografia," pp. 358-59, and Moretti, "Problemi," pp. 27-28.

2. See Wuilleumier, pp. 44, 473-74, and Georges Vallet, "Métropoles et Colonies: Leurs Rapports Jusque Vers la Fin du VIᵉ Siècle," in *Metropoli e Colonie di Magna Grecia: Atti del Terzo Convegno di Studi sulla Magna Grecia* (Naples, 1964), pp. 216-18. This volume will be cited hereafter as Convegno 3.

3. See Toynbee, *Some Problems,* pp. 217, 289, and Moretti, "Problemi," pp. 34-35. Cartledge (*Sparta and Lakonia,* pp. 154-57) argues convincingly that the change in the Spartan social system, far from being sudden, was a gradual sixth-century phenomenon, that its austerity has been exaggerated, and that the arts by no means died out entirely at Sparta.

4. See Wuilleumier, pp. 44, 176; Vallet, "Métropoles et Colonies," pp. 218-19; Moretti, "Problemi," pp. 36-38; Pierre Lévêque in "Il Dibattito," Convegno 10, p. 203; Claude Mossé in "Il Dibattito," Convegno 10, pp. 188-90; and Emil Condurachi in "Il Dibattito," Convegno 10, pp. 211-12.

5. See R. A. Higgins, *Greek Terracottas* (London, 1967), pp. 27-28.

6. See Bérard, *Colonisation Grecque,* pp. 171-72.

7. See Georges Vallet, "Les Routes Maritimes de la Grande Grèce," in *Vie di Magna Grecia: Atti del Secondo Convegno di Studi sulla Magna Grecia* (Naples, 1963), pp. 132-33 (to be cited hereafter as Convegno 2), and his "Métropoles et Colonies," pp. 223-24; also John Boardman, *The Greeks Overseas,* 2nd ed. (Harmondsworth, Middlesex, 1973), pp. 163, 179. Sparta was still producing good painted pottery, if not excellent bronze work, in the first half of the sixth century; see Martin Robertson, *A History of Greek Art* (Cambridge, England, 1975), Vol. I, pp. 136-37, and Cartledge, *Sparta and Lakonia,* pp. 136-37. Around 525 some Spartan bronzesmiths emigrated to Taras; see Cartledge, pp. 156-57.

8. On this great hoard (Inv. 1874), consisting of about 600 coins, see Colin Kraay, *Archaic and Classical Greek Coins* (Berkeley and Los Angeles, 1976), pp. 44, 63, 81, 90, 109, 165, 185. Doubt has been cast on the authenticity of the hoard; see, for example, Attilio Stazio, "La Documentazione Numismatica," Convegno 3, p. 117. Kraay, however, considers the deposit genuine. Margaret Thompson points out that it may very possibly represent the loot and/or pay of a mercenary soldier who had served abroad, rather than profits from trade; see her "Hoards and Overstrikes: The Numismatic Evidence," *Expedition,* Vol. 21, no. 4 (Summer 1979), p. 40.

9. See Moretti, "Problemi," pp. 32-33.

10. See David Randall-MacIver, *The Iron Age in Italy* (Oxford, 1927), pp. 213-18, 221-24, 331-32, and Moretti, "Problemi," pp. 31-33. Moretti adopts Randall-MacIver's dates for the beginnings of these wares.

11. See Strabo, 6.1.15. Anti-Dorian feeling on the part of the Achaean Sybarites has been questioned as a motive; see Bérard, *Colonisation Grecque,* p. 176.

12. For the opinion that Sybaris was destroyed by nature (possibly a tidal wave) rather than by Croton, however, see Oliver C. Colburn, "Return to Sybaris," *Expedition*, vol. 18, no. 2 (Winter 1976), p. 9.

13. See Boardman, *Greeks Overseas*, p. 193.

14. See Wuilleumier, pp. 267-68; D. Mustilli, "Civiltà della Magna Grecia," Convegno 3, p. 33; Ernst Langlotz, "La Scultura," Convegno 10, pp. 225-27; and Robertson, *History of Greek Art*, Vol. I, p. 115.

15. See Langlotz, p. 221, n. 2.

16. The process is superbly described by R. A. Higgins in *Greek Terracottas*, pp. 1-4, and James Chesterman in *Classical Terracotta Figures* (Woodstock, N.Y., 1975), pp. 15-17.

17. See Wuilleumier, pp. 254-55, 395-96, 425-27; Higgins, *Greek Terracottas*, pp. xlix-1, 36, 54-55, and his "Tarantine Terracottas," Convegno 10, pp. 268-70; Roland Martin, "L'Architecture de Tarente," Convegno 10, pp. 319-20; Chesterman, pp. 18-19; and Joseph Coleman Carter, *The Sculpture of Taras* (Philadelphia, 1975), p. 28.

18. See below, chap. 6, n. 12.

19. See Martin, "L'Architecture de Tarente," pp. 321-22; Lo Porto, "Topografia," pp. 361-68; and W. D. E. Coulson, "Taras," in *The Princeton Encyclopedia of Classical Sites* (Princeton, 1976), p. 879. Martin makes the point that Taras, like Marseille, Ampurias, Elea, Smyrna, and Phocaea, developed an *emporion* and was oriented toward commerce, whereas cities such as Metapontum, Locri, and Gela were oriented toward exploitation of an extensive agricultural area.

20. See Kraay, *Archaic and Classical Greek Coins*, pp. 202, 318-20, 323, 325-26, 328. In "Caulonia and South Italian Problems," *Numismatic Chronicle*, 20 (1960), pp. 73-78, 81, Kraay considers the various possible source of silver for the Greek cities of southern Italy and concludes that the importation of foreign coins for the purpose of overstriking has been unjustifiably emphasized. In his later article, "Hoards, Small Change and the Origin of Coinage," *Journal of Hellenic Studies*, vol. 84 (1964), 76-91, Kraay suggests that "since . . . there appear to have been no local sources of silver sufficient to supply the S. Italian mints, the metal had to be acquired from abroad either as loot or in exchange for products or services" (p. 77). Kraay rejects as sources for the origin of coinage both foreign trade and local (retail) trade and speculates that coinage originated for the convenience of a state's government (see pp. 82-91). South Italian coins in the late sixth and early fifth centuries B.C. "circulated without restriction" within South Italy but not beyond it (p. 77).

21. Kraay, "Caulonia and South Italian Problems," pp. 73-74, dismisses the theory that the spread fabric with incuse reverse was designed to facilitate the overstriking of imported coins.

22. See Wuilleumier, p. 52. Writing in 1939, Wuilleumier dates the adoption of coinage by the Italiot Greeks around 550, which would now be considered perhaps twenty years too early.

23. See Herbert A. Cahn, "Early Tarentine Chronology," in *Essays in Greek Coinage Presented to Stanley Robinson,* C. M. Kraay and G. K. Jenkins, eds. (Oxford, 1968), pp. 59-61, 66-67; Attilio Stazio, "Aspetti e Momenti della Monetazione Tarantina," Convegno 10, pp. 157-58; G. K. Jenkins, *Ancient Greek Coins* (New York, 1972), p. 66; and Kraay, *Archaic and Classical Greek Coins,* pp. 174-75, 203.

24. This identification was first proposed by the Duc de Luynes. See his "Médailles de Tarente relatives à l'Apollon Hyacinthien," in *Annales de l'Institut de Correspondence Archéologique,* Vol. II (1830), pp. 337-40. See also Oscar E. Ravel, *Descriptive Catalogue of the Collection of Tarentine Coins formed by M. P. Vlasto* (London, 1947; reprint ed., Chicago, 1977), nos. 70-72.

25. See Reginald Stuart Poole, *A Catalogue of the Greek Coins in the British Museum: Italy* (London, 1873; reprint ed., Bologna, 1963), p. 165.

26. Pausanias, 3.1.3. and 3.19.2-3, mentions this tomb.

27. See Wuilleumier, pp. 40-42.

28. See in particular Cahn, "Early Tarentine Chronology," p. 66, and Stazio, "Aspetti e Momenti," p. 152.

29. The substitution of Eros for Hyacinthus is that of Léon Lacroix. See "Hyakinthos et les monnaies incuses de Tarente" in his *Études d'Archéologie Numismatique* (Paris, 1974), pp. 23-35.

30. For the identity of this figure see below, pp. 32-33.

3

# The Fifth Century:
# Taras Assumes Importance

Taras expanded territorially to only a limited degree in the latter part of the sixth century and the beginning of the fifth. On the perimeter of its land the native peoples—watchful, pugnacious—were strong enough to resist attempts at appropriation of their property.[1] The colony was presumably still ruled by a king and was dominated by a vigorous military aristocracy, devoted to war as a way of life. Possessions of this aristocracy—the necessities of athletes, such as bottles of oil to spread on the body and strigils for scraping it clean—have been recovered from a group of tombs called the Athletes' Tombs, the oldest of which date from the late sixth and early fifth centuries. The athletes buried here seem to have excelled in the costly and therefore aristocratic sport of chariot racing.[2] It would have been men like these that led the city in her chronic clashes with the barbarians.

Herodotus tells a story that casts a little light on these obscure years of Tarentine history. There was, he says, a distinguished physician from Croton named Democedes who became a slave of King Darius of Persia. Darius dispatched him to Greece to inquire into the strengths and weaknesses of the Hellenes, whom he planned soon to conquer. He sent fifteen Persians along with Democedes, apparently to make sure that the Greek returned to Persia with the information, instead of staying in Greece. The party, after garnering useful details on the coast, sailed on to Italy, where Democedes was to visit his father and brothers at Croton. Like other vessels coming from Greece, their two triremes and a cargo ship docked in the harbor at Taras. It was about 492 and Aristophilides was king—the only Tarentine ruler since Phalanthus, it may be recalled, whose name we know. He welcomed Democedes and, willing to do a fellow Greek a service, had his guards take the Persians into custody as spies. (These were probably the first Persians ever seen in the city, though Tarentine sailors could have encountered Persians in

Plate 3.    Silver stater, c. 470-450 B.C. Obv.: figure r. on dolphin. 22 mm. *ANS/SNG* Part I, No. 827. *Courtesy of the American Numismatic Society, New York*

the cities of the East.) With his keepers in custody, Democedes hurried off to Croton. But the Persians, whom Aristophilides evidently could not hold for very long, chased him and seized him in the marketplace at Croton. Timid Crotoniates, impressed by the Persians' threat that Darius might enslave their city in retaliation, were in favor of giving Democedes up; but their braver fellow citizens prevailed. For these Western Greeks, perhaps, a threat from so remote a place as Persia did not mean much.

The disappointed Persians therefore set sail without Democedes, but they did not proceed very far: they were shipwrecked before getting clear of the heel of Italy, the Iapygian peninsula, and the Iapygians made slaves of them. A Greek named Gillus, who had been banished from Taras and lived among the Iapygians, persuaded these barbarians to let the Persians go, and they eventually returned to Darius. Gillus accompanied them, and Darius promised to grant him any wish because he was their savior. He said he wanted to be restored to his native city, Taras. Darius sent him back to Italy in the company of men of Cnidus, since that city in Asia Minor was traditionally a friend of Taras. But even the Cnidians could not negotiate successfully with the Tarentines concerning Gillus. Standing firm for the second time against the power of Persia, the Tarentines refused to readmit their exiled citizen. Darius gave up on the small Western problem and turned to his main business, the conquest of Greece.[3]

Herodotus's story is of course weighted in favor of the Western Greeks, whose resourcefulness and love of freedom he sets off against the strength of the Persian autocracy, just as he will contrast the intelligence and independence of their cousins the mainland Greeks with the brute power of imperial Persia in the coming war. Partisan though Herodotus's account is, however, it may have some validity as a suggestion of how these Western Greeks really did look at things. Herodotus lived among the Greeks of southern Italy when he wrote the story down, and we must therefore give some credit to his assessment of their character.

He does not say why Gillus had been exiled or give a specific reason why Taras refused to take him back; but the man's friendship with the Iapygians could not have helped his case. Otherwise, Herodotus's story does little to illuminate Taras's relations with its non-Hellenic neighbors in this period. Almost the only direct evidence we have regarding those relations is that in commemoration of what must have been an especially important victory over the Messapians, the branch of the Iapygians who lived on the Italian heel and among whom Gillus had spent his exile or would soon spend it, the city commissioned the Peloponnesian sculptor Ageladas to fashion a statuary group to be set up in the sanctuary of Apollo at Delphi. Made of spoils taken from the Messapians after the battle, the group consisted of bronze horses and captive women. Conjectures as to the date of this sculpture have ranged between about 520 and 468. The second date is certainly too late, the first one too early.[4]

So proud of its victory over the Messapians, Taras had to suffer humiliation from these Iapygian peoples about 473.[5] Boundary disputes between the Greeks and the barbarians had apparently escalated into a decisive battle, certainly one of the greatest fought up to this point in Greek Italy and, according to Herodotus, the most serious defeat a Greek people had ever been handed. The Tarentines were helped by Rhegium.[6] The Iapygians had the help of barbarian friends, so that their army, according to Diodorus, totaled more than 20,000 men. We do not know the strength of the allied Greek army. Herodotus says that 3,000 of the soldiers of Rhegium remained on the field of battle; he does not number the Tarentine dead. The Rhegians who were still alive scattered in one direction, the living Tarentines in another, both groups chased by barbarian divisions. The Iapygians slaughtered still more Tarentines before the disabled Greeks could reach their city.

This calamitous defeat, in which much of the aristocracy must have fallen, evidently left the remaining Tarentines dissatisfied with a government that could lead them to such a disaster. At least, Aristotle relates the defeat to a change in government that occurred soon afterwards.[7] We do not know whether Taras still had a king in 473 or even whether Aristophilides was a king about two decades before that, as Herodotus says he was; but after 473 the government became a democracy of sorts. Aristotle does not indicate whether the revolution at Taras was violent or pacific. Later in the *Politics* he comments on Tarentine democracy, but it is impossible to determine whether all of his comments refer to the years right after the change.[8] The rich Tarentines, he says in admiration, let the poor share in the use of their possessions, and

Plate 4.   Silver stater, c. 470-450 B.C. Rev.: Hippocamp r. 19.5 mm. *ANS/SNG* Part I, No. 837. *Courtesy of the American Numismatic Society, New York.*

as a result the poor and the rich were not antagonists. The state officials were elected—some by vote and some by lot. Aristotle reasoned that election by lot would satisfy the desire for popular participation while election by vote (which implied the possibility of dismissal for maladministration) would ensure responsible government. Who the voters were— whether the whole citizenry or only a part—Aristotle does not reveal.

Athens, most glorious and prosperous of Greek victors over the Persians, may have influenced the new Tarentine constitution. But we cannot be sure what this would have meant with regard to who composed the electorate or whom they elected, or whether the strategi (generals) retained considerable power, or whether (as at Athens) there was a *boule* or council with a frequently changing membership which proposed business for the voting citizens to approve or reject. Nor do we know the extent to which the Tarentine merchant class, gaining in prestige throughout this period, profited by the constitutional revisions. In any case, the democratization of Taras was a part of a reaction going on throughout the Greek world in the fifth century against the regal and tyrannic regimes more characteristic of the sixth.[9] Plutarch relates a folk anecdote, which may indicate the powers of the strategus this early in the democracy but may also be very untrustworthy. There was, he says, a Tarentine strategus named Dino. The citizens voted against him on a certain issue. When the herald proclaimed the defeat of Dino's opinion, Dino simply raised his right hand, declaring, "This is stronger."[10]

There is no doubt that Taras prospered as a democracy. It was probably in the 460s that the city commissioned another statuary group to be set up in the sanctuary of Apollo at Delphi, this time to commemorate a great victory over the Peucetians, the barbarians to the north. From Pausanias's description it seems to have been a more elaborate group than the former one. Two sculptors, Ageladas of Argos and Onatas of Aegina, worked on it. There were statues of foot soldiers and horsemen.

Plate 5.    Silver stater, c. 420 B.C.
Obv.: Figure on dolphin
l.; beneath, squid. 20 mm.

A Iapygian king named Opis, who had assisted the Peucetians and had been killed, was shown lying on the battlefield. Phalanthus himself, and Taras the son of Poseidon, stood in exultation on his corpse, and nearby was the friendly dolphin that had rescued Phalanthus from shipwreck on the voyage to Italy.[11]

It may have been about this time—or it may have been earlier, in connection with the border skirmishes leading up to the great battle of 473—that Taras conquered a Iapygian town called Karbina. The victorious Greek soldiers proceeded to rape the barbarian girls, the young women, and the boys. Although this conduct would have had many precedents in Greek warfare, the violation of propriety angered Zeus. He struck the soldiers dead with lightning. In Taras, pillars or *stelai* were set up at the doors of the houses where these men had lived. On the anniversary of the disaster the Tarentines would sacrifice at these pillars to Zeus Kataibates, or Zeus Descending in Thunder and Lightning.[12]

In the mid-fifth century Taras had to contend with a new threat, not from barbarians but from a Greek intruder. When in 510 Sybaris was destroyed, the citizens still alive apparently fled to the Sybarite colony of Laus. There seems to have been an attempt to revive Sybaris, but Croton destroyed the new city soon after 476, and the refugees fled this time to the Sybarite colony of Posidonia. In 453 the Sybarite descendants in both Laus and Posidonia combined to revive their ancestral city again—a testimony, perhaps, to the strong sense of belonging to one's own particular polis that existed in the Western Greek as in the Eastern Greek world. Croton, still an enemy, almost extinguished the young colony several years later. The dogged Sybarites, however, appealed to Athens. Not averse to establishing a base of influence in the West, Athens helped to found Sybaris once more in 446. In 444 it strengthened this city by sending additional colonists not only from Athens itself but from other Greek cities. (The most distinguished colonist was Herodotus, who migrated there from Attica, where he had been living for the past

Plate 6.    Silver stater, c. 460-443
B.C.  Seated figure 1. with
staff and distaff. 21 mm.

several years. He would write his history at Sybaris and stay there till he died.) The new citizens wisely put themselves on good terms with Croton. As might have been expected, however, they did not live peacefully with the people already settled at Sybaris, those who, presumably, could claim actual Sybarite ancestry. About 440 the newcomers chased out these older inhabitants. The ancient location, now possessed entirely by Athenians and other Greeks not descended from the Sybarites, was renamed Thurii in honor of a local spring.[13]

The city stood about 134 kilometers (approximately eighty miles) south of Taras, close enough for a conflict of interests. The conflict apparently began almost at once, as Taras looked jealously at the intervening land. The fact that Taras was Dorian and Thurii a creation of Ionian Athens may have been another source of hostility. The general who led the Thurian troops against Taras was, however, an exile from Sparta. Thurii received no explicit help from Athens. Taras, which must have been especially vigorous and self-confident at this point in its life, won the war. The two cities were now on sufficiently good terms to join in the sponsorship of a new colony, but the colony's affiliations were to be largely with Taras.[14]

This joint foundation was on the coast of the Gulf of Taranto in the Siritide, the land once controlled by the long-destroyed city of Siris. Almost immediately—about 433/432—it was moved inland a short distance and given the name Heraclea, City of Heracles—not an original name, since several cities in the older Greek world were also called after the embattled hero. The coastal colony functioned as its port. Greeks had settled on the acropolis at the site of Heraclea as early as the end of the eighth century, about the time Phalanthus and his followers had settled Taras.[15] But this early attempt at colonization had apparently been of little significance. Under Tarentine patronage Heraclea would flourish, and its location, about halfway between Taras and Thurii, would protect Tarentine interests this far to the south. The fact that Heraclea

Plate 7.   Silver stater, c. 420 B.C.
1.          Rev. of No. 5. Seated figure
            with dog, staff, distaff.

had a body of ephors is often taken to mean that Taras had one too and had influenced the young Heraclean constitution in this respect. Such an inference may or may not be justified. A better proof of Tarentine influence is probably the fact that the Heracleans, like the Tarentines, spoke Greek with a Doric accent.[16]

The power of Taras was now growing markedly, while the power of some of its rivals was on the decline. Croton, for instance—probably deprived of some of its territory by the establishment of Thurii, and harassed by Lucanian and Bruttian barbarians—could not hold onto its early hegemony. Metapontum, squeezed by Taras to the north and Heraclea to the south after 433, came under the domination of Taras.[17] The Tarentine population was increasing too. About the time Heraclea was established, Taras built a great eastern wall to protect the expanded city.

Although Taras, like the other Italiot Greek colonies, did not become very actively involved in the Peloponnesian War, emotionally it sided with Dorian Corinth and with its own mother Sparta against Athens and the Ionians. It must have watched the progress of the struggle in the old Greek world with considerable partisan sympathy; and when the war came to Magna Graecia, it made its feelings clear. It refused to receive the ships and men of the great Athenian armada of 415 which, sailing down the coast of Italy, needed to touch land for fresh water, food, and other supplies. But it received the Spartan general Gylippus in 414 on his way to take command at Syracuse; and after he had been driven out to sea by a storm on the Italian coast, it received him again so that he could repair his ships.[18] Later, after the Athenian catastrophe at Syracuse, Taras along with Locri contributed vessels to the Dorian cause.[19] The final defeat of Athens in 404 must have given the Tarentines strong reason to rejoice.

Plate 8.    Silver stater, not much before 400 B.C.  Rev. Seated figure l. with strigil and oil jug. 22 mm.

The naked dolphin rider that replaced the mysterious kneeling figure as a type on Tarentine coins first appeared as an incuse device on an issue on which the kneeling figure, also incuse, occupied the obverse. Very soon, however (after an incuse issue on which he occupied both sides), the dolphin rider was given the obverse. This occurred perhaps as early as 510 B.C., possibly even before. With one exception he would remain on the obverse for the next several decades (plate 3). The kneeling figure never reappeared.

With this issue of about 510, Taras abandoned the incuse style, as the other Italiot Greek cities, sooner or later, would also do. The dolphin rider, depicted in relief, had one arm stretched out in front as if he were hailing the land where the new city would be located. On the reverse was a succession of devices, also in relief—a hippocamp or sea monster (half horse, half dolphin), then a wheel, then a head, and then a hippocamp again, which alternated with the head as the years approached midcentury. Before the hippocamp gave place to the wheel as a reverse type, the flan, which had remained broad in the earliest hippocamp strikings, became thicker and less broad, although the coins were still staters, too valuable to be used for everyday purchases. On some of the later issues the dolphin rider stretched both arms forward in a gesture of greeting; or, if only one arm was held out in front, he carried a cuttlefish in the other hand.[20]

With the dolphin rider as with the kneeling figure, we run into the problem of more than one plausible identification; and again our knowledge of Tarentine thought at so early a period is too meager to make us sure how a Tarentine citizen would have interpreted the type. When he looked at one of these coins, he might have seen Phalanthus or he might have seen Taras himself.

Pausanias, in describing the statuary group set up at Delphi in gratitude for victory over the Peucetians, said that it included a dolphin because a dolphin had rescued Phalanthus from shipwreck on the way to Italy (10.13.10). Assuming that this part of the Phalanthus legend was already current by about 510 B.C., the coin type could certainly have been an illustration of the story. On the other hand, and also according to Pausanias, when Phalanthus and his followers came to Italy they found a river and town named Taras after a local god, and they said that this god was a son of Poseidon by a nymph of the vicinity (10.10.8). It would have been appropriate to use as a badge of the city the being whose name the city bore and, since he was the son of the sea god, to picture him on the back of a dolphin.

There is speculation as to the very ancient connotations of Taras and Phalanthus. It has even been suggested that Taras started off as a Dorian lightning god, since *teras* (Dorian *taras*) may have signified lightning.[21] As was remarked in Chapter 1, Phalanthus too may have been a supernatural being rather than an historical Spartan who led a group to found a city—perhaps even, like Hyacinthus, some pre-Dorian deity if not a version of Hyacinthus himself.[22] Or he was possibly a manifestation or aspect of Poseidon and for that reason a rider over the sea on a dolphin; and perhaps, early in Tarentine life, worship of him was supplanted by the actual worship of Poseidon through the seagod's son, Taras. In that case the legend that the founder was driven from the new city and died at Brundisium may have represented the rejection of the cult of Phalanthus in favor of the cult of Taras. (The return of his ashes to Taras would signify something quite different, simply the eventual establishment of a founder cult.) Or, alternatively and finally, Phalanthus was not a manifestation of Poseidon or Hyacinthus but a full-blown god in his own right, the original dolphin god—possibly also a phallic deity, as his name might indicate.[23]

None of these speculations, interesting as they are as possible insights into the religious beliefs of the early Tarentines, is provable, and none of them helps much toward establishing the identity of the dolphin rider. Scholarship as a whole, however, prefers Phalanthus to Taras.[24] It is conceivable that Tarentines themselves practiced a dual indentification, associating the figure on their money with either Taras or Phalanthus at pleasure. Certainly he acquired a dual signficance later on if not this early. By the fourth century at the latest, Phalanthus and Taras had become inextricably fused or confused.[25]

The first of the reverse types, the hippocamp, is understandable enough on the coinage of a maritime city (Plate 4). The wheel, four-spoked and apparently standing for a chariot, may allude to a traditional Tarentine athletic event, possibly held in honor of the eponymous god since the Western Greeks tended to honor river gods with chariot races. Or it may allude to the Dioscuri, Castor and Pollux (Polydeuces),

Plate 9. Silver stater, mid-fifth century B.C. Rev.: Naked horseman 1. 22mm.

whose cult had been carried to Taras from Sparta and who, in later Tarentine art, were sometimes shown in chariots.[26] The head is the most obscure of these reverse types. It may or may not be female; if it is, the female exudes masculine strength. Various candidates have been suggested: Phalanthus (for whom the Tarentines developed an important cult), Artemis, and Aphrodite. But the most popular candidate is Satyra, the local nymph (a daughter of Minos in one legend), who was loved by Poseidon and became the mother of Taras.[27]

Fairly early in the fifth century there appeared on the obverse of some Tarentine staters a new figure. This was a seated male of austere mien, bearded, naked to the waist, the lower part of his body draped in a himation. He held a large cantharus or drinking cup and a distaff. The dolphin rider, both arms reaching out in front, was relegated temporarily to the reverse. The coin had a broad flan and a guilloche border.

On later coins, often with a considerably smaller flan, the seated male was transferred to the reverse and the figure on the dolphin rode across the obverse as usual, to right or to left, with one or both arms outstretched (Plate 5). The seated male, now deprived of his beard, was depicted in a style that became increasingly less austere—more classical, more relaxed, more graceful; and Tarentine die engravers attained a remarkably high degree of art in the depiction of this figure. He was given various attributes in addition to the earlier ones—a dove perhaps, or a panther cub, a dog, a staff, a strigil and an oil jug (Plates 6-8). Some of the later coins had an olive wreath for a reverse border; others had a beaded border or no border at all.[28]

In the nineteenth century this seated figure was generally thought to be the Demos or People of Taras, and the coins were therefore said to mark the establishment of democracy at Taras after the disaster of 473. This attractive identification has died a lingering death; it is now no longer considered a possibility.[29] If the figure was not the Demos of the city,

Plate 10.  Silver hemilitra, c. 500-430
B.C. Obv.: Scallop shell.
7.5 mm.

perhaps the Tarentines viewed him as the oecist or founder—in other words, Phalanthus—or as Taras himself. The consensus today is that the Tarentines would actually have understood him to be Taras, possibly as eponymous founder, more likely as eponymous hero.[30] As with the dolphin rider, however, there may have been, even this early, a tendency to combine the two identifications—a tendency which, for all we know, the religious practices of the city may have supported.

The initial issue, with Taras seated on the obverse rather than the reverse, probably occurred about 480, while coin types in general were still austere. The issue could not have continued very long, as few examples of it remain. There was a break of perhaps fifteen years before the seated Taras was moved to the reverse. As for the pieces with an olive wreath as a border, far from marking the change to a democracy after the defeat of 473, they cannot have been struck much before 445, since one of them was overstruck on a Corinthian stater dating from about 450. The seated Taras continued to be used on Tarentine coins until perhaps 430 or 425.[31]

The attributes associated with the seated Taras provide glimpses into the concerns of the city in the fifth century. One of the two oldest attributes, the distaff, must have celebrated the textile industry, which played a significant part in its financial development. Given the tendency of Greek states to use their coins propagandistically, the distaff may even be interpreted as a civic advertisement. The coin apparently credits the eponymous hero as founder or patron of the textile industry, just as his other early attribute, the cantharus or wine cup, presumably implies a libation poured by the hero for the city's well-being.[32]

The staff that the seated hero holds in so many representations very likely signifies his staff of office as the eponymous ruler of the polis; and possibly there is also an allusion to the shepherd's staff, or in other words to the flocks in the Tarentine countryside, which provided the wool for the textile industry. The aryballus or oil flask and the strigil or

Plate 11.   Silver drachm c. 475-450
B.C. Obv.: Forepart of hippocamp r. Côte Collection,
No. 60 (this coin). 15.5 mm.
No doubt because the eth-
nic(retrograde) appears under the hippocamp, Ravel
in the Côte Catalogue prefers to designate this
side the reverse. But see
*ANS/SNG* Part I, Nos. 845-
848.

scraper, which frequently appear in combination on late issues, present the hero as athlete, ready to oil and scrape his body in connection with exercise or actual games. The reference may be to games in honor of Taras himself.

The cantharus may have carried for Tarentines a connotation aside from that of a libation for the prosperity of the state. A cult of the heroized dead was particularly important to the religious life of the city; in some respects it was part of Taras's Spartan heritage. On Spartan sepulchral reliefs, the heroized dead frequently held out a cantharus.[33] Together with veneration of the heroized dead in general, there flour-ished in many Greek cities the worship of the semidivine hero who had died, such as Lycurgus of Sparta or Theseus of Athens. According to a local myth, Taras had ruled many years over the pre-Greek city until, in the midst of a sacrifice to his father Poseidon, he fell into the river Taras and drowned. Since the citizens could not find his body, they assumed that he had gone to join his father and started worshiping him as a hero to whom divine honors should be paid.[34] If the seated figure on the coins was intended by his engravers as Taras, he was therefore Taras the heroized and deified dead, the object of religious ceremonies in the state. Although he occasionally sits on a *klismos*, a graceful chair with curved back and legs, his usual seat is the *diphros* or stool, traditionally assigned to the gods and the heroized dead in Greek art. Aside from the cantharus and the *diphros*, other attributes that occur with the seated figure also suggest his chthonic or underworld nature. He is sometimes shown playing with or feeding a panther, associated at Taras with departed heroes. Sometimes he holds a dove, symbol of the soul.[35]

The question of why a particular coin type was abandoned is as prob-lematical as why it was adopted. We do not know who within the Taren-tine government was responsible for determining coin types; we do not know whether more than one workshop existed simultaneously at

Plate 12.  Rev. (in Côte, obv.) of No.
11. Female head (Satyra?)
r.

Taras, each having its special assignments. But about the middle of the century, for one reason or another, a new type began appearing on the reverse of Tarentine staters, and it would be retained when engravers ceased to carve the seated figure. This new type was a naked horseman (Plate 9). It would eventually be moved to the obverse.[36] Unlike the seated figure, it would continue to satisfy the Tarentines. Along with the dolphin rider, which would then occupy the reverse, it would represent the city until late in the third century; and in the variety of attributes and symbols accompanying it and the disposition of the horseman himself (riding fast, standing still, crowning the horse or jumping off) the type would far surpass the seated figure and exceed even the dolphin rider in invention and diversity. During the fourth and third centuries, just as Athens would be known for its owls, Taras would be known for its horsemen.

In addition to staters, Taras began quite early—possibly before the end of the sixth century—to issue silver coins of smaller denominations, probably intended for daily purchases in the market, perhaps also to be used along with the staters in paying troops. Among the earliest of these were litrae (only slightly heavier than the obol, which itself was equal to about 1/12 of the stater) with a scallop shell on the obverse and a four spoked wheel on the reverse, and the infinitesimal quarter-obols, equaling one-sixth of a litra, with the same types or, occasionally, the wheel on both sides. Again the wheel may have alluded to chariot races in honor of the heroized Taras, or to the Dioscuri. The scallop shell, obviously a maritime reference, suggests a favorite food of the Tarentines (Plate 10). There were thirds of starters and diobols (worth one-sixth of the stater) with maritime types on both sides—a dolphin and usually a scallop shell on the obverse, a hippocamp on the reverse. The forepart of the hippocamp occupied the reverse of drachms struck, probably, in the second quarter of the fifth century (Plate 11). A head, presumably female and maybe that of Satyra, occurred on the obverse of some of the smaller coins and also of the drachms (Plate 12). Sometimes the head was incontrovertibly male and may have represented Taras. From perhaps the coming of democracy down to the beginning of the Peloponnesian War, there were quarter-litrae with the city denoted by a large T on both sides, and trihemiobols (worth ⅛ of a stater) with both sides occupied by the four-legged stool of chthonic association. Trihemiobols of the mid-fifth century and beyond bore a club and bow on the obverse (probably denoting Heracles) and, on the reverse, the distaff that stood for the city's textile industry. Other tiny coins had on the obverse a vase, perhaps also chthonic in its significance.[37]

# Notes to Chapter 3

1. Carter remarks that Taras's "relations with the indigenous tribes of Apulia (Messapians, Daunians, Peucetians) were characterized by unrelenting hostility" (*Sculpture of Taras*, p.7). The city was protected by "an arc of Hellenized towns not more than twenty kilometers distant" (p. 7, n. 4).

2. See Moretti, "Problemi," pp. 39–40.

3. Herodotus, 3.129–38.

4. The sculpture is described by Pausanias, 10.10.6. For discussion as to date, see Ettore Pais, "The Alliance between Rhegium and Tarentum against the Iapygians," in his *Ancient Italy: Historical and Geographical Investigations in Central Italy, Magna Grecia, Sicily, and Sardinia,* C. Densmore, trans. (Chicago and London, 1908), pp. 34–35; Wuilleumier, pp. 54–55; and Moretti, "Problemi," p. 29.

5. See Hherodotus, 7.170, and Diodorus Siculus, 11.52. The date 473 has been much questioned, but no better date has been arrived at. It is derived from Diodorus's statement that skirmishes between Tarentines and Iapygians reached the point of open war during the archonship of Menon at Athens and the consulships of L. Aemilius Mamercus and G. Cornelius Lentulus at Rome. For doubts as to the date see especially Pais, *Ancient Italy*, p. 37. Moretti ("Problemi," p. 40) and Coulson ("Taras," *Princeton Encylcopedia*, p. 879) are among those who accept 473 as approximately correct, though for Moretti 467 is possible. Wuilleumier prefers 467 (p. 57).

6. For the conjecture that the Taras-Rhegium alliance was due to Rhegium's desire to counter the growing political and economic power of Syracuse, see Pais, "Alliance," *Ancient Italy*, pp. 29–34; R. Hackforth, "Sicily," *Cambridge Ancient History*, Vol. V (Cambridge, England, 1935), pp. 148–50; and Wuilleumier, pp. 55–56.

7. See *Politics*, 5.3.7–8.1303A.

8. See *Politics*, 6.5.9–14.1320B.

9. See Moretti, "Problemi," p. 40. For valuable comments and conjectures on the revision of the Tarentine constitution, see especially Wuilleumier, pp. 177–79; Moretti, "Problemi," pp. 45–46; Paolo Enrico Arias, "Rapporti e Contrasti dalla Fine del VI a.C. al Dominio Romano," Convegno 3, pp. 141–42; and Pierre Lévêque in "Il Dibattito," Convegno 10, pp. 203–205. Lévêque in particular considers possible Athenian influence.

10. Plutarch, *Quaestiones Graecae*, Question 42, in *The Greek Questions of Plutarch*, W.R. Halliday, trans. (Oxford, 1928, reprint ed., New York, 1975), p. 179. Halliday relates the anecdote tentatively to this period of Tarentine history but remarks (p. 180) that a somewhat similar anecdote is told of Abraham Lincoln.

11. See Pausanias, 10.13.10. See also Pais, *Ancient Italy*, p. 35; Vlasto, *Taras Oikistes,* p. 55; Wuilleumier, pp. 57–59; and Moretti, "Problemi," p. 29.

12. Klearchos, fragment 9, *apud* Athenaeus 12, p. 522D. See the discussions in Wuilleumier, pp. 53–54, and in Arthur Bernard Cook, *Zeus: A Study in Ancient*

*Religion*, Vol. II (Cambridge, England, 1925), p. 29. Cook considers it "fairly obvious that death by lightning is regarded not as a disaster, but as an honour. . . ."

13. For numismatic evidence for this chain of events see Kraay, *Archaic and Classical Greek Coins*, p. 173. The more traditonal view that Athens sent its contingent of settlers after the Sybarites had been driven out is that of F.E. Adcock in *Cambridge Ancient History*, Vol. V, pp. 168–69.

14. Diodorus Siculus, 12.23 and 12.36.4; Strabo, 6.14.1. See Arias, "Rapporti e Contrasti," pp. 239–40, and Kraay, *Archaic and Classical Greek Coins*, p. 184.

15. See R.R. Holloway, "Herakleia," *Princton Encylcopedia*, p. 384.

16. See Vlasto, *Taras Oikistes*, p. 144; Wuilleumier, pp. 61–62; and Bérard, *Colonisation Grecque*, pp. 197–98.

17. Vlasto (p. 144) goes so far as to say; "The Tarentines thus reduced Metapontum almost to vassalage." But even if this is true, it could not have occurred as early as the Athenian expedition of 415–413 against Syracuse, when Metapontum, choosing to honor an alliance with Athens in the face of obvious Tarentine objection, donated two triremes and 300 javelin men to the Athenian armada (Thucydides, 7.33.4–5). Kraay ("Caulonia and South Italian Problems," pp. 80–81) affirms that Metapontum was hurt by the war between Taras and Thurii since it lay in disputed territory, but that it recovered after 430.

18. Thucydides, 6.44.2 and 6.104.1-2; Diodorus Siculus, 13.3–4. It is significant that when the Athenian fleet was just setting out for Sicily, Hermocrates proposed to the assembled Syracusans that they use Taras as a naval base (Thucydides, 6.34.4–6).

19. See Thucydides, 8.91.2.

20. On the chronology of these issues see especially Cahn, "Early Tarentine Chronology," pp. 59–71, and Kraay, *Archaic and Classical Greek Coins*, pp. 175, 203. Cahn dates the incuse coinage (including the type with the dolphin rider incuse) ca. 520–510, the first issue with the dolphin rider and hippocamp both in relief ca. 510–500, the first issue with a smaller flan ca. 500–490, the issue with wheel reverse ca. 490–480, the issue with a head on the reverse ca. 480–470, and the revival of the hippocamp reverse (alternating with the head) ca. 470–460. Kraay (p. 175) in large degree agrees with Cahn's chronology but, on the basis of a hoard buried in 450 at the earliest and containing examples of all these issues, decides later (p. 203) that this dating is approximately ten years too early. In "Caulonia and South Italian Problems" (p. 80) Kraay had felt that Taras did not begin coining until after 510 and made the point that the incuse fabric had never really become established there. On the basis of overstrikes on coins of Acragas, Ulla Westermark dates the wheel series to ca. 480–470 and the series with the head to after 470; see her article "Overstrikes of Taras on Didrachms of Acragas" in *Greek Numismatics and Archaeology: Essays in Honor of Margaret Thompson*, ed. Otto Mørkholm and Nancy M. Waggoner (Wetteren, Belgium, 1979), pp. 287–93. For staters with the dolphin rider incuse, see Ravel, *Collection... Vlasto*, nos. 62–69, for coins with the dolphin rider and the reverse type both in relief, nos. 73–161.

21. See Cook, *Zeus*, Vol. II, pp. 31–32, discussing H. Usener, "Keraunos," *Rheinisches Museum*, Vol. LX (1905). The association of Taras with a Iapygian town and river, of course, argues against this originally Dorian connotation.

22. See Cahn, "Early Tarentine Chronology," pp. 67–68.

23. See Eunice Burr Stebbins, *The Dolphin in the Literature and Art of Greece and Rome* (Menasha, Wisc., 1929), pp. 65–66, for discussion of these last two theories: The first is that of Franz Studniczka, *Kyrene* (1890); the other is that of Usener. Vlasto is aware that on some of the coins the dolphin rider is ithyphallic but suggests that this may be just a pun (*Taras Oikistes*, p. 134).

24. See Stazio, "Aspetti e Momenti," pp. 152–53. Vlasto (pp. 6–8) approves of Studniczka's preference for Phalanthus. Wuilleumier (pp. 36–37) points out that Taras's character as a Iapygian river god would not make the dolphin especially appropriate to him. Bérard, among other modern scholars, refers to the figure without comment as Phalanthus (*Colonisation Grecque*, p. 170, n. 5). Cahn also terms him Phalanthus but describes him as "assimilated with the Greek Pantheon as Poseidon's son" ("Early Tarentine Chronology," p. 68). On the other hand, Lacroix categorically identifies the figure as Taras the eponymous founder of the city, commenting that a historical founder (which he considers Phalanthus to be) did not appear on the coins of other cities of the Greek West, that he has his hands outstretched in joy at seeing the new territory which has been granted him by his father, and that the dolphin, instead of having rescued him from a shipwreck, has been charged with helping to realize the divine design by carrying the young Taras to this territory (*Monnaies et Colonisation*, pp. 90–91, 94–96).

25. See Wuilleumier, p. 38, and Cahn, p. 68.

26. See Cahn, p. 69.

27. For discussion see Arthur J. Evans, *The "Horsemen" of Tarentum* (London, 1889), pp. 2–3; Vlasto, p. 69; Wuilleumier, pp. 372, 480; and Cahn, p. 70.

28. For these coins see Ravel, nos. 162–257.

29. The identification was proposed by Raoul-Rochette in his "Essai sur la Numismatique Tarentine," *Mémoires de Numismatique et d'Antiquité* (Paris, 1840), pp. 197–256. Among other distinguished numismatists, L. Sambon followed Raoul-Rochette; see his *Recherches sur les Anciennes Monnaies de l'Italie Méridionale* (Naples, 1863; reprint ed., Bologna, 1967), p. 123 (but on pp. 112–13 Sambon refers to the figure simply as "personnage assis"). Evans in 1889 called the figure Demos (*"Horsemen,"* pp. 3–4), and even though he thought of Taras as another possibility, Taras on these coins would, in his view, have to be considered as representative of the democratic revolution (pp. 11–12, 32–33). Vlasto in 1922 (*Taras Oikistes*, pp. 2–5, 28–29) attacked the identification with the Demos, however, citing scholars from Barclay V. Head on (*Historia Numorum*, 1887) who questioned its validity. Although Wuilleumier did not relate the earliest appearance of the figure to the democratic revolution (since he dated the earliest appearance ca. 485 and dated the revolution ca. 467), and although he followed Vlasto in not identifying the seated figure as the Demos, he, like Vlasto himself (*Taras Oikistes*, p. 55–58), did associate the olive wreath that

bordered some of the later issues with this revolution (pp. 57, 177, 372–73). A political significance for at least some of these pieces retained enough seduction so that Cahn felt it necessary to state as late as 1968: "Neither the victories over the Messapians and Iapygians, nor the institution of democracy ... can be traced on coins. Coinage had its own law" (p. 73). Stazio in 1970 pronounced on the death of the Demos identification ("Aspetti e Momenti," p. 155).

30. Vlasto calls Taras "the eponymous founder or 'oekist' " (p. 4). Cahn (p. 71) objects to terming an eponymous hero an oecist; and certainly the oecist was Phalanthus. Kraay (*Archaic and Classical Greek Coins*, p. 175) agrees that although the seated Taras is "sometimes called an oecist," he is not one. Lacroix claims that the figure represents Taras not as eponymous founder but as heroized ancestor of the Tarentines (*Monnaies et Colonisation*, pp. 97–98), and this view has considerable attractions. Wuilleumier (p. 177, n. 2) identifies the figure as Phalanthus rather than Taras.

31. See Cahn, pp. 71–72; Stazio, p. 158; Kraay, *Archaic and Classical Greek Coins*, pp. 175–76; and Kraay, "Caulonia and South Italian Problems," p. 61, establishing that the staters with olive wreath border could not have been struck before ca. 445. Vlasto in 1922 had proposed 485 as a date for the first appearance of the seated figure, but he tentatively brought the terminal date for the figure down as far as 380 (pp. 11–13, 22, 28–29, 199–203). Sydney P. Noe in *The Coinage of Caulonia* (New York, 1958), p. 61, supports Vlasto's date of ca. 485 for the beginning of the type. Evans ("*Horsemen*," p. 4) had preferred 420 as a terminal date.

32. See Vlasto, p. 9; Cahn, pp. 71–72; and Kraay, *Archaic and Classical Greek Coins*, p. 175. In Cahn's view the distaff may also refer to some forgotten myth; the cantharus, to a Dionysiac aspect of Taras. Lacroix is not surprised that the figure holds so feminine an instrument, saying that it represents Taras as the bringer of the arts of civilization to his city (pp. 98–99).

33. See, for example, George Steinhauer, *Museum of Sparta* (Victoria, Spain, n.d.), p. 13 and figs. 42 and 43. The fact that the seated figure held a large cantharus in his earliest appearance on Tarentine coins strongly supports Lacroix's indentification of him as the heroized Taras.

34. See Herodotos, 6.38.

35. I am indebted largely to Vlasto's speculations on the chthonic nature of the seated Taras. See *Taras Oikistes*, pp. 8–9, 25–26, 40–41, 63, 178–79, 214, 225, 232–33.

36. Evans, "*Horsemen*," pp. 29–31, dates the earliest appearance of the horseman type ca. 450; Vlasto (pp. 109–10), ca. 460; Wuilleumier (p. 375), midcentury; Kraay (*Archaic and Classical Greek Coins*, pp. 176, 183), ca. 445/440. For the coins see Ravel, *Collection ... Vlasto*, nos. 297–348.

37. For these small coins and others see Ravel, nos. 155–61, 1105–1203, 1730–57.

# 4

# Syracuse
# and
# Archytas

There were barbarian takeovers in other parts of Italy. About 423, Sabellian peoples, the Lucanians, entered Capua near the west coast; and in 421 the Lucanians seized the Greek foundation of Cumae on the western shore close to Naples and sold many of the citizens into slavery. Before the end of the century the Lucanians also made the old Sybarite colony of Posidonia on the western littoral their victim. Greeks in southeastern Italy realized that their own cities would in time be imperiled by the Lucanian expansion; some of them, such as Croton, would in fact suffer badly. But for the moment Taras was spared the time to improve its industry and trade.

The traditional sympathy between the Dorian cities of Taras and Syracuse continued into the fourth century. In the early part of the century Taras had as its friend the strong Syracusan tyrant, Dionysius the Elder (406/5–376). Not satisfied with combating Carthage or with extending his power over much of Sicily, Dionysius worked to achieve political and economic control in southern Italy as well—and even, in fact, waged successful war against the Etruscans in the northwest and established trade relations with the Veneti on the Adriatic. About 392 a number of South Italiot Greek cities banded into a league directed mainly against the Lucanians; in so far as we know, Taras and Locri had no part in this league. In 390 Dionysius attacked Rhegium on the Italian side of the Strait of Messana; if he took it he would gain mastery of the strait itself. The Rhegians, with the help of the Greek cities belonging to the league, repulsed him; and he proceeded to ally himself with the Lucanian barbarians against his fellow Greeks. Locri was his friend and an important base of operations for him; since Taras was also his friend, Taras prospered while his Syracusan army and his Lucanian allies

Plate 13.   Silver stater, c. 380-1345 B.C.
Obv.: Naked horseman r.
on standing horse. 18 mm.

devastated the other Greeks. In 389/388 Dionysius crushed Thurii, just about destroyed Locri's neighbor Caulonia, ravaged Hipponium, moved the surviving citizens of Caulonia and Hipponium to Syracuse, and exacted a war indemnity from Rhegium. He had, however, won the gratitude and support of other Greek cities by his clemency after defeating their combined armies: he released the prisoners he had taken and did not even require ransom. In 387/386 he attacked Rhegium again, took it, and made slaves of the citizens too poor to pay the ransom demanded. In 379 he took and plundered Croton.

The extent to which Taras was actually controlled by Dionysius during this period is not ascertainable. With the Lucanians as his allies on the western side of the Italian peninsula, with Iapygians and Messapians on the eastern side as his allies also, with the Strait of Messana in his hands, with Locri looking out for his interests and inimical Greek cities severely debilitated, he must have exercised a great deal of authority both direct and indirect. Taras retained its independence and had his help; but Tarentine autonomy was surely qualified, much as the city flourished.

In 388, in the midst of the troubles in Italy, the Greek world rested from war to compete in the Olympic Games. Dionysius entered many four-horse chariots, symbols of his wealth, and provided pavilions of bright cloth interwoven with gold. He also dispatched professionals to the games to recite his own poems, of which he was proud. But the audience laughed at his poetry and rifled the pavilions. Some of his chariots bumped into others; some ran off course. After the games, the ship carrying his humiliated representatives back to Sicily was wrecked near Taras. Eventually the sailors succeeded in reaching Syracuse, where they said that Dionysius's poetry was so awful that it had caused the poor showing of the chariots and the wreck of the ship.[1] It is a rather safe guess that the Syracusan sailors had been helped after the shipwreck by their allies and fellow Dorians, the Tarentines. The Syracusans may

Plate 14.   Silver stater, c. 400 B.C.
Rev,: Dolphin rider r. At
1., ethnic retrograde. 20.5
mm.

have even tried out at Taras the sarcastic story about Dionysius's poetry. If they did, the Tarentine populace, not accustomed to tyrants, perhaps enjoyed this ridicule of the autocrat who was officially their friend. This is of course a tissue of conjecture, but in view of Taras's geographical position, importance as a port, and political relationship to Syracuse at the time, it is a conjecture that is tempting.

Dionysius died in 367, his strength having been sapped by two unsuccessful wars against Carthage. About this time Archytas was elected strategus at Taras. The city must have been at the apogee of its power. This was probably the period that Strabo was referring to when he said that Taras had the largest fleet in the Western Greek world and could put thirty thousand foot soldiers into the field, along with three thousand horsemen and one thousand cavalry commanders (6.3.4). Archytas, like Epaminondas at Thebes or Pericles at Athens, was a man who could personify the high point of a polis. He was an intellectual, and the ancient world seems to have admired his thought as well as his actions. Unfortunately, he is far less well recorded than his friend Plato or his admirer in the next generation, Aristotle. We are left with an impression of his excellence—little more.

Married, he owned many slaves and may therefore be assumed to have been rich. He liked to play with the sons of his slaves—not for sexual amusement, apparently, but just because he had the capacity to relax from the business of life with children.[2] We know hardly anything about the nature of slavery at Taras in the first half of the fourth century B.C.—not even whether the majority of slaves were fellow Greeks or barbarians. Whoever they were, Archytas seems to have been a kind taskmaster. An incident involving one of his slaves, recounted by both Cicero and Diodorus Siculus, suggests not only that he tried to avoid severity but that he was careful to control his passions so that he would not do things he might regret later. On a visit to his estate he saw that the slaves had carried out none of his orders. Fighting against his rage, he

Plate 15. Silver stater, c. 380-345 B.C. Obv.: Naked horseman crowning standing horse l.; beneath horse, Palladium. 18 mm.

told the man whom he had appointed overseer, "This is all your fault. I'd have you whipped to death if I weren't so angry."[3] In another story told by Cicero, Archytas is said to have spoken at length—really lectured—about the bad effects of lust.[4] Somewhat more doubtful is a remark on the necessity of friendship which Circero attributes to "Archytas, I think." Whoever the speaker was, he said that if a man could ascend into the sky and a get a near-hand view of the awe-inspiring glory of the stars, he would not be happy unless he had someone to whom he could talk about what he had seen.[5] Whether it was made by Archytas or not, the observation is certainly Greek.

Archytas was strategus at Taras seven times. The office was annual. It is thought that he succeeded himself without interruption and that his administration extended from about 367 to 360, but other administrations conceivably intervened. According to Diogenes Laertius the Tarentines made an exception for him: "the law excluded all others from even a second year of command."[6] An entente with Syracuse, now ruled by Dionysius the Younger, son of the great Dionysius, was evidently an important aspect of his government. He may even have provided Dionysius the Younger with bases in Apulia from which the Gauls, on Syracusan instigation, launched attacks against a developing and potentially dangerous Rome.[7] Once he resigned his office because of popular disapproval of his policies. Diogenes Laertius (8.82) does not particularize as to what had caused this reversal of feeling or reveal whether the resignation occurred in his last term of office, though presumably it did. All he says is that without Archytas to lead it, the Tarentine army immediately suffered a defeat.

As strategus, Archytas was commander in chief of the Tarentine military forces against enemies such as the Lucanian barbarians. The office was the highest in the state; Archytas could influence the civil policies of Taras as well as the military policies and could speak for the state in transactions with foreign powers—Syracuse, for instance. Scholars are fond of citing the strategus Dino, who, it may be remembered, declared that his fist was stronger than the wish of the people. We do not know whether Dino—if there ever was such a man—lived in the fifth century or the fourth, but as a political anecdote suggesting the authority of the strategus, the story is of some value in the absence of anything else.[8]

Pythagoreanism, which had of course arisen at Croton in the late sixth century, was centered at Taras by the fourth, and Archytas was a Pythagorean. The philosophy as an organized school was in its final stage. Archytas may have been its chief exponent at Taras. As a Pythagorean, he presumably valued aristocracy as the best form of government, may possibly have practiced vegetarianism because of the sect's belief that the consumption of dead flesh was an unclean habit, and certainly emphasized fields of learning to which harmony was important, such as music, mathematics, and physics. The theory that he applied Pythagorean principles of harmony to the government of Taras is very attractive but it is, unfortunately, no more than a theory. So is the idea that when Aristotle described Tarentine aristocrats as sharing their possessions with the poor, he was thinking of the administration of Archytas.[9]

The man apparently wrote a great deal, but most of his writing does not survive and passages sometimes attributed to him may not be by him at all. There are, for instance, fragments of a work *On Law* (*Peri Nomo kai Dikaiosynas*), possibly by Archytas, possibly produced as late as the first century A.D.[10] Whether Archytas wrote *On Law* or not, it was Pythagorean in outlook, relating law to harmony and advocating control of the passions as the source of virtue (one is reminded of Archytas's remark to the overseer as reported by Cicero); preferring aristocratic government to democratic and oligarchic or tyrannic governments as based on the highest excellence; conceiving of the citizens in general as frequently ignorant of what is best for them; considering the religious and moral concerns of legislation as more important than its practical concerns; stressing the necessity for public conscience and heartfelt custom if written laws are to work; advising punishment by shame as more effective than punishment by fine; valuing a simple, even strenuous existence and decrying a life of luxury; and defining the true magistrate as a man not only wise and powerful but law-abiding and humane.[11]

The work is in large degree idealistic, assuming a natural law which human law must approximate as nearly as possible. There is occasional mention of Sparta as exemplary in one respect or another—understandable enough if the treatise was actually produced in the Spartan colony of Taras, but also indicative of the admiration in which Sparta was held by so many fourth-century Greeks. The most we can say is that

Plate 16.    Silver stater, c. 400 B.C. Obv. of No. 14. Naked horseman on standing horse l., with shield.

*On Law* seems to have expressed ideas which Archytas would probably have endorsed.

Fragments of some mathematical and scientific writings, *Peri Mathematon*, are the only works attributed to Archytas which are likely to be genuinely his. From them, and from occasional allusions in other ancient authors, we can gain some idea of his contributions to these fields. He established the mathematical relationships underlying the diatonic scale (containing five whole tones and two semitones), the chromatic scale (proceeding entirely by semitones, in other words sharps, flats, and naturals), and the enharmonic scale (having the same pitch as in the tempered scale but differently noted, as G sharp/A flat). In mathematics he defined arithmetic proportion or progression, with equal intervals between the numbers (as 8/6/4/2); geometric proportion, in which the relationship of the first number to the second is in the same proportion as the relationship of the second number to the third (12/6/3 — 12 is 2 x 6 as 6 is 2 x 3); and harmonic proportion, in which the first number is larger than the second by the same fraction as that by which the second number is larger than the third (6/4/3, proceeding from right to left: 1/3 minus 1/4 = 1/12; 1/4 minus 1/6 = 1/12). Diogenes Laertius tells us that he discovered how to double the volume of a cube by using two split cylinders to determine the lengths of the edges of the doubled cube.[12] Like other Pythagoreans he probably also speculated on astronomy; and the remark on the glory of the stars with which Cicero somewhat doubtfully credits him may therefore have a factual origin.

But far-ranging as Archytas's thinking was, it must, like that of Archimedes a century and a half later, have been directed fairly often to some practical end. He was very much interested in mechanics. He created clever mechanical toys, such as a wooden dove capable of flight. He invented the screw and pulley.[13] Plato apparently considered his learning too practically oriented to have much philosophical siginificance. Plutarch explains that in Plato's view geometry is a spiritual

Plate 17.  Silver stater, c. 380-345
B.C. Obv.: Vaulting horse-
man l., holding shield with
l. hand, reins with r. 19
mm.

discipline derived from God the Divine Geometrician and helping a
man to rise above mundane matters and achieve "a complete purifi-
cation and a gradual deliverance from sense-perception." Archytas and
Plato's own pupil Eudoxus, Plato thought, tied geometry too closely to
the earth by doing such things as "setting out to remove the problem of
doubling the cube into the realm of instruments and mechanical devices, as if they were trying to find two mean proportionals not by the
use of reason but in whatever way would work."[14] Enraged at such a
debasement of geometry, Plato reproached Archytas very gravely.

Whether or not Plato ever did give Archytas a reprimand of this kind,
it is certain that the two learned men knew each other well. Evidently
they also admired each other's intellectual powers.

Plato could have met Archytas as early as his first visit to Syracuse,
about 388/387 B.C., two decades before Archytas became strategus at
Taras, as Plato's ship presumably made the stop at Taras as usual for
vessels coming from Greece. More likely, however, Plato and Archytas
did not meet until later—perhaps in 367, when the Athenian traveled to
Syracuse for the second time and when his ship would again have put in
at Taras on the way.[15] The story of Archytas now becomes involved with
the story of Plato at the Syracusan court.

Dionysius the Younger, who succeeded his father as tyrant of Syracuse in 367, had not been brought up in princely fashion. The father,
afraid that the son might try to seize the throne if he was groomed for it,
had had him poorly educated and had excluded him from affairs of
state. The young Dionysius had amused himself with debauchery and
with making little wagons and pieces of furniture out of wood. Now in
control at the age of thirty, he submitted for the moment to the counsels
of his uncle Dion, but he would soon throw off Dion's influence.

Apparently fairly intelligent, with pretensions to learning if not with
great talent, he wished to make his court an intellectual center on the

Plate 18.   Silver stater, c. 380-345 B.C. Rev.: Dolphin rider aiming trident at tunny. 19.5 mm. *ANS/SNG* Part I, No. 909. *Courtesy of the American Numismatic Society, New York.*

model of Athens itself. His uncle Dion, a follower of Plato, was by far the more capable of the two men as well as the more idealistic about government. It was largely because Dion held a position of such influence at Syracuse that Plato had decided to pay a second visit to the city, where the monarch expected him to gild its court with intellectual splendor.

Dionysius's accession to power, Plato's second visit to Syracuse, and Archytas's first term as strategus at Taras all occurred about 367/366. It may have been this early that Plato was instrumental in bringing about an entente between the new Syracusan monarch and the head of the Tarentine state, Syracuse's natural ally in any case.[16]

Plato had Dionysius study geometry and no doubt talked with him philosophically. But if he entertained any idea of turning the tyrant into a philosopher king, he soon gave it up. The young ruler, reveling in his new authority and devoted to extravagance and sensuous living, was a poor student of Platonism. Instead of ripening into a philosopher king, he acted on unreasonable fear and exiled Dion, of whom he was suspicious and jealous. Plato tried to persuade him to recall Dion, failed at this, and sailed back to Greece in disgust.

During the next few years Dionysius dealt with affairs of state in a rather more competent manner than might have been expected. He founded colonies in Apulia on the east coast of Italy to protect shipping against the piracy endemic in the area. He helped the Tarentines in a war which, under Archytas's leadership, they were waging against his father's old allies, the Lucanian barbarians. He sent Archytas a marvelous candelabrum with a light for every day of the year—a demonstration, perhaps, of the Syracusan's habitual magnificence.[17] Meanwhile he did not forget intellectual glitter. He gathered philosophers around him, and tried vainly to excel them at their own profession. He composed what purported to be a handbook of Platonic doctrine, and he carried on a campaign to bring Plato back to Syracuse. Although he distrusted Plato as the friend of Dion (still in exile), he realized how much the philosopher could contribute to his court's veneer of culture.

Plato did not want to come, but persuasion eventually proved too much for him. It was reported that Dionysius had now grown sincerely interested in philosophy. Dionysius persuaded Archytas, who was evidently paying a visit of state to the Syracusan court, to advocate Plato's return; and Archytas, who after all was Dionysius's ally, went so far as to vouch for the king's philosophic inclinations and to send a fellow Pythagorean or so to Athens to talk with Plato on the matter. The king himself wrote to Plato, urging another vist and implying that only if Plato was in Syracuse could Dion be forgiven. It was probably the hope of helping Dion that decided Plato. Of secondary importance was the possibility that the tyrant was finally ready for training in the idea of kingship. Dionysius dispatched a trireme to carry Plato to Sicily. The arrival of the famous Athenian, now in his upper sixties, must have been something of a triumph for the monarch.[18]

But the situation rapidly deteriorated. Opportunistic philosophers surrounding Dionysius, such as a pseudo-Socratic named Aristippus who catered to the king's love of pleasure, made life hard for Plato at court. Dionysius's attitude and policy toward Dion did not change, and the tyrant resented Plato's persistent support of his absent friend. He may even have suspected that Plato was conspiring to bring about a revolution. He moved Plato from the Syracusan acropolis to the citiadel, where the mercenary soldiers lived. These soldiers had been told that Plato was their enemy, and they were consequently his. The philosopher, by now a virtual prisoner in the mercenaries' quarters, was afraid that they would kill him.

And so he wrote to the only man who could save him—Dionysius's influential friend, Archytas. The Pythagorean, probably repentant over his own part in inducing the philosopher to make the trip west, sent to Syracuse a thirty-oared ship. It sailed on some diplomatic pretext, but the real purpose of the voyage was to rescue Plato. Aboard was a Tarentine named Lamiskos, friend of both Plato and Archytas. Lamiskos was to request the Syracusan tyrant—apparently in the name of the Tarentine strategus—to let the philosopher depart in peace.[19]

If Diogenes Laertius is to be believed, the vessel also carried a letter from Archytas to Dionysius requesting Plato's release. The letter is almost certainly as spurious as most other writings ascribed to Archytas, but part of it deserves to be quoted as reflecting the connotations which the salvation of Plato would acquire among the Greeks. Here was the duly elected Tarentine magistrate addressing the Sicilian autocrat in terms of heroic reprimand:

You will do well to remember the zeal with which you urged us all to secure

Plate 19.   Silver diobol, after 380 B.C. Obv.: Head of Athena l., wearing helmet decorated with Skylla. 13 mm.

Plate 20.   Rev. of No. 19. Heracles r. wrestling lion.

Plato's coming to Sicily, determined as you were to persuade him and to undertake, amongst other things, responsibility for his safety so long as he stayed with you and on his return. Remember this too, that you set great store by his coming, and from that time had more regard for him than for any of those at your court. If he has given you offense, it behoves you to behave with humanity and restore him to us unhurt. By so doing you will satisfy justice and at the same time put us under an obligation.[20]

If this is not by Archytas, one might wish that it was.

The mission succeeded. Dionysius, apparently unwilling to go against the wish of an important political friend—and probably glad for the chance to get rid of Plato anyway—allowed his guest to sail. Presumably the thirty-oared ship carried Plato to Taras, where he visited his friend and deliverer—a much closer approximation of the philosopher king than Dionysius.

Dealers in ancient coins are fond of calling the period from 380 to 345 the Age of Archytas. They derive the term from Sir Arthur Evan's invaluable piece of numismatic scholarship, *The "Horsemen" of Tarentum*.

Plate 21.  Silver diobol, after 380
B.C. Rev.: Heracles astride
lion, seizing him by tail.
11.5 mm.

Although Archytas was in office during only seven years of this period, the term is justified as denoting, roughly, the time when he was influential in Taras, intellectually if not politically, and the time when Taras perhaps enjoyed its greatest prosperity. It is numismatically justified because after 345 Taras started calling in mercenaries to help in its wars, and its coinage was then modified to reflect the presence of those mercenaries.

But during the latter part of the Age of Archytas some of the citizens must have sensed that a change was coming about. Archytas's resignation presumably occurred not long after the rescue of Plato in 361, and almost immediately the city suffered a severe military defeat.[21] During the next fifteen years or so, the barbarians would grow increasingly distressing. The ravages of Dionysius the Elder—his near-destruction of Caulonia, Hipponium, and Rhegium, his emasculation of Croton and Thurii—had left Taras with the oppresive honor of leading Hellenic civilization almost single-handed against the native hordes. Within the city, factions may have been causing more and more unrest; the rich and the poor perhaps found it increasingly difficult to unite against a common enemy.

Coinage, however, maintained a high standard of art throughout the period. On the basis of style alone it would be impossible to determine which issues came soon after 380, which ones were produced during Archytas's administration, and which were struck close to 345. Two styles are distinguishable: one compact and almost severe, the other more expansive and much more sophisticated, even elaborate. But this stylistic disparity may indicate two ateliers working simultaneously rather than a difference in time.[22]

The figure on horseback, which had been introduced as an alternate reverse type around the middle of the fifth century, and which had gradually replaced the seated figure, had been moved to the obverse of the silver staters during the last quarter of the century, and he would continue to hold this preeminent place for the two remaining centuries

Plate 22.   Silver diobol, c. 272-235 B.C. Obv.: Helmeted head of Athena 1. 11 mm.

of Tarentine coinage, with the reverse usually occupied by the dolphin rider[23] (Plate 13). Whoever the dolphin rider was originally supposed to be, after he was transferred to the reverse he was probably identified with Taras, son of Poseidon and eponymous hero—certainly by outsiders and very likely by Tarentines themselves. This was partly because the word "Taras" or its abbreviation "Tar" customarily appeared with him on the reverse—intended, perhaps, as no more than the ethnic of the city, but inevitably associated with the figure it accompanied[24] (Plate 14).

The horseman had not originated as a military type. Naked rather than protected by armor or even a shield, carrying a whip (if anything at all) rather than a spear, he was agnostic—an athlete representing games held at Taras. On the whole he retained his agnostic character in the fourth century—especially during the Age of Archytas, when he sometimes crowned his horse with the wreath of victory[25] (Plate 15). The question predictably arises, however: did the Tarentines, in addition to seeing in him an equestrian athlete, recognize him as Taras or Phalanthus? They may have; but surely, in a city that stressed horse races and other equestrain sports as much as Taras did, any official equivalence with either of these figures must easily have been forgotten by people looking at the naked cavalier as they had watched him recently in the games.

The association, however, was more than simply athletic: it was also chthonic. There was a hippic cult of the underworld at Taras; a chthonic sanctuary excavated in the latter part of the nineteenth century contained terra-cotta votive figures of horsemen similar to figures on the coins. On a number of the coins of this period the naked horseman was shown with a shield—sometimes simply riding, sometimes vaulting from his mount (Plates 16-17). These coins evidently picture a kind of athletic contest practiced by the Tarentines and by other Western Greeks, in which a man carrying a shield would jump from a fast-moving horse and run along beside it, possibly even remounting it

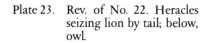

Plate 23. Rev. of No. 22. Heracles seizing lion by tail; below, owl.

before the end of the race. Depictions of such a figure among the terra-cottas in the chthonic sanctuary suggest that the race had to do with the cult of the dead, and that it was meant to honor deities of the under-world or heroized ancestors. Here, then, is another instance of the Tarentines' engrossment with the matter of death.[26]

Some of the horseman obverses in the first half of the first century, however, unlike earlier ones, must have had a military implication. The Tarentine cavalry perhaps even this early was earning a reputation as outstanding. When the rider wore a helmet and carried both shield and spear, he must have had reference to the city's wars against its barbaric enemies. As for the attributes accompanying the dolphin rider on the reverse, they suggest aspects of Tarentine life. On some coins, for example, the dolphin rider aims a trident at a cuttlefish or a tunny (mackerel); here the city seems to be advertising the fishing industry so important to its economy (Plate 18).

Taras had been issuing diobols, worth 1/6 of the stater or didrachm, sporadically since early in the fifth century. Most of the earliest diobols had a dolphin and a scallop shell on the obverse and a hippocamp on the reverse.[27] During the Age of Archytas the production of diobols was enormous.

At some time during this period—perhaps during Archytas's ad-ministration, although we do not know—the Tarentine-dominated colony of Heraclea became the seat of a league of Italiot Greek cities whose object was to resist the barbarians. Other cities in this confedera-tion were Croton, Thurii, Metapontum, and Elea; but it was fitting that since Taras was the leading member, Taras's satellite should be the political center.[28] Heraclea, which had been issuing diobols since about 433 (the time of its foundation), stepped up production of these coins after 380; but it was from Taras that most of the diobols came. They bore identical types at both cities—on the obverse the helmeted head of Athena, on the reverse Heracles wrestling with the Nemean lion—the huge beast, ravager of the Peloponnesian countryside, which could not be killed by any instrument made of stone, bronze, or iron, and which Heracles consequently had to strangle to death (Plates 19–21). Before they started appearing at Taras, both types had already appeared on Heraclean diobols.[29]

It is generally assumed that these numerous pieces, which were imitated by other cities in Greek Italy, were a federal coinage, issued under the auspices of the league for use by the cities in the league. While they must have represented the league and certainly circulated freely among those cities, however, they were perhaps only semi-official as a federal currency.[30] In any case they surely proved useful in minor commercial transactions for which the didrachms or staters would have been inconveniently large. During the fourth century, coins were employed in more and more transactions that, in an earlier period, would have been conducted through barter. The popularity of the diobol not only during the Age of Archytas but far beyond it testifies to its usefulness[31] (Plates 22–23).

Although the coin bore no inscription indicating that it represented a league of cities, its largely federal nature is suggested by the fact that both its obverse and reverse types brought to mind the city where the league had its seat. An Athena head was a familiar type on Heraclean money, and the reverse, of course, depicted the hero from whom the city took its name. The die engraver at Taras responsible for most of these diobols managed to include a remarkable amount of sharp detail in a very small area; tiny as they are, the coins are artistically distinguished. Such artists, like engravers of ring stones or seals, may have been myopes, whose defectively close vision was an advantage if not a necessity for near-microscopic work.[32] The Athena head is executed in high classical style. On the reverse Heracles and the lion are shown in a variety of positions—the hero, not yet triumphant, grappling with a still-ferocious beast in standing or kneeling posture, sitting on him, trying to choke him, fending off his jaws, grabbing his tail. The interesting suggestion has been made that the reverse was supposed to symbolize the struggle which the Greek cities were waging against brutal barbarism.[33] That struggle would become fiercer than ever in the second half of the fourth century, and Heracles would have to look around for help.

# Notes to Chapter 4

1. See Diodorus Siculus, 14.109.1–5.

2. See Aelian, *Varia Historia*, 7.14, and Athenaeus, *Deipnosophistai*, 12.519B.

3. Cicero, *De Re Publica*, 1.59–60. The story of Diodorus Siculus (10.7.4–8) is less full but to the same purpose.

4. Cicero, *De Senectute*, 12.39–41.

5. Cicero, *De Amicitia*, 23.88.

6. Diogenes Laertius, *Lives of the Eminent Philosophers*, 8.79, R. D. Hicks, trans. Loeb Classical Library, *Diogenes*, Vol. II, p. 393. See also Diogenes Laertius, 8.82, and Strabo, 6.3.4.

7. This is, at any rate, a conjecture of Arnold J. Toynbee. See his *Hannibal's Legacy: The Hannibalic War's Effects on Roman Life*, Vol. I (London, 1965). pp. 26–27.

8. For conjectures on the powers of the strategus see A. Delatte, *Essai sur la Politique Pythagoricien* (Liège and Paris, 1922), pp. 70–71; Arias, "Rapporti," pp. 242–43; Moretti, "Problemi," pp. 46–47; and Carter, *Sculpture*, p. 8. Arias considers the Tarentine "democracy" an extremely limited one, in great degree an oligarchy, with much power in the hands of the strategus.

9. For exploration of these conjectures see Wuilleumier, pp. 70, 181–82, 583–84; but see also Moretti, "Problemi," pp. 49–50. Delatte points out that in any case the sharing of wealth with the poor was a practical political act intended to further a harmonious relationship between the two classes and had no moral or religious implications (*Essai*, pp. 198, 259–60). The relevant passage in Aristotle is *Politics*, 6.3.1320B.

10. On the authenticity of these fragments see especially the discussions in Delatte, pp. 71–75, 121–24, and Wuilleumier, pp. 576–77. Delatte is too eager to ascribe doubtful passages to Archytas. Certain other fragments attributed to Archytas are available in *Iamblichus' Life of Pythagoras . . . Accompanied by Fragments of the Ethical Writings of Certain Pythagoreans in the Doric Dialect*, Thomas Taylor, trans. (London, 1926, reprint ed., 1965, from ed. of 1818), pp. 154–60, 174–76, 180–81. Most of these passages of loquacious philosophy are presumably from a work called *The Good and Happy Man*; others are presumably from *On Ethical Erudition* and *On Disciplines*. They are too questionable to deserve discussion.

11. For the fragments of *On Law* and illuminating discussions of them see Delatte, pp. 79–121.

12. Diogenes Laertius, 8.83. See an interesting explication of this discovery in Herbert Westren Turnbull, *The Great Mathematicians* (New York, 1962), p. 23. For an excellent discussion of Archytas's musical, mathematical, and scientific contributions see Wuilleumier, pp. 577–84.

13. This, at any rate, is accepted as fact by Mustilli, "Civiltà," p. 18.

14. Plutarch, *Moralia: Quaestiones Conviviales*, 18.718E, E. L. Minar, Jr., F. H. Sandbach, and W. C. Helmbold, trans. Loeb, *Moralia*, Vol. IX, pp. 121–23. See

also Plutarch, *Lives*, "Marcellus," 14.5–6.

15. Cicero mentions only that Plato visited Archytas; see *De Finibus*, 5.87. As Taylor remarks, "Plato and Archytas were already friends in 367 . . . and we do not know how much earlier" (A. E. Taylor, *Plato: The Man and His Work* [London, 1949], p. 542).

16. See Plato, *Epistulae* VII, 338C, and Plutarch, *Lives*, "Dion," 18. Wuilleumier (p. 71) places the entente this early, whereas R. G. Bury dates it anywhere between 367 and 362; see his Introduction to *Plato*, Loeb, Vol. VII, p. 387.

17. Athenaeus, 12.545A.

18. See Plutarch, "Dion," 18.2–3, and Plato, *Epistulae* VII, 338A-C, 339A-E.

19. See Plato, *Epistulae* VII, 349E-350B.

20. Diogenes Laertius, 3.22, R. D. Hicks, trans. Loeb, *Diogenes*, Vol. I, p. 297.

21. See Diogenes Laertius, 8.79.

22. Evans (*"Horsemen,"* pp. 47–49) thinks the styles reflect two workshops, Wuilleumier (pp. 376–77), that they represent earlier and later artistic standards. Even coins preceding the Age of Archytas issues, however—for instance, many of those with the seated figure on the reverse—can be called sophisticated in style. To designate one style as less advanced than the other may, at any rate, be to judge too subjectively if not too subtly.

23. Kraay, *Archaic and Classical Greek Coins*, pp. 183–84.

24. Like other scholars, Bérard (*Colonisation Grecque*, pp. 170–71, n. 7) and Cahn ("Early Tarentine Chronology," p. 68) point out that Aristotle himself was confused in this regard. The confusion must have been widespread.

25. On the horseman as agnostic, see especially Evans, pp. 12–14; Wuilleumier, p. 234; and Kraay, *Archaic and Classical Greek Coins*, p. 190. The fact that he sometimes carried a shield on issues of this perod may have been related to games as much as to military maneuvers.

26. For a descriptive list of the horseman didrachms of the Age of Archytas see Evans, pp. 57–63. Evans discusses the chthonic associations of the horseman, pp. 16–19. On leaping from a horse as an athletic event, see H. A. Harris, *Sport in Greece and Rome* (Ithaca, N.Y., 1972), pp. 158–59, 181. See also Agnes Baldwin Brett, *Catalogue of Greek Coins* (Boston: Museum of Fine Arts, 1955, reprint ed., New York, 1974), nos. 57 (Taras) and 299 (Motye in Sicily). Staters attributed by Ravel to the Age of Archytas occur in *Collection . . . Vlasto*, nos. 349–497.

27. See Ravel, nos. 1127–32. Ravel assigns to the years 380–334 rare diobols with a bridled horse on the obverse and a dolphin rider on the reverse (nos. 1225–31), or with a helmeted head of Athena on the obverse and Heracles seated on either a rock or a lion on the reverse (nos. 1232–35).

28. See Wuilleumier, pp. 62, 70–71.

29. For Tarentine diobols on which Heracles wrestles the lion, assigned by Ravel to the period 380–334, see Ravel, nos. 1236–1347. The type had started

appearing on Heraclean diobols around 410; see Kraay, *Archaic and Classical Greek Coins*, pp. 185-86.

30. Stazio ("Aspetti e Momenti," pp. 167-68) maintains that these diobols were not strictly a league coinage. Kraay (*Archaic and Classical Greek Coins*, p. 193) calls them "virtually a federal coinage."

31. Just as the reverse type continued to be Heracles battling the lion, the obverse type was usually the head of Athena in profile. For other obverse types—the head of Heracles facing or in profile, the head of Apollo Karneios— see Ravel, nos. 1348-57, 1359. For diobols assigned to the third century, still with the head of Athena and in the majority of cases still with the Heracles-and-lion reverse, see nos. 1360-1472.

32. For this very plausible theory see Leonard Gorelick and A. John Gwinnett, "Close Work Without Magnifying Lenses?" *Expedition*, vol. 23, no. 2 (Winter 1981), pp. 27-34, and no. 4 (Summer 1981), pp. 15-16.

33. This is the suggestion of Kraay, *Archaic and Classical Greek Coins*, p. 193.

# 5

# The Mercenaries

In the middle of the fourth century B.C., in spite of native peoples growling at the borders and (probably) some internal unrest as well, life in Taras must have been particularly pleasant. The city was rich. On its fertile territories it grew fruits and vegetables, herded sheep, and grazed horses. From its waters it took fish, prawns, and scallops. Its merchant fleet carried its products far and wide—the woolen textiles colored with its crimson dye, the multitudinous ceramic products. With the decline of the pottery industry in Athens, the Western Greeks had begun to manufacture pottery on their own in great quantity, and Taras was already one of the most prolific centers of production. Artistically the city was very active, as artisans decorated the clay vessels in an increasingly elaborate style, carved limestone sculptures, cast small figures in bronze, made gold rings and necklaces for the living and terra-cotta figurines for the dead. The prosperous enjoyed amenities imported as well as domestic, and at the theater the prosperous and the poor alike could watch the tragedies of Euripides. The expansion of the city illustrates its material success. Taras in the fourth century was comparable in size to Athens.

According to ancient authors, the good life had a softening effect. Strabo comments disapprovingly (and not very plausibly) on the Tarentines of this bountiful period: ". . . Because of their prosperity, luxury prevailed to such an extent that the public festivals celebrated among them every year were more in number than the days of the year." Polyaenus, writing in the second century A.D., relates an anecdote which, while probably untrue, suggests the reputation the Tarentines were acquiring. A Tarentine had gone into military service under Philip II of Macedon; but the king, made of sterner stuff than these Italians, stripped him of his command "because he used warm baths: saying, 'You seem a stranger to the Macedonian customs; which do not indulge the use of warm water even to a woman in child-bed.' " Whether or not the Tarentines were becoming self-indulgent, their city bred no more men like Archytas. Strabo remarks that devotion to luxury caused the Taretines to be "poorly governed."[1]

One proof of their poor government, in Strabo's moral opinion, was the fact that they called in foreign generals to conduct their wars. But Strabo was perhaps unduly scandalized. The employment of foreign mercenaries was of course by no means uncommon in the Greek world of the fourth century B.C. and was to become customary after Alexander the Great. Between 344 and 280 Taras would hire external help five times—a record which, for the period, is not extraordinary. Modern historians, like Strabo, may overestimate the significance of this record. No doubt an influential element in the city no longer felt fully confident that Taras could fight its own wars; no doubt there were people who would have preferred to let others fight while they themselves rolled in abundance and conducted business. (After all, Taras had the wealth to pay for its security.) But young Tarentine males still underwent military training and still took part in battle, sometimes alongside mercenaries brought by commanders from abroad, sometimes not. Besides, the pressure on Taras from native Italian peoples, ultimately from Rome, would grow more and more intense as the city took on its shoulders the championship of all Italiot Greeks. Taras's chronic requests for outside help do not imply that the city had given up on helping itself; they imply, rather, that its situation was becoming desperate.

Its appeal in 344 was to a general who was not even entirely foreign: Archidamus, another Dorian Greek, who had been one of the two kings in the Spartan dyarchy since about 360. The relationship between Taras and its mother city is largely a matter of guesswork. For a long time there could not have been much trade between them. Sparta's rigorous self-sufficiency, of course, discouraged commerce with the outside world in general; for that reason Sparta still used iron sticks instead of coins. But Tarentine sympathy for the Spartan/Syracusan side in the Peloponnesian War indicates the endurance of the Dorian tie. An appeal to Sparta was, on sentimental grounds, easy to justify.[2]

A little is known of Archidamus's career before his going to Italy. In 362, while his father, Agesilaus II, was still king, he fought bravely against the Thebans, who, having defeated Sparta drastically in 371, were attacking it again under the great Epaminondas. In 356, when the Phocians committed the outrage of seizing the sanctuary of Apollo at Delphi so that they could use Apollo's wealth to finance a war against Thebes, they did so with Archidamus's approval if not his actual help. According to Pausanias (3.10.3), he sacrilegiously took his share of the sacred money, and his wife, bribed by the Phocians, persuaded him to send Spartans in support of Phocis against Thebes. Later, however, he became disenchanted with the Phocians and withdrew his support from them.

When the Tarentine envoys came to Sparta with their request for help in 344, the Spartans put ships and men under Archidamus's direction. But he was diverted by another appeal—this time from Lyctus, a Cretan city which considered itself Dorian and which had been devastated by mercenaries hired by its unfriendly neighbor, the ancient city of Cnossus. How long it took Archidamus to settle the Cretan problem is not known, but when he had settled it, he proceeded to Italy.[3]   What he did in Italy is no clearer than when he got there. Diodorus Siculus says that Taras had called him in for assistance in a war against the Lucanians—bellicose, partly Hellenized members of the Sabellian group of Italic peoples, relatives of the Samnites who would cause such trouble for Rome, users of the Oscan tongue, extraordinarily energetic during this period, when they grew in power at the expense of others. (The territory now called after them stretched from the Bay of Taranto to Italy's western coast.) Plutarch, on the other hand, says that Archidamus fought the Messapians, the people of Illyrian provenance located south of Taras in Italy's heel.[4] He appears to have died in 338, fighting outside the walls of a settlement called Manduria in Messapian territory; so perhaps he dealt with the Lucanians first, then with the Messapians.[5] Pausanias, saying only that he was killed by "the foreigners," adds that his body was not buried: Apollo was still angry at him for his part in the robbing of Delphi (3.10.5).

In the ancient world, although coins came to be used more and more for commercial transactions, the immediate cause of their issue was frequently war: they were struck as soldiers' pay. This may have been true even of the earliest coins, Lydian electrum pieces of the late seventh century. Gold coins in particular seem to have been struck as payment for troops. It has been thought that during Archidamus's presence in Italy, Taras for the first time produced gold coins—staters, less often hemistaters, diobols, and obols—which must have been intended for the men that Archidamus had brought with him to help fight Taras's battles.

The gold issues were struck not on the local standard used for silver but on the Attic standard, which Philip of Macedon employed for the gold coins that he turned out in great quantity to finance his wars. The wide diffusion of Philip's coins helped to make the Attic standard for gold a truly international one, acceptable throughout the Greek world; Taras's gold coins of Attic weight would consequently be more useful to mercenary troops than would pieces whose weight adhered to a local standard only. No matter where their various wars or intervals of peace carried the mercenaries, they could spend their money easily, as soldiers like to do. For this reason, during the remainder of the fourth century,

Plate 24.  Gold stater, c. 344-338 B.C.? c. 320 B.C.? Female head r., wearing stephane and veil. Dolphin in front; behind, E. 17.5 mm. British Museum, *Guide to the Principal Coins of the Greeks* (1932, rpt. 1959), III. C. 7. *Courtesy of the British Museum.*

whenever Taras struck gold coins it would employ the Attic standard.[6]

The various denominations of gold coins which were apparently struck for Archidamus's soldiers all bore the veiled head of a goddess on the obverse—possibly Hera or Aphrodite, conceivably Posidon's wife, the sea goddess Amphitrite, perhaps Demeter or even Persephone, who, as queen of the dead, would have been especially appropriate for a city where chthonic religion was so prominent (Plate 24). Amphitrite would seem to be least suitable, since the eponymous founder Taras was Poseidon's son not by her but by the local nymph, Satyra. Whomever the head represented, it was in considerable degree modeled after the profiles of the nymph Arethusa, which had for a long time decorated Syracusan money and which were admired and more or less imitated at Locris Opuntii in Greece itself.

The reverse of at least one issue of gold staters, presumably the first, was more original. It showed Poseidon, identified by his trident, seated on a stool and inclining his head toward a boy who, standing in front of him, reached up his arms in a gesture of supplication (Plate 25). The boy was evidently Poseidon's son, Taras himself, and the scene has been interpreted as having an obvious meaning for Archidamus's men. The worship of Poseidon was rather prominent in the Peloponnesus, and the god on the coin could therefore be identified with Sparta, parent of Taras the city and its helper now against its enemies. To make the identification even clearer, above Poseidon shone a star. Stars were symbols of the Dioscuri, Castor and Pollux, originally pre-Dorian heroes, patrons of Sparta. A bow on Poseidon's lap indicated that Sparta's answer to its child's appeal was military.[7]

For the reverses of other gold staters the Tarentine moneyers had recourse to varieties of the horseman figure used on the obverse of the silver: the naked young rider crowning his horse with a wreath as if after a victory in the religiously oriented games celebrated by the city, or

Plate25. Rev. of No. 24. Poseidon
seated l.; boy r. with arms
raised.*Courtesy of the British
Museum.*

charging in the city's defense, armed with lances and a shield. (It may be
remembered that for a while after his introduction the horseman had
always been an athletic figure, never a military one. Now he was fre
quently a warrior.) On the reverses of hemistaters Taras rode the dolphin
as on silver coins. On diobols he knelt, holding a ball of wool and the
distaff that represented the city's textile industry. The small area of the
obol accommodated a cantharus.

The silver coins of the period were of course used for business within
the city and commercial transactions with other Greek cities in Italy.
Some of the staters bore on the obverse the victorious athlete crowning
his horse, with Nike or Victory flying up from behind to crown the
athlete, and others showed a groom, down on one knee under the horse,
examining a forefoot which had apparently been injured in the race
(Plate 26)—a delightful type, evidently inspired by staters of Ambracia
in Greece, on which a groom knelt to examine Pegasus's hoof. These
latter staters showed the dolphin rider on the reverse armed with a
shield, and in other ways too the silver coinage of this period sometimes
alluded to war. An especially fine stater, for instance, depicted on the
obverse the military horseman that occupied the reverse of some of the
gold—charging, lancing downward at some enemy not shown, carrying
two spare lances and a shield (Plate 27). On the reverse of this coin the
dolphin rider, possibly with head bowed in grief, contemplated a crested
helmet which he held in one hand. On either side of him shone a star—
again representing the Dioscuri, whose cult was vigorous at Taras as at
Sparta[8] (Plate 28).

The silver staters carry such letters as Ϝ, ϜA, M, Φ, KA, ΦI, AP, or
API. Letters also occur on the gold coins. These are probably the abbreviated signatures of magistrates responsible for particular issues.[9]

In the absence of dates or of explicit political references on ancient
coins—and even the scene of Poseidon and young Taras on the gold
staters cannot really be called explicit—numismatists can resort to

Plate 26. Silver stater, c. 344-338 B.C.? after 330 B.C.? Obv.: Nude horseman r.; groom examining horse's forefoot. 19 mm. *ANS/SNG* Part I, No. 962. *Courtesy of the American Numismatic Society, New York.*

various criteria in trying to determine a date for a certain issue. The style of the engraving is perhaps the most dubious criterion. Style may not change much for a considerable period. Besides, the new artistic principles of a cultural capital such as Athens—the esthetics of sculpture, for example—might or might not be reflected fairly early in the coin dies of a more "provincial" area. Conversely, the die engravers in a "provincial" city might be more imaginative, even more eccentric, than those working for a metropolis cautious about altering the traditional designs that had helped to make its coinage widely accepted and trusted. Athens itself evidently required the engravers of its dies to retain the so-called Archaic eye (facing eye in the side view of a face) long after other artists at Athens, as well as engravers of coin dies in cities such as Syracuse, had abandoned it.

Political events that would have affected the coinage of a certain city can be very useful: if we know that a city was destroyed or at any rate taken over by an enemy in a particular year, it is a fairly safe assumption that the city's coinage stopped or at least changed drastically in that year. This of course still leaves the *terminus a quo* up in the air.. And political events less final than the conquest of a city—even a drastic change in the form of government—may be more misleading than anything else, seducing a numismatist into false assumptions. The change to a democracy at Taras in 473 is an example of this.

Hoard burial has considerable value. If it can be established that a hoard must have been buried prior to a certain date (and this is not always easy), all the coins in it must obviously have been struck sometime before that date. Coins which, on the basis of previous knowledge, one might have expected to find in the hoard but are noticeably lacking were presumably struck after.

The signatures that occur on many coins, often in abbreviation, are helpful. Two coins with the same signatures must be closely related in time even if their designs, their denominations, and the metals of which they are composed are different.

Die linkage is extremely important in establishing sequence. Suppose obverse die *A* was used with reverse dies *a* and *b*, and obverse die *B* was used with reverse dies *b* and *c*. Then, if obverse die *A* shows wear or a worsening die break with reverse die *b* and if obverse die *B* shows wear or a worsening die break with reverse die *c*, the sequence must be *Aa*, *Ab*, *Bb*, *Bc*.

Overstrikes are also very significant. In the ancient world it was not unusual for one city, perhaps without an adequate supply of silver on hand, to overstrike its own devices on silver coins of another city. If the date of the coin underneath can be ascertained, the date of the over- strike can at least be approximated.

All of this is a gross oversimplification of a study which is still far from the exactitude of a science. There are perhaps few areas of intellectual endeavor whose pronouncements are more open to qualification and revision than ancient numismatics, especially Greek numismatics.

Using two of the above criteria—signatures and overstrikes—the distinguished numismatist G. K. Jenkins has recently undermined the structure of issues traditionally assigned to the period of Archidamus.[10] The generally accepted sequence of silver issues within this coinage—a sequence for which Sir Arthur Evans is responsible—is, he says, sub- stantially correct. But the gold staters and smaller gold denominations, he points out, carry abbreviated signatures ($\Phi$, $\vdash$, M, K,) similar to signatures on silver staters (in other words, didrachms) placed late in the sequence, and this would suggest that the gold too belongs late in the sequence. There are, however, instances of silver staters both early and late in the sequence that have been overstruck on staters (didrachms) of Corinth: one with the obverse depicting a young rider crowning his horse and crowned in turn by a flying Victory; one whose obverse shows a groom picking a pebble out of the horse's hoof (both of these early in the series); and one with a boy on the obverse crowned by Victory as he rides a prancing horse which another boy, standing in front, embraces (rather late in the series). The Corinthian didrachms involved are at present believed to have been struck sometime between 340 and 330. If this dating is right, and if we allow a few years for circulation of the Cor- inthian coins before they got to Italy, the overstrikings at Taras probably did not occur until 330 or after. The issues late in the Archidamus sequence may not have been struck until around 320, and the gold coins bearing similar signatures were probably struck about the same time. In other words, none of these gold or silver coins traditionally assigned to the period of Archidamus, who died about 338, could really date from that period. Jenkins even doubts that on the reverse of the gold staters a

Plate 27.   Silver stater, c. 344-334 B.C.? after 330 B.C.? Obv.: Horseman charging l., lancing downward, equipped with two spare lances and shield. Beneath horse, ΚΑΛ. 21 mm.

bow is lying on Poseidon's lap. What sometimes looks like a bow is, in his opinion, just a fold of drapery, not a symbol of war.

Jenkins's whole thesis, of course, collapses if the dating of the underlying Corinthian coins to approximately 340/330 proves to be wrong. At present, however, it is a very appealing argument. The Poseidon-and-Taras scene on the gold staters is certainly explicable as Poseidon granting the city of Taras to Taras, his son, without any reference to Sparta.[11] As for the stars of the Dioscuri that occur on some of the coins of this group, they need not refer to Sparta either, since the cult of the Dioscuri flourished at Taras as well as at the mother city.

About 334, four years after the death of Archidamus, Taras called on King Alexander the Molossian for help against the Messapians of the heel of Italy and the Lucanians. This particular Alexander was the brother of Olympias, sorceress wife of Philip of Macedon. Philip had put him on the throne in Epirus, the mountainous land across the Ionian Sea from Italy. Alexander was ambitious to make Epirus an important power, and to that end he married, late in 336, his niece Cleopatra, daughter of Olympias and Philip. He was now allied to the Macedonian royal house through his wife as well as his sister.[12]

His nephew, brother-in-law, and namesake Alexander, Cleopatra's brother and Olympias's son, had become king in Macedon on the assassination of his father, Philip, at the Molossian's wedding to Cleopatra. The young Alexander, of whom much had been expected since his boyhood, was already making a name for himself throughout Greece. In 334, the year when the uncle sailed to Italy, the nephew would cross to Asia on the whirlwind course of conquest which would establish his divinity and earn him the title "the Great."

According to the Roman Aulus Gellius, who wrote in the mid-second century A.D., the Molossian king, en route to Italy to fight the Romans,

Plate 28.   Rev. of No. 27. Dolphin rider r. carrying helmet; star on each side. Beneath dolphin, API.

said that he was going against the Romans as a nation of men, but the Macedonian was going against the Persians as one of women.    But this ungenerous remark was surely never made, the Molossian monarch probably had no intention of engaging the Roman republic in war; as a matter of fact, he entered into a treaty with Rome.[14] Writing in the days of Rome's strength, Aulus Gellius no doubt found the great empire convenient for carrying out a neat literary parallel: two men named Alexander, nephew and uncle, one heading east for conquest and the other heading west, one opposed to a vast Oriental monarchy, the other opposed to the rising Occidental power.

The Molossian's jealousy of the Macedonian's reputation may have been overstressed by modern scholars as well as by Aulus Gellius. It is perhaps too tempting to apply hindsight: to look at the spectacular progress of Alexander the Great from 334 on and assume that his uncle must have been tremendously envious. There is no doubt,   however, that whether or not the Molossian burned to surpass his nephew in conquest, it was personal ambition that prompted him to grant the Tarentine request for help. He seems to have reasoned, even from the beginning, that once he was in Italy he could create an empire for himself there. Helping the Tarentines was reduced to a pretext.

We do not know much more about Alexander's Italian campaigns than we do about Archidamus's. Presumably Alexander fought the Messapians, traditional enemies of Taras; he doubtless also took on the Lucanians and their relatives the Samnites, enemies of Rome, as well as the Bruttians, who, from the very bottom of Italy's heel, were exploding against the Greek cities. He seems to have defeated a combined army of Lucanians and Samnites in a great battle near Posidonia and, as mentioned before, to have concluded a treaty with Rome. Livy, not an extraordinarily reliable source, credits Alexander with recapturing Heraclea from Lucanian conquerors, taking the Apulian town of Sipontum, seizing Consentia and probably Terina from the Bruttians, and capturing other towns in Lucanian and Messapian territory.[15] Whatever he may have done, he must have been more successful than Archidamus. Presumably he proceeded from the eastern part of southern Italy toward the western coast, toward Posidonia; and presumably his western progress necessitated the treaty with Rome.

Alexander's ambitions and his victories, however, had ruptured relations with his employer. He was not content to subordinate his aims to the wishes of Taras; and the Tarentines resented his use of their appeal as a device to further his private dream of empire. When he began taking steps to transfer the seat of the anti-barbarian league from Tarentine-dominated Heraclea to Thurii, all pretense of amity between himself and the Tarentines must have vanished.

In the short view, Alexander had materially helped the Italiot Greeks by coping with the barbarians as the Greeks by themselves surely could not have done. But, in the long run, his break with Taras had also aggravated the situation by stirring up mutual animosities among the Hellenic cities—animosities which would have to be suppressed if the Hellenes were ever to win out against the native peoples. The less powerful Italiot Greek states, such as Metapontum or Thurii itself, had been obliged to look to Taras for leadership against the barbarians even though they might be jealous of its power. Alexander's split with Taras provided them with a rallying point—himself—and with the hope that they would not need Taras any longer..

It was therefore perhaps fortunate for Greek unity that he died soon after, probably in the autumn of 331.[16] His empire, just before his death, was by no means secure: the Lucanians and Bruttians had joined together against him. Even Lucanian exiles, who had apparently been fighting on his side, now thought of returning to their own people. They asked their countrymen to take them back if they could deliver Alexander's body, quick or dead. It had been raining insistently, and the rivers of southern Italy were swollen. The Lucanians had surrounded the part of Alexander's army commanded by the king himself; but Alexander broke through the blockade with his troops, personally killed the Lucanian ruler, and prepared to plunge into a river where the bridge had been washed away. Livy tells us with delight, and probably without foundation in fact, that the oracle of Zeus at Dodona in Epirus had warned Alexander to beware of the city of Pandosia and the waters of the Acheron. There were a Pandosia and an Acheron in Epirus, and it was partly to get away from them, Livy says, that Alexander had come to Italy. But he was now near the Italian city of Pandosia and the river he was about to cross was called—not quite the Acheron, but the Acheros. Alexander heard a soldier cry out the river's name. He paused, afraid.

One of his attendants remarked that the river had to be crossed—there was no other way. Seated on his horse, the king entered the water. He had almost reached the other side when a Lucanian exile threw a javelin. Alexander fell into the river, dead. His body floated downstream, and the Lucanians fished it out.

What happened to it, in Livy's account, is as dramatic as its death. The Lucanians cut it in half at the waist. They sent one half—Livy does not say which one—to the city of Consentia, in the territory of the Bruttians toward the western side of Italy's toe. But they kept the other half to have fun with, setting it up as a target and throwing javelins and stones at it. A Lucanian woman, instead of contentedly watching it deteriorate under this barbaric vengeance, rushed forward to stop the proceedings. She shouted that she hoped to use the remains to ransom her husband and sons, prisoners of the Greeks. Obviously she would have a hard time doing this if there were nothing left except a bloody mess. Her countrymen ended their sport.

Livy does not inform us whether her husband and sons were ever ransomed. The mutilated half of the corpse was taken to Consentia, where, under the woman's supervision, the body was cremated. The bones were then given to the Greeks at Metapontum. They were shipped across the Ionian Sea to Epirus and eventually reached the king's widow Cleopatra, sister of Alexander the Great, and the dead man's own sister, Olympias, mother of Alexander the Great. In such a manner did the second mercenary helper of Taras come home.

If Jenkins is right, some of the coins discussed in connection with Archidamus were of course struck even later than Alexander the Molossian. Silver staters or didrachms which have as a symbol in the reverse field an eagle with folded wings are perhaps most likely to have been struck during Alexander's presence. The bird of Zeus was an Epirot symbol, associated with the oracle of Zeus at Dodona, which, in Livy's account, had warned Alexander against the city named Pandosia and the river called Acheron. It had occurred on Molossian coinage immediately preceding Alexander, and he himself had put it on his bronze.[17]

The horseman lancing downward was, as might be expected, a frequent obverse type on coinage struck at Taras under Alexander the Molossian—coinage of military reference (Plate 29). An interesting variant of the dolphin rider on the reverse, however, was his appearance as a child inclining definitely to fat (Plate 30). This unhandsome representative of the city was apparently supposed to be Taras in his aspect as Iacchos, son of the chthonic Dionysus and of Persephone, goddess of the underworld. Similar figures of chubby children, made of terra-cotta,

Plate 29.   Silver stater, c. 334-331 B.C.
Obv.: Horseman charging
r., lancing downward,
equipped with spare shields
and lances. Beneath horse,
ΣΙΜ. 19.5 mm.

were deposited in Tarentine tombs. This coin type is, then, another instance of the Tarentine preoccupation with death, or rather with the afterlife.[18]

Tarentine gold staters and half-staters, perhaps to be identified as struck during the period of Alexander the Molossian, bore on the reverse the Molossian symbol of the thunderbolt, Zeus's weapon as the eagle was his bird. The pieces had on the obverse the head of a goddess or (on some of the staters) that of Heracles. The reverse of the half-staters showed the dolphin rider; of the staters, Taras holding a trident and driving a biga or two-horse chariot, or the horseman equipped for action with javelin and shield and spearing downward. On the obverse of third-staters appeared the head of Athena in a Corinthian helmet, perhaps with reference to the Italiot league at Heraclea. Taras again drove his chariot across the reverse. Smaller gold had the head of Helius on the obverse and the thunderbolt as principal reverse type.[19]

But in addition to these Tarentine coins, Alexander had coins minted in his own name in Italy, perhaps to pay his troops but also for distribution throughout the southern part of the peninsula as he expanded his holdings there. Before coming to Italy he had already struck silver staters bearing the oak-crowned head of Zeus on the obverse, a thunderbolt and (as symbol) the tiny head of an eagle on the reverse. Engravers located mainly at Taras, perhaps also at other cities in his new realm such as Metapontum, now produced obverse dies for both gold and silver coins (staters and half-staters) repeating the Zeus head, reverse dies repeating the thunderbolt; and Croton may have struck bronze coins with the eagle and thunderbolt types. The eagle with folded wings appeared as a symbol on his silver coinage. The smaller issues (gold obols, silver diobols) used the thunderbolt as reverse type and had the facing head of Helius on the obverse, as on small coins struck in the name of Taras. The reverses all bore inscriptions identifying the money as Alexander's, not Taras's.[20]

Plate 30.  Silver stater. Rev. of No. 29.
Dolphin, rider l., carrying
distaff; eagle in l. field,
waves below. Beneath dol-
phin, ΦΙ.

The political situation in the two or three decades following the death of Alexander the Molossian was one of shifting alignments, confusion, perhaps even indirection. One factor that emerges clearly from it, however, is the growing tension between Taras and Rome.[21] Taras was now menaced not only by the continued hostility of its barbarian neighbors but by the economic competition of the Roman state—a state which, in Hellenic pride, Tarentines may not have considered greatly different from the barbarians themselves. As the richest and most powerful Greek foundation on Italian soil, Taras watched and feared the expansion of the republic on the Tiber.

The Lucanians and Apulians allied themselves with Rome, under-taking to help it against the Samnites. Meanwhile the Romans besieged the small Greek city of Palaeopolis, a suburb of Naples. The Palaeopoli-tans had been guilty of unfriendly acts against Romans living in the surrounding region of Campania. But the Tarentines, worried about Roman encroachment on the partly Greek-settled Campania, where Taras had trading interests, had promised to help Palaeopolis. The Palaeopolitan leaders, however, seeing their city suffer under siege, decided to surrender to Rome. The Tarentines, angry at Palaeopolis for what they considered a betrayal and shocked at the Lucanians and Apulians for befriending Rome, apparently resorted to trickery. Livy. at any rate, says that they paid some young Lucanians to lash one another's bodies and then claim that the Romans had committed this outrage. According to Livy,. the Lucanian people were temporarily deceived by the story and broke their alliance with Rome.[22]

Almost inevitably the war against Palaeopolis had involved the ad-joining city of Naples. According to Dionysius of Halicarnassus, the Samnites sent men to help Naples but the Neapolitans did not feel comfortable with these barbarian allies and thought about making peace with the Romans on Roman terms. Taras immediately sent

Plate 31.    Gold stater, c. 315-314 B.C. Obv.: Head of a goddess r., wearing earring and necklace; dolphin in front. Under neck truncation, KOΙ/. 16 mm. *ANS/SNG* Part I, No. 1031. *Courtesy of the American Numismatic Society, New York.*

envoys, who promised Naples a fleet if it would carry on the war. But Taras's diplomacy was unsuccessful. Naples became a Roman federate in 327, and the Tarentines saw their sphere of economic influence impaired.[23]

About 325 the Syracusan democrat Agathocles, exiled from his city in his middle thirties because of his opposition to its tyrants, came to southern Italy. There, with a band of adherents, he led the life of a military adventurer, taking advantage of whatever wars offered themselves (in Bruttium, apparently), gaining the tactical experience that would prove useful to him later. For a while he hired himself out to Taras. But the Tarentines, probably remembering their recent troubles with Alexander the Molossian and suspecting that Agathocles was also just using them for his own ambitious ends, soon dismissed their third mercenary captain.[24]

Meanwhile the Roman problem had not diminished—nor would it. Rome was embroiled with the Samnites in Apulia, the part of Italy starting just north of Taras and continuing on up the eastern side of the peninsula. Badly defeated at the Caudine Forks in 321, the resilient Romans prosecuted the war just the same. They were too close to Taras for comfort. Just as the Neapolitan peace with Rome several years earlier threatened Tarentine interests on the western coast in Campania, the Roman troops in Apulia threatened Tarentine interests in that area. Again Taras tried diplomacy, and again Taras failed. About 320 it sent ambassadors to the Roman camp to suggest that the republic and the Samnites make peace. The envoys even warned the Romans that Taras itself would go to war against whichever side did not opt for peace. But the Roman consuls, who had examined the entrails of a sacrifice and had consulted the sacred chickens, answered that the omens favored war. The consul Lucius Papirius Cursor dismissed the Tarentines "with exclamations on the folly of a nation which, powerless to manage its own affairs, because of domestic strife and discord,

Plate 32.   Rev. of No. 31. Dioskouroi
mounted l. Above, ΔΙΟΣ-
ΚΟΡΟΙ. In exergue, ΣΑ.
*Courtesy of the American Nu-*
*mismatic Society, New York*

presumed to lay down the limits of peace and war for others."[25] Rome
made the town of Luceria in northern Apulia a permanent military base,
the war continued (interrupted by a truce in 318-16), and Tarentine influence in Apulia was jeopardized.

Papirius's reference to "domestic strife and discord" at Taras is of
course the invention of Livy, patriotically denigrating Rome's enemies
for the delight of Roman readers. But it may reflect an actual situation.
The probability that civil dissension troubled Taras after the period of
Archytas has already been mentioned. There were a land-based aristocratic party and a democratic party composed of fishermen, farmers,
other workers; and perhaps their ideological disagreements, aggravated
by the Roman menace and the barbarian menace and the insincerity of
the mercenary chieftains, had by this time escalated to acrimony. The
chronic question of whether to call on mercenary help surely generated
discord. It was perhaps the democrats who had favored hiring Agathocles
since Agathocles was a democrat himself, driven off by the Syracusan tyrants; and it was perhaps the aristocrats who had favored his dismissal.

Agathocles had done well since then. In 317 he himself had become
tyrant of Syracuse, and he wished to bring as much of Sicily as possible
under his control. About 315/314 the Sicilian cities of Acragas, Gela,
and Messana, urged on by exiled Syracusans who were enemies of
Agathocles, decided to go to war against him and, like Taras, invited a
foreign mercenary to lead their troops—Acrotatus, son of a Spartan
king. On the way to Sicily, Acrotatus stopped at Taras and tried to
persuade the Tarentines to help him in the coming conflict. The Tarentines debated the matter. An appeal from a Spartan was of course hard to
resist. Taras decided to contribute twenty ships to Acrotatus's forces.[26]

The decision came to nothing. Acrotatus sailed on to Sicily while the
Tarentines were still getting the fleet ready, and in Sicily he lived pleas-
urably and expensively, had his chief Syracusan ally killed, and in

general alienated the people who had asked him to come. His former friends eventually tried to stone him, but he escaped in the dark and made his way back to Greece. The Tarentines, who had dispatched the twenty ships by this time, recalled them.

The curious aspect of the matter, however, is the reversal of roles. Until the recall of the fleet, Taras was helping a mercenary; the city itself was answering an appeal for military aid. It must have felt strong enough to do so—or at least the prevailing party must have felt that it was strong enough. We do not know how the Tarentines expected to benefit by the arrangement with Acrotatus, aside from earning the sentimental satisfaction of granting assistance to a prince of Sparta. But Livy's implication that Taras was too ridiculously weak to be taken seriously by the Romans—"powerless to manage its own affairs," as he has the consul Papirius say—loses credibility in the light of the Acrotatus affair. Taras realized it was beset by enemies; but the city was not "powerless," for internal reasons or others.

The designs for Tarentine silver and gold in the latter part of the fourth century may occasionally lack the strength of earlier designs, but in the musculature of the figures, the variety of poses attempted, and the imitation of action, they are among the most distinguished types produced in the Greek West. The head of a goddess on some of the gold staters traditionally attributed to the period of Acrotatus's expedition, with one or two dolphins in the field as on coins of Syracuse, was of especially lovely style (Plate 31). Other gold staters had a noble head of Heracles wearing the mane of the lion he had killed. Taras rode the two-horse chariot on the reverses of staters with the Heracles head. Reverses of the other staters depicted the Dioscuri, nude and mounted on magnificent horses—the two brothers riding side by side, one of them crowning his steed—an obvious reference to Sparta, center of their cult and home of Acrotatus[27] (Plate 32). On the most remarkable silver didrachm, and one of the most beautiful issues, the dolphin rider not only carried a palm branch in his left hand, suggesting the peace that comes with victory, but had his right hand outstretched, as if he was greeting somebody (Plate 33). The horseman on the obverse of this coin raised his right hand, again as if in salutation (Plate 34). It is probable that both the dolphin rider (by this time surely identified with Taras) and the horseman were welcoming Acrotatus to Italy. The letters on the reverse—ΣΥΜ—may stand for an official but may also be an abbreviation of ΣΥΜΜΑΧΙΚΟΝ and stand for the alliance into which Taras had entered to defeat the Syracusan tyrant.[28]

After Acrotatus's fiasco the Tarentines apparently did well enough by themselves for a decade or so. Meanwhile Rome handed the Samnites a crushing defeat in 304, and in the same year Agathocles made himself king at Syracuse. In 303 Taras turned once more to Sparta for help against the Lucanians. This time the hired general was Cleonymus, younger brother of Acrotatus. Fierce, violent, autocratic, he had been excluded from the Spartan throne in favor of a nephew. He was as ambitious as his brother and, like Acrotatus, saw in the appeal from Taras a chance to improve his fortunes.

Cleonymus came to Taras with 3,000 mercenaries and proceeded to gather a greater force: about 5,000 more mercenaries, perhaps 20,000 Tarentine citizens as foot soldiers, and 2,000 Tarentines as cavalry. These figures, incidentally, illustrate the fact that even when Taras employed a foreigner as military chief, the city itself could still expect to do much of the fighting; the charge of softness was to that degree unmerited. The Messapians rallied to Cleonymus, as did South Italiot Greeks from cities other than Taras. With this formidable army he seems to have intimidated the Lucanians into a treaty of peace with the Tarentines. The only South Italians who did not come over to him were the citizens of Metapontum, still a flourishing place if one can judge from its abundant coinage. Cleonymus sent the Lucanians against Metapontum, attacked the city at the same time with his own troops, entered it as a forceful friend, and, according to Diodorus Siculus, demonstrated his authority by demanding over 600 talents of silver and, as hostages, 200 well-born girls with whom he lived in luxury. He thought of invading Sicily in imitation of his brother and defeating Agathocles in his new kingship, but for the present he satisfied himself with sailing to the island of Corcyra (now Corfu), on the eastern side of the Ionian Sea twelve miles off the coast of Epirus, and taking possession of it. From Corcyra he could dominate Taras's trade routes with the Illyrian coast and with Greece, and he could also lend ships to the Iapygians and Peucetians for piratical actions whose profits he would share. In addition he had a base for future mercenary/military operations in Greece. It may have been during Cleonymus's sojourn in Italy that the Romans, intimidated like the Lucanians, agreed to a treaty favorable to Taras, which stipulated that they would not sail their ships north of the Lacinium Promontory. This made the waters north of the cape, specifically the present Gulf of Taranto, Tarentine territory, free from disturbance by Roman vessels.[29]

As Cleonymus might have expected, the Tarentines and the Lucanians took advantage of his absence in Corcyra to revolt against his authority. He returned to Italy and, if we can believe Livy, seized an otherwise unknown town called Thuriae (not Thurii) in the country of the Sallentini in the peninsula's heel. But the Romans, according to Livy, defeated

Plate 33.  Silver stater, c. 334-330 B.C. or later. Rev.: dolphin rider with r. hand outstretched, carrying palm branch in l. hand; behind, helmet. Beneath dolphin, ΣΥΜ. 20 mm.

him and drove him back to his ships. Livy may actually be crediting Rome with a victory won by the Lucanians, the Tarentines, or both. If Rome did in fact defeat Cleonymus at Thuriae, the republic was helping the Tarentines against the former employee who was now their enemy. Rome may have felt that this was a wise thing to do—that as a Greek who wished to establish dominion in southern Italy, Cleonymus threatened Roman interests more than the Tarentines did. In any case, Cleonymus and his fleet withdrew up the Adriatic to the country of the Veneti, where in later years would rise the city of Venice.[30]

The reaction against Cleonymus's authority brings up the question of just what authority Taras's mercenary generals did have and, beyond that, what the whole relationship was between the city and its foreign helpers. We possess very little information to apply to these questions, and the answers that may work for one general do not necessarily work for the others.

Although it is usually assumed that all the mercenary commanders were hired—that money was paid for their services—even this assumption may not be justified in all cases. There may have been other forms of compensation instead of money or in addition to it. Diodorus Siculus, it is true, uses the term "mercenaries," which must imply money, for Archidamus's soldiers, and he says about Agathocles: "While among the Tarentines he was enrolled in the ranks of the mercenaries." In connection with Cleonymus, he remarks that the "Tarentines sent money and ships" (apparently to transport the Spartan's troops to Italy).[31] Nonfinancial arrangements are not mentioned, but that does not mean that there were none. The territorial ambitions of Alexander the Molossian make it possible that his agreement with Taras was more sophisticated than a simple money deal. It may have included political provisions, for instance. As for Cleonymus, it is conceivable—no more than conceivable, since there is no evidence—that one of the conditions

Plate 34.   Obv. of No. 33. Horseman
r., r. hand raised. Beneath
horse, ΣA.

of his coming to Italy was a promise on Taras's part that he would control Metapontum, a condition to which Metapontum, presumably dominated by Taras at the time, had agreed simply because Taras made it do so. Metapontum's later resistance to him would therefore have been resistance to this agreement.

Then there was the matter of quartering and feeding the foreign troops while they were in Italy. When the soldiers from abroad did not happen to be on campaign, presumably they lived either in Taras itself or on land belonging to the city, to the inconvenience of Tarentines if nothing more. On campaign they must have taken their food from the countryside, but again, while marching through Tarentine territory, they would have eaten and drunk at the expense of its inhabitants. This could not have improved relations between the mercenaries and their employers.

That Taras retained its autonomy under all these commanders is suggested by the fact that it continued to strike its own coins, although we cannot be sure that it struck them in all the years when the foreigners were present, and although it did strike silver and gold in the name of Alexander the Molossian as well. All the generals must have exercised supreme military control at Taras, over Tarentine troops as well as their own; we do not hear of any Tarentine generals. The office of strategus was still in existence at Taras, however, and it would be helpful to know the division of powers between a strategus and a foreign commander.

Agathocles, in exile from his own city, was probably not in a position to make a deal with Taras that was very advantageous to himself or to exert much authority there except military authority; and the Tarentines dismissed him because "he was suspected of revolutionary designs."[32]. Archidamus, their first mercenary general, seems to have pleased them the most; from the little that we know, he did not presume on his position. But Alexander the Molossian evidently appropriated more authority than the city felt he should have, and when he attempted to

Plate 35. Silver stater, c. 302-281 B.C. Obv.: Nude horseman (ephebe), crowning stationary horse. Behind, ΣA: beneath horse, ΑΡΕΦΩΝ in two lines.

move the seat of the Italiot league from Heraclea to Thurii, he was interfering inexcusably with Tarentine politics. His empire in South Italy was at best vaguely defined, with variable borders. Whether he interpreted it as including Taras, or the extent to which he conceived of Taras as subject to him, can only be guessed. Strabo says that he tried to get the seat of the league transferred "out of enmity" toward the Tarentines, which would suggest that a rupture had already taken place and that whatever authority he had exercised in the city had already come to an end.[33] Whether he took the initiative in bringing about this rupture, or whether the Tarentines provoked him to it, is again unanswerable on the basis of the records.

With Cleonymus the Tarentines had to resort to open revolt, profiting by their general's absence from the city. His authority over them until that time seems to have been considerable. Diodorus Siculus says that Cleonymus "made slaves of those who had trusted in him," and surely Diodorus is thinking of the Tarentines among others.[34] Strabo's view is quite different. According to him the Tarentines were demanding and contumelious: ". . . Even to those whom they called in they could not yield a ready obedience."[35] Strabo, however, is not referring specifically to Cleonymus. His purpose, besides, is to prove that Taras declined after the Age of Archytas. The term "a ready obedience" is unclear anyway; he may mean military obedience or he may mean submission of other kinds. But it is possible that until the advent of Cleonymus—even during the period of Alexander—Taras did tend to act in an arbitrary way toward those it had called in for help, rejecting their attempts to dominate and perhaps even showing a quarrelsome disposition. The city was, after all, a proud one, greatest in Greek Italy. Some of the Tarentines must have felt a certain sense of humiliation in having to ask for mercenary assistance in the first place, even more in having to do what the mercenaries told them to do.

Plate 36.   Silver stater, c. 302-281
B.C. Obv.: Horseman rid-
ing sideways l., with shield.
At r., EY. 21.5 mm.

Southern Italy at this period lay as a vulnerable land whose charms attracted men greedy for power. Soon after the turn of the century Agathocles looked at it again. He took and pillaged Croton about 296, seized Hipponium in the western part of the toe about 295, subjected to his influence Metapontum on the east coast, Naples and Elea on the west. His relations with the more powerful city of Taras are unclear. He may have enlisted once more as a mercenary general for the metropolis, this time against the Bruttians, tribesmen of the Italian heel who were showing their muscle.[36] But it is probable that, as ruler of the Syracusan empire, he would not have wished to expose himself a second time to the indignity of rejection by a democracy. He operated against the Bruttians in any case—and without having achieved anything lasting, left Italy to its own devices.

Around 291 the Romans, in the course of a new war undertaken against the Samnites, founded a military colony at Venusia, on the eastern side of the divide, only two days' march from Taras itself. With their colony at Luceria to the north of Venusia and somewhat to the west, they were now positioned to interfere with Tarentine interests in the north. By occupying Rhegium they gained control of the Strait of Messana and imposed themselves between the Greeks on the eastern side of Italy and those on the western side. It was with such problems to face that Taras entered upon the second decade of the third century.

Evans groups under his Period VI the coins struck at Taras that may be attributed to the years 302-281. The silver staters or didrachms were the last Tarentine coins of the traditional weight of about 123 to 130 grains or perhaps slightly over 8.2 grams, on the average; in approximately 281, the coins would undergo a weight reduction. Signatures were now carried out to a fuller extent—sometimes completely—on the obverses of most of the didrachms, under the horse's belly.[37]

Plate 37.   Gold drachm, c. 302-281
B.C. Obv.: Female head
(Satyra?) 1. Ethnic retro-
grade; to r., ΣA. 13 mm.
*ANS/SNG* Part I, No. 1033.
*Courtesy of the American
Numismatic Society, New
York*

As for the types, the horseman (or boy) in a number of variations
still occupied the obverse—crowning his horse, accompanied by a
standing Nike who (as on some pieces customarily attributed to the
period of Archidamus) seized the horse's forelock, vaulting from his
mount with shield in hand and sometimes a javelin as a participant in
Taras's games, spearing downward as defender of the city, or armed
with helmet and shield (Plates 35-36). On the reverse the dolphin
rider carried objects such as a cantharus or an ear of grain, a little Nike
or a distaff. On one reverse he placed a knee on the dolphin's back as
if rising to a standing position; and on another he threw a javelin at
Taras's enemies.[38]

Gold coins were still struck: staters with the head of a goddess on
the obverse and an androgynous child crowning his horse on the
reverse, and sometimes with a little Nike flying up with a wreath;
drachms with a female head (Satyra?) on the obverse (Plate 37) and
Taras riding the dolphin on the reverse while holding a trident and
receiving a little Nike; and diobols with the laureate head of Apollo
on the obverse and, on the reverse, Heracles struggling with the lion
as on the silver diobols struck for the Italiot league.[39] Dolphins
around the head of the goddess on the staters constituted an imitation
of Sicilian silver coins on which dolphins were similarly placed,
probably those which had been struck by Agathocles from 317 to
about 305.[40]

But a new denomination was introduced around the year 300—the
silver half-stater or drachm. We date it to this period because the
inscription IOP on the reverse also occurred on some of the gold staters
and silver didrachms. The obverse bore the helmeted head of Athena
with a stone-throwing Scylla decorating the helmet (Plate 38)—a type
perhaps indebted to Heraclea or Thurii or even to Elea on the west
coast, where the helmeted head of Athena had characterized the

Plate 38.   Silver drachm, c. 302-281 B.C. Obv.: Head of Athena r., helmet decorated with Scylla. 14.5 mm.

Plate 39.   Rev. of No. 38. Owl facing. To r. IOP.

coinage from the mid-fifth century. On the reverse—as also on coins of Elea—an owl stood on an olive spray (Plate 39). The puzzling aspect of these silver drachms is that their weight was considerably less than half that of the didrachms. In this respect they anticipated the reduced weight that would characterize the didrachm after 281. Evans tentatively suggested that these drachms, like the diobols, may have been intended for circulation not in Taras itself but in other cities which were members of the Italiot league and which may have reduced their own weight standards before Taras reduced hers. Or, possibly, the cheapening of the coinage which was setting in at Taras manifested itself first, unofficially, in the new denomination and did not become official until it was applied to the didrachm around 281.[41]

# Notes to Chapter 5

1. *Geography,* 6.3.4, Horace Leonard Jones, trans., Loeb, *Strabo,* Vol. III, p. 115; Polyaenus, *Stratagems of War,* 4.2.1, R. Shepherd, trans. (London, 1793; reprint ed., Chicago, 1974), p. 134. On the size of Taras see Wuilleumier, pp. 173-74, 185, and Carter, *Sculpture,* p. 8.

2. Vallet maintains that the Tarentines appealed to Archidamus as the leader of a strong military force rather than as a fellow Dorian ("Métropoles et Colonies," p. 221), and no doubt Spartan power weighed heavily with Taras.

3. Evans in 1889 surmised that Archidamus did not land in Italy "till shortly before 338" (*"Horsemen,"* p. 64). Most modern scholars prefer an earlier date. Wuilleumier, for instance, suggests 344 or 343 (p. 79); Woodhead, about 342 (*Greeks in the West,* p. 100). See Diodorus Siculus, 16.62.

4. See Plutarch, *Lives,* "Agis," 3, and for the supposed involvement with the Lucanians, Diodorus Siculus, 16.62.4, 16.63.2.

5. For discussion see especially Pais, *Ancient Italy,* pp. 100-101, and Wuilleumier, p. 80.

6. See Stazio, "Aspetti e Momenti," pp. 169-71.

7. See Evans, p. 67; Wuilleumier, pp. 204-205, 381-82; and Kraay, *Archaic and Classical Greek Coins,* pp. 191-92. See Ravel, *Collection . . . Vlasto,* nos. 1-9, for gold coins usually attributed to the period of Archidamus.

8. Evans, pp. 74-76, suggested that this type was struck in honor of the fallen Archidamus and that the dolphin rider so pensively contemplating the helmet was mourning the death of the hero. The dolphin rider, however, may not have been intended as the sad figure that he is sometimes said to be. Anyone looking down at a helmet would have to "bow" his head a little. See Ravel, nos. 498-563, for silver staters usually attributed to the period of Archidamus or the next few years.

9. See Kraay, *Archaic and Classical Greek Coins,* p. 191; also Evans, pp. 28-29, 67-74, and Wuilleumier, pp. 378-82. Evans thought the signatures were those of die engravers.

10. See G. K. Jenkins, "A Tarentine Footnote," in *Greek Numismatics and Archaeology,* Otto Mørkholm and Nancy M. Waggoner, eds. (Wetteren, Belgium, 1979), pp. 109-14.

11. For a similar interpretation of the Poseidon-and-Taras reverse, previous to Jenkins, see Lacroix, "Monnaies et Colonisation," pp. 92-93. Lacroix's analogy, a hymn by the third century Alexandrian poet Callimachus in which Zeus grants Athena many cities, may not help his case, but the case is a strong one without it. Lacroix also points out that Evans's attribution of these coins to the period of Archidamus is by no means certain. See also Andrew Burnett, "The Coinages of Rome and Magna Graecia in the Late Fourth and Third Centuries B.C.," *Schweizerische Numismatische Bundschau (Revue Suisse de Numismatique),* 56 (1977), 108-109.

12. On the dates see especially Pais, *Ancient Italy,* pp. 92-100, and Wuilleumier, p. 82.

13. Aulus Gellius, *The Attic Nights,* 17.21.32-33, John C. Rolfe, trans. Loeb, *Gellius,* Vol. III, p. 283.

14. See Livy, 8.17.8-10.

15. See Livy, 8.24.4. For speculations on Alexander's campaigns see especially Pais, pp. 102-109, and Wuilleumier, pp. 83-87.

16. The date is Wuilleumier's, p. 88. For an account of his death we must depend on Livy, 8.24.7-17.

17. See Evans, pp. 87-88, and Kraay, *Archaic and Classical Greek Coins,* pp. 190-92. Anticipating Jenkins, however, Burnett says that "the association of the eagle with Alexander should be dropped" ("Coinages of Rome and Magna Graecia," p. 108).

18. See Evans, pp. 88-92. On the basis of a picture on an Apulian krater, Evans even relates the distaff held by Taras on these coins not to the city's woolen industry, which of course it generally advertised, but to a chthonic cult. See also Ravel, *Collection . . . Vlasto,* nos. 564-80.

19. See Ravel, nos. 10-20.

20. See Wuilleumier, pp. 383-84, 490-91; Pierre Lévêque, *Pyrrhos* (Paris, 1957), pp. 427-28; Kraay, *Archaic and Classical Greek Coins,* p. 192; and Ravel, nos. 1864-74. M. P. Vlasto in "Alexander, Son of Neoptolemos, of Epirus," *Numismatic Chronicle,* 5th ser., Vol. VI (1926), 154-231, classifies the coins struck in Alexander's name and assigns most of them to Italian mints, a few to Epirus.

21. The tension may have been more Tarentine than Roman. Léon Homo, maintaining that Rome's policy toward the Italiot Greeks had in large degree been one of friendship since long before the Pyrrhic wars, makes the point that, confronted with enemies such as the Samnites and their Sabellian relatives, Rome wished to count on the neutrality rather than the hostility of the Greek cities. See his *Primitive Italy and the Beginnings of Roman Imperialism,* V. Gordon Childe, trans. (New York, 1926), pp. 200-201.

22. See Livy, 8.22.5-10, 8.25.1-13, 8.27.1-3. But see also the healthy skepticism of Wuilleumier, pp. 90-91. The whole story may be a fabrication to cover up a failure in Roman policy.

23. See Dionysius of Halicarnassus, 15.5.1-6; also the comments of Wuilleumier, pp. 89-90, and Moretti, "Problemi," p. 52.

24. See Diodorus Siculus, 19.4.1-2.

25. Livy, 9.14.5, B. O. Foster, trans., Loeb, *Livy,* Vol. IV, p. 213. Livy's account of this embassy (9.14.1-5) is no doubt partly imaginative, but there is no reason to reject the whole thing. See M. Cary, *A History of the Greek World from 323 to 146 B.C.* (rev. ed., 1951; reprint ed., London, 1972), pp. 177-78.

26. For this decision and Acrotatus's subsequent career in Sicily, see Diodorus Siculus, 19.70.1-8, 19.71.1-7. I have followed Wuilleumier's speculations on the

two parties (pp. 182-83). Wuilleumier, however (p. 93), wishes to transfer Taras's proposal for a Roman/Samnite peace to the time of the Acrotatus affair. On the parties see also Moretti, "Problemi," p. 42.

27. See Evans, pp. 16, 100; Wuilleumier, p. 385; and Ravel, nos. 21-23.

28. These are Evans's suggestions, pp. 95-97. There seems to be no good reason to dispute them. See Ravel, nos. 651-53.

29. See Diodorus Siculus, 20.104, 21.4. For commentary see especially Evans, pp. 136-37; André Piganiol, *La Conquête Romaine*, 4th ed. (Paris, 1944), pp. 119, 133-34; Cary, *History of the Greek World*, p. 178; Tenney Frank, "Pyrrhus," *Cambridge Ancient History*, Vol. VII, 640-41; and Wuilleumier, pp. 94-95, 185.

30. See Diodorus Siculus, 20.105, and Livy, 10.2.1-15; for commentary, in addition to references in the preceding note, see Wuilleumier, pp. 95-96.

31. Diodorus Siculus, 16.63.2 (Charles S. Sherman, trans.), 19.4.1 (Russel M. Geer, trans), 20.104.2 (Geer, trans.). Loeb, *Diodorus*, Vol. VII, p. 415; Vol. IX, p. 237; Vol. X, p. 419.

32. Diodorus Siculus, 19.4.1, Geer, trans.

33. Strabo, 6.3.4, Horace Leonard Jones, trans. Loeb, *Strabo*, Vol. III, p. 115.

34. Diodorus Siculus, 20.104.4, Geer, trans., Loeb, *Diodorus*, Vol. X, p. 421.

35. Strabo, 6.3.4.

36. See Cary, "Agathocles," *CAH* VII, 635; Frank, "Pyrrhus," *CAH* VII, 641; and Wuilleumier, pp. 96-97.

37. See Evans, pp. 26-27, 116, 121, 124-25, 129-30, and Wuilleumier, pp. 385-86. There is no basis for Evans's speculation that these signatures may be those of officials who also engraved the dies.

38. For didrachms attributed to the period 302-281, see Ravel, nos. 666-709.

39. See Evans, p. 130; Wuilleumier, pp. 386-87; and Ravel, nos. 24-27. Ravel nos. 21-23 are gold coins attributed to the period of Acrotatus.

40. See Burnett, "Coinages of Rome and Magna Graecia," pp. 109-110. At least, coins such as this, Ravel no. 24, with three dolphins and with the head facing left rather than right, are presumably the ones to which Burnett is referring, and which he dates ca. 310-290, though he does not distinguish them from Ravel nos. 21-22, on which the head faces right and there are only one or two dolphins in the field. Ravel dates no. 24, ca. 302 B.C. It should be noted that Burnett slightly modifies Evans's chronology, so that Evans IV (344-34) becomes 335-20, Evans V (334-302) becomes 320-300, and Evans VI (302-281, misprinted as 302-231 in Ravel) becomes 300-280. See Burnett, pp. 115-16.

41. See Evans, pp. 125-28, 138-39; Wuilleumier, pp. 203-204, 386; Stazio, "Aspetti e Momenti," pp. 173-77; Kraay, *Archaic and Classical Greek Coins*, p. 193; and Ravel, nos. 1047-57.

# 6

# Life in the City

We probably know as much about life at Taras as at most cities in the Greek world before the end of the fourth century B.C. Its coinage is one reason for this; its abundant pottery is another; the enormous amount of stone sculptures and ceramic figures remaining from it is a third. Many of its finest works of art were appropriated by the Romans and have long been lost. Its greatest buildings are yet to be excavated; some of the temples on what was the acropolis must lie under churches erected in Christian times. But, especially in its numerous graves, enough of ancient Taras is left to give us an idea of the work and play, preoccupations and beliefs of its people in late Archaic, Classical, and early Hellenistic times.

Religion is surely the best channel by means of which to approach the life of a Greek city. Evidence of traditional, expectable worship may be mentioned first. At Taras there are marble heads of Athena from the fifth century, clay figurines and vase paintings from the fourth century depicting her, as well of course as her head on the diobols struck in the city for the Italiot league, her head and her owl on the drachms starting about 300 B.C.[1] Hera was less popular but appeared occasionally on vases and may have had her temple at Taras. Poseidon, as god of the sea, must have received considerable attention in a city where many of the ordinary people sailed merchant ships or fished the nearby waters, and where his son by the local nymph Satyra was the eponymous hero, credited with the founding of the original town before the coming of the Spartans. Remains of an archaic Doric temple on the acropolis—two heavy columns and blocks of the stylobate on which they stood—are customarily assigned to him although they may belong to another deity, perhaps Persephone.[2] Artemis appeared frequently on vases and in the form of clay figures, mostly from the fourth century. Hecate, associated with the underworld, appeared on vases as companion of Artemis or of Persephone and Hades, whose chariot she sometimes preceded. Ares,

the god of war, figured now and then on vases and perhaps was represented by a bronze statue remaining from the fifth century, but Tarentines
seem to have been no fonder of him than were Greeks in general. His
lover Aphrodite, patroness of sex per se, was extremely popular in
Hellenistic Taras and must have been honored earlier as well. Nike
(Victory) was seen on many coins of the fourth century as well as the
third, sometimes bringing a triumphal wreath to the dolphin rider and
sometimes, with no reference to war, bringing a wreath to a horseman
(or boy) who had won a race in the games. From the fourth century on,
Asclepius, god of physical well-being, appears to have been venerated at
Taras as in other parts of a world increasingly concerned with material
matters such as health.[3]

One of the most fascinating aspects of Greek religion is its local
variations and emphases. The Tarentines, for example, had a ceremony,
strange to other Greeks, in which they sacrificed an ass to the Winds.
Although the choice of an ass is unclear, the Winds—especially those
which in summer blew from the northwest down the Adriatic—were of
course important to a city where navigation was a business. The love
god Eros received perhaps an unusual amount of respect at Taras—on
the earliest staters, if the kneeling figure is actually Eros rather than
Hyacinthus, on later vases, and in clay statuettes. Whether or not the
god on the coins was supposed to represent Eros and not Hyacinthus to
Tarentines around 500 B.C., the Spartan colonists had carried over from
the Peloponnesus in the early years the cult of Amyclaean Hyacinthus,
accidentally killed by a fond Apollo. In the absence of any evident
remains of temples and shrines, we can sometimes guess at the location
of these structures by the location of votive deposits; such deposits
indicate a tumulus of Hyacinthus outside the eastern wall of the lower
city. The worship of Apollo, god of music, was favored by the Pythagoreans and, partly for that reason, Apollo may even have displaced his
unintended victim in the favor of the Tarentines. He apparently had his
temple on the south side of the lower city, near what was in classical
times a necropolis.[4]

It may be recalled that sometime in the first half of the fifth century,
according to Athenaeus, the Tarentines in the course of their wars
against the Iapygians attacked and sacked the city of Karbina and then
sexually assaulted its young women and children. Athenaeus claims
that Zeus punished the offenders by striking them dead with lightning;
and at Taras the citizens set up pillars in front of their houses, one pillar
for each man who had been killed. In later years, on the anniversary of
the disaster, the Tarentines would sacrifice on the pillars to Zeus Kataibates, god of thunder and lightning. There seems, then, to have been a

definite pillar cult at Taras, perhaps of ancient Dorian origin, with the pillar functioning as an altar. There may even have been a persuasion that the god himself lived in or on a pillar.[5] But in the years when Alexander the Molossian was in Italy, the cult of the Epirot Zeus, the oak-crowned god of the great oracle at Dodona, may have received emphasis at Taras; his head on coins struck at this time would certainly have supported an attempt to popularize the Epirot form of his veneration.[6]

Among lost works of art of which the Tarentines were particularly proud, we know of two that had reference to Zeus. One, commissioned in the first half of the fifth century, was a sculptural group executed in marble by a certain Pythagoras of Rhegium. It showed Zeus as the bull, carrying Europa on his back to Crete. The other was commissioned from the superb artist Lysippus, court sculptor to Alexander the Great. An enormous figure in bronze, apparently portraying Zeus armed with the thunderbolt, it stood about sixty feet high, protected against strong winds by a nearby column, according to Pliny the Elder, and dominating the Tarentine agora or marketplace. In the natural style of the later fourth century, it seems to have provided the model for the Colossus of Rhodes, created in the next generation by Lysippus's pupil Chares. It has been suggested that the column protecting the statue against gusts signifies a persistence of the pillar cult into the later fourth century.[7]

Although Dionysus did not appear on Tarentine coins except occasionally through attributes such as a bunch of grapes carried by the dolphin rider, he was among the favorite gods of the city, frequently depicted on vases or in terra-cotta. The strong appeal of the god of wine, with the power to transform people's thinking processes, to flood people with joy, to raise them to ecstasy, to get inside people as few other deities did, was obviously one reason for his popularity. So was his relation with the theater, to which the Tarentines were devoted.[8] But another reason for the worship of Dionysus at Taras, at least in the classical age and later, was his association with the cults of the dead. In southern Italy he was identified with or assimilated to Hades, lord of the underworld, from classical times on. It may be recalled that on some of the silver coins struck in the period of Archidamus, Taras appeared as Iacchos riding the dolphin—a chubby child, son of this chthonic Dionysus and Persephone. Votive deposits dating from the sixth to the third centuries suggest a sanctuary to Dionysus/Hades in a part of the lower city where there were tombs in Archaic and Classical times.[9]

Hermes seems to have attracted the Tarentines partly because of his function as conductor of the souls of the dead. They represented him quite often in their statues and on their vases. In terra-cotta statuettes of the fifth century, he sometimes had a ram slung across the back of his neck. On the vases he accompanied Heracles, invader of the underworld, or he turned toward Persephone as if to show her the way out.[10]

Heracles himself, as a Panhellenic hero, may have been venerated at Taras from an early date, although evidence of his popularity does not occur until the second half of the fifth century. In the later fifth century and especially the fourth, he was a frequent subject of Tarentine art—in bronzes and terra-cottas, in funerary limestone sculpture, in scenes on vases—conquering the Nemean lion or wearing its mane and jaws as a headdress, defeating the Amazons, battling giants and centaurs and monsters, or raised to immortal status and seated next to Zeus. The Tarentines in the later fourth century commissioned Lysippus to create a bronze statue of him as of Zeus. Of tremendous size like the Zeus, it showed Heracles seated on the lion skin, which was spread over the basket where he had put the bull manure when he cleaned the Augean stables as one of his labors. This was the weary hero, resting his head on the palm of his left hand. Like Dionysus/Hades or Hermes, Heracles was important to the Tarentines because of his relationship with death and the life beyond. Limestone reliefs in the city's great cemetery celebrated him as victor over death—a title which he must have held not only because of his invasion of Hades but because of his own apotheosis. Vases depicted him subduing the infernal dog Cerberus and rescuing Theseus from the world of the dead. In spite of all the emphasis on Heracles in the visual arts, however, the city seems not to have had an official Heracles cult until toward the end of the century—perhaps not until the arrival of Cleonymus of Sparta.[11]

The worship of Persephone—Kore the Maiden—was naturally prominent at so chthonically oriented a city. Whether or not the Archaic temple on the acropolis traditionally ascribed to Poseidon was actually hers, she certainly had a sanctuary in the southeastern part of the lower city, where terracotta deposits from the seventh century on have been found in abundance, representing the goddess standing or enthroned. One of the best-known pieces of Tarentine art, a marble statue of a seated goddess, severe yet gracious, dating from the late Archaic period, is perhaps a representation of the lady of the dead. The part-Dorian settlement of Locri Epizephyrii, situated on the eastern side of Italy's toe, had built a sanctuary to Persephone in the sixth century which may have exerted some influence on her veneration at Taras.[12] But her main appeal for Tarentines, as perhaps for Athenians, was her connection with the renewal of life. She was the goddess who rose from the dead; with her return to earth the grain sprang up from under the surface, and fruit trees burst into bloom. She came to promise immortality for those who served her. Persephone's mother, Demeter, goddess of grain and the reproductive cycle, presider over childbirth, sorrowing searcher for her child, was of course important also to the Tarentines though perhaps less so than to their neighbors in grain-growing Metapontum, who often placed her portrait on their coins in the fourth century.[13]

The Tarentines honored the Dioscuri, the divine brothers, as their ancestors had done at Sparta, where the two royal houses traced their descent from Castor, the tamer of horses, and Pollux, the boxer. The symbols of the Dioscuri that sometimes appear on coins—their stars— may refer to their cult at Taras as well as their cult at Sparta. In the sixth century and later they were depicted in Tarentine sculpture at a banquet table, along with canthari and amphorae. These representations, bringing to mind the funeral feast, had a chthonic implication. In terra-cotta reliefs of the fourth century, constructed as shrines and with suspension holes, the brothers sacrificed at an altar, reclined at a table, hunted, drove a chariot, or, like the agonistic figures on some Tarentine coins, jumped from their horses.[14] They must have had importance for the Tarentines for other reasons too—during the Peloponnesian War, for instance, because they had once conquered Athens, or during most of the life of this great trading city, because they were patrons of navigation. But their most significant aspect was their connection with immortality. Pollux, who could claim Zeus as his father, was immortal to begin with. Some believed that Castor's parentage was entirely mortal— that he was the child of the Spartan royal house. But according to the legend, an arrangement was worked out with Zeus whereby the brothers (or half-brothers) shared immortality. One day Castor would be under the earth and Pollux in the upper air; the next day Pollux would descend and Castor would rise. This alternation of death and afterlife must have meant a good deal to the Tarentines.

As might be expected, the chthonic association made Orpheus also important to the Tarentine mind. He was depicted on vases of the fourth century as descending into Hades and speaking to Persephone, perhaps introducing initiates of his cult to the great goddess of the world below, perhaps playing his lyre while the deserving dead were rewarded and sinners were punished. Orpheus was evidently celebrated not only for his attempt to bring Eurydice back to life but as an authority on the underworld, teacher of its secrets to initiates, among whom must have been some of the Tarentines themselves.[15] Like other South Italiot Greeks, the Tarentines were drawn to the Orphic mysteries.

The most noteworthy aspect of Tarentine religion, then, was its preoccupation with a life after death—a preoccupation which was largely responsible for the special place held in the city's art, thought, and worship by deities and immortals such as Dionysus/Hades, Persephone, Heracles, Hermes, Orpheus, and the Dioscuri. Another instance of this same preoccupation is the unusual emphasis on cults of the dead in this city.

Cults of the dead had been a part of Greek religious life since the Bronze Age. Those dead a long time—renowned military chieftains such as Agamemnon, legislators such as Lycurgus, founders of cities such as Phalanthus himself, legendary figures who in actual fact may never have existed—were revered as heroes. They had achieved a semi-divinity; they had their shrines and their formal veneration. The recently dead—relatives, friends, people within one's memory or the memory of one's immediate ancestors—were another matter; but they too could become the objects, not of formally organized worship, but of worship of a sort. If elaborate tombs were raised in their honor (as happened at Taras) and if offerings were made to them, the living who erected those tombs and contributed those offerings invested the deceased by those very acts with a suprahuman character. The living at least regarded them as possessing an afterlife in which they could use offerings and from which they could grant favors when propitiated.[16] Because they received food and drink from the living which they enjoyed at their banquets, the dead may even have had an obligation to do all in their suprahuman power to ensure the fertility of the earth in return—to sponsor and promote the productivity of the soil in which they lay.[17] Pythagoreanism, with its emphasis on immortality, no doubt fostered the semideification of the dead as it filtered down into the popular consciousness. The very appearance of the city was a constant reminder of death and an afterlife. Not outside the walls as at most Greek settlements, but inside as at Sparta, lay a city of the dead—a vast and elaborate necropolis where those who had passed from life could be remembered, honored, propitiated.

There have been found at or near modern Taranto thousands of statuettes in the local yellow or pale orange clay, dating from the sixth to the third century, portraying a reclining male. Among about 30,000 statuettes from the deposit of Fondo Giovinazzi, most are of this figure. He is nude to the waist, sometimes bearded and sometimes not, and (from the fifth century on) sometimes accompanied by a female figure and less often by a child. He lies on a banquet couch, or once in a while on an animal such as a ram. He may hold a lyre, a cantharus or another vessel, or an egg—an obvious symbol of the renewal of life, as in the Dionysiac mysteries.[18] We can occasionally identify more than one reclining figure as having been made in the same mold, since they are identical except that one perhaps wears a beard, added after he came out of the mold. Clearly the statuettes, which were manufactured for deposit in sanctuaries, had associations with an afterlife, but the question of whom the male figure or the whole group represented has bothered scholars in the past. Either the figures depicted underworld divinities—

Hades/Dionysus, Persephone, and their child Iacchos, the chthonic family—or they depicted, more symbolically than realistically, a dead and heroized Tarentine, his wife, and their son, at a funeral feast. Scholarly opinion today generally interprets them as divinities of the underworld.[19]

Among the wealth of evidence for a preoccupation with an afterlife in Tarentine religion are terra-cotta disks, evidently sometimes buried with the dead person to aid him on a journey to the other world. Some of them have relief pictures that can be associated with deities of chthonic significance—for instance, the caduceus of Hermes, the club of Heracles, the grapes of Dionysus—or that may even suggest a celestial ascension of the soul.[20] On stone reliefs meant as decorations for tombs, the dead man could be abstractly portrayed as a heroized figure, half-draped or in heroic nudity, with a staff in his hand or perhaps with a serpent. A relief showing a favorite pastime of heroes, the hunt, may have depicted the activities of the blessed. Limestone scenes of abduction, especially if they concerned the rape of Persephone or if the "victim" was, like Ganymedes or the South Italian vegetable goddess Thalia, carried upward by a deity, surely signified immortality. Sculptures of Heracles' defeat of death made the same point. Groups depicting a procession of sea creatures brought to mind the journey of the soul toward a new existence. Most of these sculptures were made in early Hellenistic times, but they illustrate the continuity of a state of mind that had characterized Tarentine life since the Archaic Age.[21]

The question of why Tarentines placed their deceased relatives and friends inside the walls in the eastern part of the lower city, rather than relegate them to the environs as most Greeks did with their dead, evidently perplexed some ancients as well as modern scholars. Polybius claimed it was in obedience to an ancient oracle (8.28[30].6-8). Scholars have pointed out that the Tarentines had a precedent in their mother city: at Sparta the dead were generally interred within the walls. Nearer at hand, the Messapians in the Italian heel did not consider it offensive to bury dead Messapians inside their towns. But space limitation may really have determined the Tarentine practice. When the graves were first dug, they were beyond the inhabited area, which was still mainly the acropolis. But as Taras increased in prosperity and population, it expanded fairly rapidly, spilling down from the acropolis and south-eastward along the peninsula of which the acropolis formed the point. The living population consequently overtook the dead. For protection a wall had to be built from the Mare Grande to the Mare Piccolo, making Taras just about impregnable but enclosing the necropolis along with the rest of the city. The dead, in other words, were incorporated because there was no choice; and once the practice had started, new graves were added. Spartan custom and possibly the custom of the Messapians provided justification.[22]

The necropolis reflected the orthogonal plan followed by both the lower city as a whole and the acropolis. The main streets crossed it at right angles and, from the classical period on, the tombs were neatly aligned according to this grid layout. The earliest graves—and probably those of the poor in later times—were only rectangular trenches (cist graves) dug into the dirt or the rock of the peninsula or, in some cases, were built of blocks on the surface. In either case they were covered with slabs of sandstone. They usually accommodated more than one corpse. Other dead persons had chamber tombs, square or oblong rooms where they lay on a funeral couch or perhaps in an elaborate sarcophagus decorated, at least in the fourth century, with gilt figures of clay and with a lid resembling the pediment of a temple. A stair descended to the chamber, and the stucco walls were often painted with scenes in fresco. The roof, consisting of stone slabs, could be either flat or pitched; in the fifth century it was supported by one or more Doric columns. Sometimes there were several chambers ranged around a colonnaded central area ornamented with sculptures in relief.

Over both trench graves and chamber tombs the living, from the middle of the fourth century on, possibly even earlier, erected facades or *naiskoi* if they had the money to do so. The *naiskoi* were small, shallow temples or shrines of the locally quarried limestone, not much over six feet high and four or five feet wide, white-pillared, covered with stucco which was often painted red, and lavishly supplied with fine limestone sculptures on the pediments, the metopes, the cornices, the capitals, the apex—sculptures representing mythological abductions or the adventures of Heracles, other reliefs representing heroic combat and heroic death, battles against Amazons, Victories, interwoven vines, flowers, and palmettes, Dionysiac processions, or mourning figures (a rare subject, however, since the Tarentine expectation of immortality precluded a dwelling on grief). All the carving for the *naiskoi* appears to have been done between about 330/325 and 250 B.C.—beginning, therefore, just after the period when Alexander the Molossian was using Taras to establish his South Italian empire, and extending well into Hellenistic times.[23] By the end of the fourth century, when Cleonymus had been driven off and the Tarentines were for the moment free of foreign helpers, the great necropolis, its straight uncrowded streets bordered by the rich little temples and facades, some of the graves perhaps marked by isolated free-standing sculptures as well, may already have reached a state of elegant extravagance, rivaling if not surpassing the city of the living in splendor. Inside the tombs, the living left vases and other offerings—vases imported from Greece in early times (Panathenaic amphorae, perhaps for athletes who had brought their city victory in the games), florid locally made hydriae and amphorae and volute kraters in the fourth and third centuries (sometimes with hollow bases, an indication that they were not meant for use by the living), and shoes such as those found hanging in an athlete's tomb, perhaps as equipment for the final journey.[24] To the tombs the living came with food for their ancestors; and for the tombs, in late Classical and Hellenistic times, they commissioned the sculptures alluding to immortality. The dead were always with the living—inhabiting their own city within the living city, inhabiting people's thoughts, commanding attention.

Although *naiskoi* are not unique to Taras, their abundance there is exceptional. It brings up the question of where the Tarentines derived the concept. *Naiskoi* could be seen in Asia Minor, though they differed considerably from the Tarentine ones. In mainland Greece, Attica had a few *naiskoi*, and they may have influenced those at Taras. The flourishing city of Cyrene on the coast of northern Africa, significantly a Dorian foundation, had many. There may also have been some influence from peoples in Italy itself; the Etruscans had been constructing *naiskoi* in the fifth century. The question is still unsettled.[25]

Many Tarentine relief sculptors, born and probably trained far from the main centers of Hellenistic art, developed local peculiarities of style—fantastically swirling draperies, very free movement of forms, and an exaggerated three-dimensionality, creating a vivid interplay of light and shadow. Whether particular sculptures had these peculiarities or were more internationally Hellenistic in style, they could be extremely beautiful. But Tarentine work could also show inadequacies or roughnesses of execution that marked it as "provincial," possibly in a pejorative sense.[26] If the stonework of Taras is judged in terms of its milieu, however, it can at least be said to have answered a need and answered it well. Tarentine sculptors were practicing a private, domestic art, not the magniloquent public art of a man like Lysippus, sculptor in bronze to Alexander the Great. During the period when Tarentine citizens were ordering these reliefs, the latter years of the fourth century and the first half of the third, there may have been close to one hundred artisans engaged in their manufacture—probably grouped in various ateliers, though we know nothing of that.[27] These men and their patrons—and presumably the dead—were satisfied with a sculpture which would make a small family monument a pleasing thing. The grandiose and the ultrasophisticated were beyond their wishes.

Even if the figure of close to one hundred sculptors working between 330 and 250 is an overestimate—and there is no good reason to think that it is—the production of limestone reliefs at Taras in this period takes on the proportions of a big business. So does the manufacture of pottery; so does the molding in clay of the reclining male figure, perhaps accompanied by female and child. So does the molding of other terra-cotta figurines, with or without funerary associations, during the fifth and fourth centuries, such as statuettes of horsemen, of sileni with horse tails and grotesquely enormous penises, and of seated female figures (not goddesses) apparently designed for a throne of wood which has deteriorated long ago.[28] So does the manufacture, during the early Hellenistic period, of clay statuettes of women seated on a rock, a block, or a chair—evidently unique to Taras—or of so-called Tanagra type figures: stylish ladies enveloped in softly falling draperies, gracefully posed in a standing position or, less often, seated—not necessarily characteristic of Taras, as similar figures were being made in Greece itself and in Asia Minor.[29] Such products, and others manufactured at Taras, were exported far and wide in the city's fleet of merchant ships, as Corinthian pottery had been exported in the sixth century and Attic pottery in the fifth. Again it was a matter of business.

Today, when Tarentine ceramic or limestone pieces come on the market at all, they are sold as art. The artisans who made them, however, would probably not have thought of themselves as artists. They might have been satisfying a customer's request for a tomb relief which would look better than reliefs on other people's tombs, or a demand for a wine cup that was decorative as well as useful. They might have been contributing clay statuettes to the cargo of a vessel bound for Sicily. They might have been designing a mold from which a number of identical votive figures would come, just as the engraver of a coin die made possible the striking of many identical coins—mass production in so far as ancient Greeks were capable of it. Any originality which they might have attempted would have been qualified not only by tradition but by a customer's particular requirements and, very likely, by the dictates of the master of the workshop.

What was true of Taras was of course true of the ancient Greek world in general, Athens and Corinth being two of many cases in point. But the business orientation of Tarentine workshops does not necessarily mean that modern dealers in artifacts are guilty of unconscionable exaggeration when they call the products of those ateliers works of art, any more than dealers in ancient coins are guilty of exaggeration when they price a Tarentine stater rather high or a Syracusan decadrachm higher. It would be hard to find any art that has not been a business—even in the nineteenth century, when the Romantic and other movements tried to set creative souls apart as too sensitive to be touched by money.

The fact that Tarentine art was anonymous does not derogate it as art either. Most vase painting at Athens was also anonymous; so would

most European art of the Middle Ages be, whether manuscript illumi-
nation, enamel work, ivory carving, or stone sculpture. So would much
of the rest of the world's art be. Greek Italy did have a handful of artists
known to us—preeminently the sculptor Pythagoras of Rhegum—but
it also had a great many very competent artisans, differing from hundreds
of very competent painters in, say, the Italy of the Renaissance less with
regard to quality than with regard to the fact that we happen to know
who quite a few of the painters were. When the Tarentines wanted two
masterpieces in bronze, they went abroad and commissioned works by
Lysippus, possibly because their civic pride would not settle for less,
more likely because their own workshops, specializing in the small-
scale items of a domestic art, were not equipped to turn out monumen-
tal bronze. There is no implication that the Tarentines considered
themselves esthetically mediocre or unable. Certainly other people did
not consider them so, to judge from their willingness to pay for
Tarentine creations.

Although the city in the Archaic and early Classical periods had
imported most of its pottery from mainland Greece, it apparently
began the systematic production of its own ceramic vessels about 430
B.C. Its early potters may have migrated from Athens, although during
the Peloponnesian War and even at the beginning of the fourth century,
they might logically have been more attracted to a friendlier city, without
Dorian connections. Tarentine entrepreneurs must have started selling
vases to other Italiot Greek cities fairly soon, and Tarentines no doubt
bought the ceramics of other cities in return. This trading activity makes
it very difficult to identify a particular vase as Tarentine on the basis of
its find spot; until recently it has even been doubted that Taras was a
center of vase production, though that doubt no longer exists.[30] The so-
called Sisyphus Painter, a first generation decorator of vases, from
whom descended both the styles now designated Plain and Ornate,
almost certainly worked at Taras.[31] From the beginning, the whole
region showed a preference for large vases, such as volute kraters,
ornamented with sometimes quite complex mythological scenes; these
scenes were often in two registers, or even three from the middle of the
fourth century. The dwindling of exports from Attica beause of the
Peloponnesian War naturally gave a great impetus to Tarentine vase
manufacture, although the city does not seem to have succeeded in
dominating the trade in red figure vases until about 370. Around the
beginning of the century, when vase production was increasing at a
rapid rate in Taras, painters also experimented with shading and high-
lighting, attempting to give a greater impression of space than their
Attic predecessors had done. By perhaps 350, the Plain Style had merged
with (or been overcome by) the Ornate, which was elaborate indeed.[32]

In the fourth century—perhaps as early as 350, probably somewhat later—*naiskoi* became a favorite subject for vase painters, and *naiskoi* continued to be shown on vases for the greater part of a century. The dead man was usually presented within the structure in idealized fashion, as a youthful, heroic figure, sometimes naked except for a chlamys or short cloak. The *naiskoi* themselves had a pair of Ionic columns, a pediment that might contain a Gorgon head, palmettes emerging from the pediment's corners, and a high base with a floral or possibly a wave or meander pattern. Although no actual *naiskoi* remain to us in their entirety, we do have enough component parts to see that the *naiskoi* on vases are simplified versions—almost stereotyped, in fact. This may be because when they first began to be depicted on the vases, they were not yet embellished with the sculptures that made them such elaborate structures in the Hellenistic period. After the Tarentines had bedecked their *naiskoi* with limestone reliefs, vase painters probably found it easiest not to alter the old formula.

The offerings carried by the living who visited the tombs were more faithfully represented: baskets of fruits and cakes, eggs and grapes for the nourishment of the dead, paterae for a libation of wine, necklaces, wreaths, and crowns, or, if the deceased was a Dionysiac initiate, perhaps a thyrsus.[33] The vases must have reproduced scenes that a walk through the necropolis would supply.

A favorite subject of Tarentine and other Apulian vase painters, from perhaps the second quarter of the fourth century on, was the theater. It was again, of course, a question of business: Tarentines, with their tremendous enthusiasm for the theater, would buy such vases. Scenes apparently based on tragedies by Aeschylus occurred fairly frequently, scenes from Sophocles less often. Scenes from Euripides were by far the most popular. Frequently, a small stage building—a temple or a palace— would provide the background for a dramatic episode on a vase. Incidents from satyr plays were sometimes depicted on pottery too, and when farcical comedy attracted large audiences in the later fourth and third centuries, comic encounters began appearing on pots.

In relating scenes on vases to drama, however, some caution is a good idea. Myths were, after all, the heritage of everybody, and a tragic scene of mythical origin on a vase did not necessarily allude to drama. It could, for instance, reflect a poetic version of a myth, or no particular version at all. Vase painters, besides, felt no obligation to depict the background exactly as it would have been seen by a theater audience; they might add fanciful details of their own invention to an actual, modest stage building. They might also depict, in the interior of an edifice, violent events which would not have been seen by an audience since, according to Greek theatrical convention, those events would have been reported by a messenger rather than acted. As for comic scenes on vases, they might be taken straight from daily life, not from a play.[34] But in spite of these reservations there is no doubt that in considerable degree Tarentine vases of the fourth century reflected one of the most popular sources of enjoyment at the city.

Apulian red figure pottery, much of it probably still manufactured at Taras, lasted into the early years of the third century. But from the middle of the fourth century, by 340 anyway, the drawing had begun to deteriorate. It became increasingly florid, and for decorative effect there were more and more touches of white, yellow, and purple, so that a restrained Attic ancestry for these Italian vases was difficult to discern. Fat, effeminate Erotes were popular. So were female heads, usually in profile but sometimes frontal or semifrontal, stylishly equipped with earrings, an embroidered sakkos or snood or an elaborate *kekryphalos* or net to keep the hair in place, and sometimes a stephane or headband with radiate decoration; these fashionable heads were hemmed in by large, looping floral designs. "Fish plates" were made in great quantity—big saucerlike dishes with depressions in the center, painted with marine creatures such as sea perch, wrase, flounder, torpedo fish, and even conch shells, usually three of these creatures to a plate. Around the middle of the fourth century there arose (apparently not at Taras itself) another kind of pottery which would be made alongside red figure ware and would last until perhaps the mid-third century. This was Gnathian ware, often ribbed in imitation of metal vessels (which would have cost more)— black in color, with fussy flowers and grape clusters, vines and wreaths and garlands painted over the black in white, purple, and yellow.[35]

Dependable or not, the pictures on pottery supply most of our information about drama at Taras. The theater is one of the Tarentine buildings that have vanished without a trace. Drama at Taras, however, must have flourished since about the beginning of the fourth century. Aeschylus evidently experienced a revival in the Western Greek world in the fourth century; again on the shaky evidence of vases, plays of his such as the Oresteia trilogy were particularly popular. The large quantity of vases whose pictures are probably illustrations of plays by Euripides has already been mentioned; on it is based the assumption that Tarentine taste in tragedy ran especially to Euripidean drama in the fourth century.[36] Among a people who wished to be entertained, there may also have arisen a taste for post-Euripidean tragedy, about which we know little except that it was sensational, pathetic, not very profound, and not very good.[37] In England enjoyment of Shakespeare declined into the Caroline preference for sentimental, lurid, psychologically sick plays. It sounds as if something of the same thing occurred at Taras, or in South Italy in general. We have little to judge by, however, except the mournful principle that the highest dramatic standards are often too demanding for playgoers to maintain.

As for comedy, it cannot be proved that the plays of Aristophanes were ever favorites at Taras, though they were generally popular in the Greek West of the fourth century. We know of two South Italiot playwrights, a certain Cratinus and an Alexis of Thurii, each of whom wrote two dramas ridiculing Tarentine Phythagoreanism, apparently in the style of Middle Comedy. The Pythagorean philosophers' addiction to vegetarianism and to flights of rhetoric, as well as a certain pretentiousness which they had acquired, seem to have provided humor, but there is of course no record of whether these plays amused Tarentine audiences or only audiences at rival cities. New Comedy was attracting playgoers at Taras by the end of the fourth century.[38]

Aside from comedies either imported from mainland Greece or based on contemporary mainland trends in drama, the Greek West, preeminently Taras, had its own kind of comedy. This is known as phlyax farce because the men who acted in it were called *phlyakes*, a term perhaps meaning something like "speakers of nonsense" or "gossips." The origins of phlyax farce were very likely not Western. There had been farcical dances in the Peloponnesus in the seventh century if not before—protodramatic Doric performances with the participants perhaps representing satyrs and giving a ribald interpretation of mythological events. Corinthian vases of the sixth century seem occasionally to have pictured such performances, with the men dressed in the padded costumes and equipped with the enormous phalluses familiar to us from Greek comedy of later times. Sometimes called Megarian farce, this type of religious reveling presumably came to Athens via the Dorian city of Megara in the Peloponnesus and had an effect on the developing Attic comedy; fragments of vases have been found in the Athenian agora which seem to show comic actors parodying mythological themes.

Colonists from various cities in mainland Greece are thought to have brought the dances to the West. At the Corinthian colony of Syracuse there lived, in the first half of the fifth century, a dramatist named Epicharmus who evidently gave this subdramatic importation a more literary form. Epicharmus's plays, unlike Attic comedy as it flowered under Aristophanes, had no chorus. They evidently took the two directions that phlyax farce was to follow in southern Italy in the fourth century. Either they ludicrously represented mythological or heroic events, as the ancient Doric dances had done, or they ludicrously represented happenings from everyday life. As the phlyax form matured, especially in southern Italy, it no doubt took on local characteristics, such as a fascination with Heracles as a bumbling glutton or an emphasis on certain low-life comic characters, the fruit seller and the servant/thief.[39]

It retained the grotesque masks, padded tights, and highly exaggerated, dangling phallus of mainland comedy. Actors playing male parts wore unusually short chitons, sometimes himations; actors representing females dressed in long chitons and himations. There was no doubt a lot of improvisation, depending perhaps on the mood and nature of the audience and incorporating physical humor. But these farces were not entirely funny. The Byzantine scholar Suidas referred to them as "hilarious tragedy," which possibly brings them close to tragicomedy. Their dual nature can perhaps be illustrated from vases: one showing Heracles murdering his own children with comic ineptitude (throwing a child onto a pyre composed of incombustible metal utensils), or one showing old Priam of Troy sitting on an altar and delivering an obviously long-winded speech to Achilles' son Neoptolemus, who, unedified, waits with drawn sword to kill him. In spite of the ludicrousness of costumes and dialogue, however, even Tarentines may have felt that this sort of thing was straining humor a little. More representative of scenes from phlyax farce may be a vase painting of an elderly, passionate Zeus, his head stuck through the rungs of the ladder he is carrying, lighted to the window of an overdressed Alcmene of Thebes by the obliging divine guide Hermes (usually, of course, the guide of souls to the underworld), or a picture of a baldheaded man who has disguised himself as the unhappy princess Antigone. As for farces based on everyday life, the case of an elderly gentleman suffering from senile lust for a young girl, or the sight of a mischievous slave being beaten black and blue for stealing some cakes, might have satisfied the Tarentine taste for a mixture of seriousness and hilarity.[40] The characters and situations of phlyax comedy were taken over or adapted by the Oscan peoples in Campania, and as Oscan or Atellan farce this type of drama had an influence on a Rome that was acquiring sophistication.[41]

It should be remembered that Tarentine dramatic entertainments, farcical treatments of Heracles or Zeus or Apollo as well as Euripidean tragedy, had a religious basis. The actors were, after all, servants of Dionysus.[42] For Taras as well as for other South Italian cities where Dionysus was conceived as Dionysus/Hades, the theater must therefore have had some connection with the prevailing concern for a life after death.

From various references we can infer a great deal about what the Tarentines were doing when they were not watching or participating in equestrian races or other religious games, tending to their dead in the necropolis, or enjoying a play. Many of them worked in the shipyards. Many more, of course, were sailors, carrying Tarentine products to

Epirus, to Greek colonies on the Illyrian coast, to Sicily and Cyrenaica, to the Greek cities in Asia Minor and even to the regions that are now Russia, or taking the products of those places to Taras, and in the process spreading the reputation of their city over the Greek world. The work was dangerous—not only because of storms but because of pirates, especially Illyrians, to whom piracy was an ancient and honorable profession and who pounced on Greek ships sailing along their coast. Their appetite had no doubt been whetted by legitimate trade, in which they acquired commodities such as ceramic and metallic wares too sophisticated for their own craftsmen to make.[43] Plutarch has a story about trade in another commodity. He mentions a Tarentine named Theodorus who, through a naval commander serving under Alexander the Great, tried to sell Alexander two beautiful boys. But the conqueror wrote his naval commander an indignant letter "bidding him send Theodorus to perdition, merchandise and all."[44] Taras of course also did much trading closer to home—with other Greek cities in southern Italy and even barbarian centers—carrying on its commerce by land as well as by water.[45] It was this kind of business in particular that the expansion of Rome imperiled.

Many members of the Tarentine upper classes must have gained their wealth through trade-related enterprises—perhaps as shipowners, even as lenders of money on a shipping venture—but we have no firsthand knowledge of these men and assume their existence only because they existed at other Greek ports. As for the landed aristocrats, we get a rare glimpse of their life in the anecdote about Archytas and his overseer. Taras's fame for sheep and horses tells us how some of them made their money.

Aristotle singled out Taras and Byzantium as cities where, on a lower level of society, the fisherman class was especially numerous (*Politics,* 4.4.1). Fishermen brought in edible sea creatures from the Mare Piccolo between the peninsula and the mainland, from the Mare Grande, and perhaps from waters beyond, among them no doubt the varieties pictured on the fish plates made in the city—flounder, sea perch, wrasse. The Tarentines also gathered scallops, as is suggested by the appearance of the scallop shell on coins as early as the end of the sixth century and in Roman verse as late as about 30 B.C.: "luxurious Tarentum plumes herself on her broad scallops," according to Horace.[46] The squid so often carried by the dolphin rider on archaic coins was another object of the fishing fleet.

In addition to providing seafood, the sheltered waters of the Mare Piccolo held the murex shells from which Tarentines extracted the dye for which the city was well known. The shade inclined more to blood red than to purple. With the dye the Tarentines colored the woolen textiles woven by the women and sold in great quantity. The textiles and the dye itself became so famous that both were referred to as Tarentines.[47] The distaff sometimes held by the seated figure on fifth century coins and by the dolphin rider on fourth century coins, whatever its associations may have been with a cult of the dead, must also have been intended to advertise the woolen industry among people with whom Taras traded. The work of gathering the murex shells, extracting the dye, and spinning and dyeing the cloth must have employed a sizable proportion of the city's population, and of course both ends of the industry—raising the sheep on Tarentine lands, and transporting and selling the finished product—employed more.

At Taras as in other Greek cities, the manufacture of cloth may have been in some degree a cottage industry, carried on in the home for home consumption, with only the excess being sold. Or much of the cloth may have been made on estates in the country. We do not know for sure, just as we have no information that limestone was turned into sculpture in workshops. There probably were workshops for sculpture, however, as there must have been for the molding of clay figurines and, in the fourth and early third centuries, the throwing, firing, and painting of pottery. Another industry at which Tarentines worked, perhaps as early as Archaic times and certainly in Classical times, was the manufacture of small bronze objects—statuettes, vases, mirrors decorated with tiny figures such as Eros or a siren on the handle, and especially a South Italian form of mirror which had an openwork plaque between disk and handle, the openwork consisting of figures in a frame of columns or of tree trunks.[48] These things were, because of their diminutive size, easily transportable for sale abroad. Pliny the Elder says the city rivaled the Greek island of Aegina in the production of candelabra (*Natural History*, 34.11).

Taras was also, in the fourth and third centuries if not before, a center for the fashioning of objects in silver and gold for consumption at home and sale abroad. Again we know nothing about workshops, but presumably they existed for these luxury items. The artistic conventions for objects in the precious metals were so nearly uniform throughout the Greek world, especially in the later fourth and third centuries, that it is virtually impossible to establish whether an object found somewhere else in Italy, or even farther afield, had been made at Taras. Relatively few such pieces have been uncovered at Taranto itself, since the Romans took whatever valuable things they could find when they looted the city in 209 B.C.

There is, however, the famous silver Treasure of Tarentum, discovered in 1896 under a Roman mosaic pavement. It contained a cup or bowl decorated in relief with sixteen theatrical masks encircling the inside and, on the exterior, floral ornamentation, sixteen horned and plumed lion heads, and a pair of sentimental lovers with a hound dog between; a pyxis or cosmetic box supported on the foreparts of three sphinxes, the lid decorated with reliefs of Zeus, Apollo, and Artemis; two more cups or bowls with interior reliefs of Dionysus and a maenad kissing; a tall, graceful, ribbed cantharus or wine cup with double loop handles, the slender stem embellished with acanthus leaves, an Eros carrying an amphora below each handle; and a *thymiaterion* or incense burner with a fluted stem, its drum covered with overlapping leaves. Because of coins accompanying the treasure, it used to be thought that these objects had been made sometime between 315 and 272 and buried for safekeeping, perhaps during the Pyrrhic Wars. Recent scholarship favors a later date, however—perhaps around 200.[49] If the later dating is correct, these pieces lie outside the limits of this chapter, but even so they suggest the luxurious living toward which the city's richer inhabitants had been leaning for several generations. Gold jewelry still extant gives some idea of the fineries available to fashionable Tarentine ladies— a splendid necklace intricately composed of rosettes from which hang buds, masks, and female heads, or earrings in the form of male heads, swans, Erotes.[50] The goldworkers of Taras, like those of Alexandria, were skilled practitioners of a delicate art, producing beautiful adornments for patronesses who could pay.

The daily life of Taras that we know least about is the life beyond the gridiron of streets and buildings crowded onto the peninsula—the activities of the fields and pastures which were, in a larger sense, part of the polis. Among the many things we do not know is the extent to which Tarentine agriculture and animal husbandry were carried on by the slaves of landed aristocrats—such as Archytas's slaves in the first half of the fourth century—or by independent farmers with perhaps a slave or two of their own. The proportions must have varied from age to age, just as the amount of land under Tarentine control varied with the city's wars against barbarian neighbors. It has to be remembered, however, that in spite of Taras's enormous commercial interests the city was, like the other Greek establishments in South Italy, ultimately dependent on the land.

Although Taras's land may not have been as good for growing cereal as the country controlled by Metapontum, some wheat and barley were cultivated. That Greek staple the olive was grown in quantity, and grapes were raised for wine. The textile industry, of course, flourished because of the sheep that grazed the pastures. As has already been mentioned, the horses which young Tarentines rode in the civic games, and which outsiders in the fourth and third centuries almost inevitably associated with Taras at war, were bred in Tarentine pastures, tended by men well aware that the city was celebrated for horses.[51] For other products of rural Taras—figs, pears, plums, edible pine cones, almonds, walnuts, and honey—we have to go to late references by Roman writers such as Virgil, Horace, and Pliny the Elder. Strabo in the first century B.C. remarked that the country around the Roman port of Brundisium "is better than that of the Tarentini, for, though the soil is thin, it produces good fruits, and its honey and wool are among those that are strongly recommended."[52] But Strabo did not like Taras very much. In the fifth, fourth, and early third centuries B.C., if not in his time, the workers in the city's fields, pastures, and orchards were taking advantage of a rich country.

A final discomforting observation. This chapter is an attempt to portray the life of a city but the portrait does not have much of a skeleton. The underlying physical structure of Taras is in large degree missing. We know that the plan of the city was, in general, orthogonal, and that the acropolis at the northwestern point of the peninsula was the oldest part. But although we can visualize what the acropolis at Athens looked like to an Athenian of, say, 430 B.C., we have hardly any ideas of what the Tarentine acropolis looked like to a Tarentine at any period. We are aware that it had two temples and probably more, but we are not even certain whom the temples honored. We know that there were an outer harbor and an inner harbor, a great necropolis toward the city's eastern extremity but within the fifth-century wall, an agora dominated by an enormous bronze statue of Zeus from the late fourth century on, and a sanctuary to Persephone in the southeastern area. But we possess only an inadequate description of the statue of Zeus, we cannot draw a picture of the sanctuary to Persephone, and we must depend on our imagination to tell us how the city would have appeared to somebody approaching it from the water. Because of the many references (on coins and elsewhere) to games involving horses, we can assume the existence, somewhere, of a hippodrome of some kind, or at least a track, but we can go no further. Literature and paintings on vases illustrate the importance of the theater to Tarentine life, but Taras's theater has not been uncovered though we know that it commanded a view of the outer harbor. Gates, the directions of particular streets, and the architecture of living quarters for rich and poor at various periods are matters of educated conjecture. We realize that Taras in the mid-fourth century was larger in both extent and population than almost any other Greek city and suspect that it must have been crowded; but this is hardly enough to hang a portrait on. Although our information about the religious, intellectual, artistic, and daily life of Taras is extensive, we cannot put that life into anything more than a shapeless setting.

# Notes to Chapter 6

1. Arias speculates that a cult of Athena came to Taras from Thurii, which would place it in the later fifth century; see "Rapporti e Contrasti," p. 247.

2. For discussion of the building's probable architecture, see especially Stazio, "L'Attività," pp. 293, 299-300, and Martin, "L'Architecture," pp. 313, 315-18.

3. For discussion of evidences of the worship of these deities at Taras, see especially Wuilleumier, pp. 407-409, 450, 478-80, 484-86, 490-93, 513-14; Mustilli, "Civiltà," p. 15; Higgins, "Tarantine Terracottas," p. 271; and Lo Porto, "Topografia," p. 377. But note also Wuilleumier's caution, p. 471, against too much reliance on ceramic products as direct reflections of the religious beliefs of the people.

4. See Wuilleumier, pp. 247-48, 452-53, 481-82, 491-92, 495; Cook, Zeus, Vol. II, p. 284, and Vol. III, pp. 105-106; Carratelli, "Storia dei Culti," p. 134; and Carter, Sculpture, pp. 9, 12.

5. For discussion of these theories see Cook, Zeus, Vol. II, pp. 29-31, 35-36, 45, 160-61, 165-66, 559, 844-45, and Wuilleumier, p. 473.

6. See Wuilleumier, pp. 473-74, and Cook, Vol. III, pp. 1055-57 (Appendix R). Cook (Vol. II, pp. 762-64) speculates implausibly that perhaps not much before the third century, the terrifying old Zeus Kataibates was almost entirely supplanted by a concept of the god as pensive, all-wise, providential.

7. See Wuilleumier, pp. 276, 281-82; Robertson, History of Greek Art, Vol. I, pp. 463-64; and Pliny the Elder, Natural History, 34.40-41. The speculation on the column is that of Cook, Vol. I, pp. 35-36.

8. See Wuilleumier, pp. 500-501, and Martin P. Nilsson, The Dionysiac Mysteries of the Hellenistic and Roman Age (New York, 1975), p. 145. Robertson (Vol. I, pp. 427-28) discusses a vase painting of ca. 400 B.C., which depicts the baby Dionysus emerging from Zeus's thigh.

9. See Wuilleumier, p. 502; Nilsson, pp. 118, 120; and Carter, Sculpture, p. 12.

10. See Wuilleumier, pp. 405, 488-89.

11. So says Arias; see "Rapporti e Contrasti," p. 247. See also Wuilleumier, pp. 522-26; Carter, pp. 17-18; and Henri Metzger, "L'Imagerie de Grande Grèce et les Textes Littéraires à l'Époque Classique," Convegno 6, p. 180. On Lysippus's Heracles, see Wuilleumier, pp. 282-83; Robertson, Vol. I, p. 473; Margarete Bieber, The Sculpture of the Hellenistic Age, rev. ed. (New York, 1961), p. 35; and Franklin P. Johnson, Lysippus (New York, 1968), p. 193. The statue was taken to Rome in the looting of 209 B.C. and, in A.D. 325, to Constantinople to adorn the circus. The Latins melted it down in 1204.

12. See Wuilleumier, pp. 248, 251, 274, 396-97, 511; Higgins, "Tarantine Terracottas," pp. 269-70; Robertson, Vol. I, pp. 201-202; and Coulson, "Taras," Princeton Encyclopedia of Classical Sites, p. 879. Stazio, "L'Attività," pp. 302, 306-308, argues quite convincingly that the temple on the Tarentine acropolis was not to Poseidon but to a goddess, and Persephone is the best candidate. Not only did there remain a tradition of veneration of a female in the area of the temple, expressed in Christian times by a church to the Virgin Mother of

Martyrs, but there also remain fragments from a statue of an enthroned goddess.

13. See Mustilli, "Civiltà," p. 15, and, especially on Demeter as a goddess of childbirth, Wuilleumier, p. 512. Interestingly, an Apulian alabastrum of 350-40 B.C. would seem to relate Eros (depicted androgynously, in a chariot) to the rebirth and immortality of women. See Margaret Ellen Mayo and Kenneth Hamma, *The Art of South Italy: Vases from Magna Graecia* (Richmond, Va., 1982), No. 56, and discussion by Adriana Calinescu, pp. 144-147.

14. See Wuilleumier, pp. 520-22.

15. See Wuilleumier, pp. 429-30, 526-28; Nilsson, *Dionysiac Mysteries,* pp. 12, 120-21; Metzger, "L'Imagerie," pp. 177-80; and Higgins, *Greek Terracottas,* p. 91. Nilsson, pp. 140-44, relates to Orphic teaching the doctrine of the cosmic egg, from which proceeded the world and all it contains.

16. See the excellent discussion of cults of the dead in Donna C. Kurtz and John Boardman, *Greek Burial Customs* (Ithaca, N.Y., 1971), pp. 297-98; also Robertson, Vol. I, p. 379. Carratelli ("Storia dei Culti," pp. 133-34) stresses the extremely deep and ancient roots of a belief in an afterlife at Taras. On cults of heroes of the Trojan War see Wuilleumier, pp. 526-29; on limestone carvings of Agamemnon set up on the tombs of relatives as helps toward conferring immortality, Carter, *Sculpture,* p. 19.

17. This is the interesting surmise of Ruth Michael Gais in "Some Problems of River-God Iconography," *American Journal of Archaeology,* vol. 82, no. 3 (Summer 1978), 364. Gais is speaking generally rather than with respect only to the Italiot Greeks.

18. See Nilsson, *Dionysiac Mysteries,* pp. 139-44, and on the figure in general, Higgins, "Tarantine Terracottas," pp. 269-70.

19. See the careful discussion of the whole matter in Wuilleumier, pp. 502-509. Wuilleumier concludes that although the figures "présentent à la fois des traits divins, héroïques et funéraires," they "doivent être les patrons divins des morts héroïsés" (p. 509). See also Wuilleumier, pp 399-403, and Chesterman, *Classical Terracotta Figures,* p. 46. Higgins states: "It is not clear who was originally represented, but at Taras he was from the first seen as Dionysus" ("Tarantine Terracottas," p. 270), and less categorically: "The woman is believed to be Persephone, the child Iacchos" (*Greek Terracotta Figures,* p. 22; see also p. 91).

20. See Wuilleumier's discussion of the disks, pp. 222-23, 542-48, and his "Les Disques de Tarente," *Revue Archéologique* (1922), pp. 26-64. By no means all the disks had a religious import, however.

21. See Carter, *Sculpture,* pp. 17-20, 88 (n. 54), and especially Cat. Nos. 1-3, 13, 16, 31, 34, 60, 75-77, 81, 107, 127, 143-44, 146, 158, 161, 167, 177, 208, 225, 237, 243, 263-65, 289, 313, 326, 330.

22. See Wuilleumier, p. 250; Lo Porto, "Topografia," pp. 362-64, 379-80; Kurtz and Boardman, *Greek Burial Customs,* pp. 181, 308-309; and Martin, "L'Architecture," pp. 324-26. Aside from the great eastern necropolis, there were other graveyards in the lower city, so that eventually, according to Wuilleumier, one-third of the lower city was occupied by the living, two-thirds by the dead.

23. On the tombs and the *naiskoi,* see Wuilleumier, p. 254; Lo Porto, "Topografia," pp. 380-81; Martin, "L'Architecture," pp. 323-24, 327-32; Coulson, "Taras," p. 380; Kurtz and Boardman, pp. 268, 270, 312-15; Margot Schmidt in Mayo and Hamma, *Art of South Italy,* pp. 24-25;and especially Carter, pp. 9, 13-23, 31-32. The dating of all the funerary sculpture to ca. 330-250 is Carter's, pp. 21-23.

24. See Kurtz and Boardman, pp. 211, 213.

25. See the discussion in Carter, p. 14. In addition to the works cited there, see, on *naiskoi* at Cyrene, Irene F. Bald, "Seven Recently Discovered Sculptures from Cyrene, Eastern Libya," *Expedition,* vol. 18, no. 2 (Winter 1976), 19.

26. Robertson calls the sculpture of the *naiskoi* "entirely provincial and second-rate, adding nothing to our understanding of the development of Greek art" *History of Greek Art,* Vol. I, p. 591). Carter, however, suggests that to set these Tarentine reliefs against the great masterpieces of Greek sculpture is to draw invidious and in some respects impossible comparisons (pp. 21, 25-26). He examines the individual reliefs with great care, attributing each to either a "Hellenistic" or a "local" tradition which in his view (pp. 25, 33-37) existed comtemporaneously. See also Langlotz, "La Scultura," pp. 218-219.

27. The estimate is Carter's; see pp. 23-24.

28. See Wuilleumier, p. 404; Higgins, *Greek Terracottas,* pp. 91, 270, 272; and Chesterman, *Classical Terracotta Figures,* pp. 17-19.

29. See Wuilleumier, pp. 410-13, and Higgins, *Greek Terracottas,* pp. 95, 126. Higgins says regarding Hellenistic figures that "local styles were almost totally merged in a Hellenistic *koinē*" and that "In Apulia itself it should be, but is not yet, possible to distinguish between the products of Taras, Egnatia, Ruvo, Canosa, and probably other centres" ("Tarantine Terracottas," p. 273). Chesterman, however, notes that "South Italian terracottas, Tarentine in particular . . . seem to wish to break away from the somewhat rigid Tanagra poses" (p. 66).

30. See Wuilleumier, pp. 443-45; R. M. Cook, *Greek Painted Pottery* (London, 1966), pp. 193-94; A. D. Trendall, "La Ceramica," Convegno 10, p. 249; and Carter, p. 15. Trendall(p. 251) not only assumes for Taras a large export of vases in the fourth century but suggests that the stylistic uniformity of Apulian pottery, especially in the second half of the century, points to "una sola fonte de ispirazione, che dovrebbe essere la città di Taranto." from which ceramists went out to the other Italian cities.

31. See R. M. Cook, p. 197, and Trendall, "Ceramica," pp. 250, 256.

32. See Wuilleumier, pp. 448, 454-56; R. M. Cook, pp. 197-98; Robertson, Vol. I, p. 430; and Trendall, pp. 250-53, 258. On the Iliupersis Painter and the Lycurgus Painter, the latter perhaps mid-fourth century, both of them definitely Apulian if not Tarentine, see Trendall, pp. 253-54, 259. See also Alexander Cambitoglou and A. D. Trendall, *Apulian Red-figured Vase-painters of the Plain Style* (Archaeological Institute of America, 1961); A. D. Trendall, *South Italian Vase Painting* (London, 1966); A. D. Trendall and Alexander Cambitoglou, *The Red-figured Vases of Apulia,* Vol. I (Oxford 1978); and most recently, Mayo and Hamma, *Art*

*of South Italy,* nos. 12-85, and discussion by Trendall, pp. 78-80. Among trade catalogs, those published occasionally by Charles Ede, Ltd., of Brook Street, London, under the title "Greek Pottery from South Italy" are particularly useful.

33. See Wuilleumier, pp. 457, 553-56; Trendall, "Ceramica," pp. 253-54, 259; Carter, pp. 15-16; and Mayo and Hamma, *Art of South Italy,* pp. 24-25 and Nos. 41, 47, 67-77.

34. For these reservations, see T. B. L. Webster, *Greek Theatre Production* (London, 1956), pp. 103-106; Metzger, "L'Imagerie," pp. 167-69; and Marcello Gigante, "Teatro Greco in Magna Grecia," Convegno 6, pp. 124-25. See also, on dates of South Italian vases related to the theater, Webster, p. 101; on allusions to tragedy on vases, Wuilleumier, pp. 457-58, 461, 613-15, and Robertson, Vol. I, pp. 430-31; on allusions to satyr plays, Wuilleumier, p. 616, and Metzger, p. 170; on allusions to comedy, below, n. 40; and in general, A. D. Trendall and T. B. L. Webster, *Illustrations of Greek Drama* (London, 1971), especially pp. 11-13, 72-113, 121-44. Using the pictures on vases with caution, Webster speculates on the appearance of South Italian theaters and their sets, concluding: "For the first three-quarters of the fourth century Apulian, Campanian, and Paestan theatres seem to have had a wooden set representing a single-storey building with a row of columns along the back, a central door ornamented with a pediment and side doors sometimes at any rate with a flat-topped porch, which could represent the roof of the house or be used as a high platform for gods. When the Athenians built their stage-building in stone, the South Italians probably followed suit" (*Greek Theatre Production,* pp. 109-110). Margarete Bieber examines variations in the depiction of stages and sets on South Italian vases; see her *History of the Greek and Roman Theater,* 2nd ed. (Princeton, 1961), p. 146.

35. See Wuilleumier, p. 461; R. M. Cook, pp. 196, 198; Trendall, "Ceramica," pp. 254-55, 262-63; A. Cambitoglou, "Groups of Apulian Red-Figured Vases Decorated with Heads of Women or of Nike," *Journal of Hellenic Studies,* 74 (1954), 111-21; and on Gnathia ware Wuilleumier, p. 464, and R. M. Cook, pp. 196, 207.

36. See Webster, p. 98; Metzger, pp. 160-61; Gigante, pp. 110-11; and Bieber, *History,* p. 129.

37. See Bieber's discussion of a post-Euripidean scene on the Medea krater at Munich (*History,* pp. 34-35).

38. See Wuilleumier, pp. 587, 616-17; Webster, p. 254; and Gigante, p. 93.

39. For the genealogy of phlyax farce see Webster, pp. 98-101, 164; Bieber, *History,* pp. 38-39, 129; Metzger, p. 171; and Gigante, pp. 87-88, 91, 114-29. Gigante discusses in detail Breitholtz's objections (1960) that the Corinthian vases may not reflect drama at all, that Attic comedy is in fact not dependent on Megarian/Dorian farce, and that there was in fact no *Ur*-comedy from which both Aristophanic and West Greek comedy in some respects descended. Gigante would also place more emphasis on local Italian elements in the phlyax plays that would, for instance, Webster.

40. On typical characters and situations of phlyax farce, most of them assumed

from scenes on vases, see Wuilleumier, pp. 460, 525, 621-26; Bieber, *History*, pp. 129-44; Gigante, p. 94; R. M. Cook, p. 196; and Robertson, Vol. I, p. 491. A. D. Trendall's *Phlyax Vases*, 2nd edition (University of London: Institute of Classical Studies, Bulletin Supplement No. 19, 1967) and Trendall and Webster, *Illustrations of Greek Drama*, Chap. IV, "Old and Middle Comedy; Phlyakes," are indispensable. See also Mayo and Hamma, *Art of South Italy*, nos. 13, 24-25, 43. The fact that the vases, while South Italian, are not necessarily of Tarentine provenance does not diminish their relevance to phlyax farce as Tarentines would have known it.

41. See especially Bieber, *History*, pp. 145-48.

42. Bieber, pp. 143-44, reminds us of this.

43. On Illyrian piracy see Stipčević, *The Illyrians*, pp. 147-48.

44. Plutarch, "Life of Alexander," 22.1, Bernadotte Perrin, trans. Loeb, *Lives*, Vol. VII, pp. 285, 287.

45. Wuilleumier, pp. 226-28, discusses this trade partly in terms of the coins of other Italiot Greek cities found at Taranto and the circulation of Tarentine coins in those cities and in barbarian settlements.

46. *Satires*, 2.4.34, H. Rushton Fairclough, trans. Loeb, p. 189.

47. See Wuilleumier, pp. 219-22.

48. See Wuilleumier, pp. 311-21; Boardman, *Greeks Overseas*, p. 193; and Winifred Lamb, *Greek and Roman Bronzes* (London, 1929), pp. 180-81. For an example of a South Italian mirror handle consisting of an openwork figure framed by tree trunks, see Summa Galleries (Beverly Hills, Calif.), Auction I (September 18, 1981), Lot No. 45. The figure in this example is Eros; the handle is probably from Locri.

49. On the earlier dating see Wuilleumier, pp. 338, 356; on the later dating, D. E. Strong, *Greek and Roman Gold and Silver Plate* (Ithaca, N.Y., 1966), p. 96. For discussion of the pieces see Wuilleumier, pp. 340-56, and Strong, pp. 95-97, 104, 106, 121. See also Wuilleumier, *Le Trésor de Tarente* (Paris, 1930). The cup with the theatrical masks, etc., disappeared from the museum at Bari during World War I.

50. See Wuilleumier, pp. 365-66, and Reynold Higgins, *Jewellery from Classical Lands* (British Museum, 1965), p. 20.

51. See Wuilleumier, pp. 213-17, and Bérard, *Colonisation Grecque*, pp. 172-73. Tenney Frank's *Economic Survey of Ancient Rome*, Vol. V (Baltimore, 1940), pp. 147, 161-62, 164-65, discusses Tarentine farming of the first centuries B.C. and A.D.

52. *Geography*, 6.3.6, Horace Leonard Jones, trans. Loeb, *Strabo*, Vol. III, p. 121.

# 7

# Famous Men

A little can be said about men whom the city must have celebrated, both those who lived in Taras and those who went from it.

When a Greek city sent men abroad to represent it, those men were, more often than not, athletes. Taras in the fifth century sent out athletes of whom it could feel very proud, men who did much for the city's image. One of these was Anochos son of Adamatas, who won both the short and the double foot race in the Olympic games; the grateful state commissioned his statue to be made by the Argive sculptor Ageladas and set up at Olympia (Pausanias 6.14.11).

The athlete Iccus attained distinction perhaps a little later, around the middle of the century. He impressed his fellow citizens and other Greeks not only with his athletic ability but with his application of chastity to sport. While he was in training, he did not risk weakening his body through sexual indulgence, and he became so notorious for restraint that later ages remembered him for it. An admiring Plato cited the report that, "spurred on by ambition and skill, and possessing courage combined with temperance in his soul," throughout his training "he never touched a woman, nor yet a boy."[1] In the early third century A.D., when Greek Taras itself was hardly more than a memory, Aelian could praise Iccus along with bulls for refraining from sex before strenuous competition:

And when a Bull that is the leader of a herd is defeated by another leader, he departs to some other place and becomes his own trainer and practices every method of fighting... particularly abstaining from sexual acts and living continently like Iccus of Tarentum.... For to him the prizes meant glory—the wild olive of Olympia, the Isthmian pine, and the Pythian laurel, admiration in his lifetime, and after death an honoured name.[2]

Of all their fellow citizens the Tarentines must have been proudest of Archytas, statesman and general, exemplar of the Pythagoreanism which they still honored when other parts of Greek Italy had abandoned it.

His friendship with Plato, his dealings with Dionysius of Syracuse, and his philosophical works and other treatises must have enhanced Taras's reputation considerably among the Greeks. Archytas had probably had as his teacher a Pythagorean named Philolaus, who was also probably a Tarentine though there is a possibility that he was born at Croton. Philolaus lived and taught at Thebes as well as at Taras. Plato had heard of him; in the *Phaido* a Theban named Cebes, a pupil of Philolaus, inquires: "Why in the world do they say that it is not permitted to kill oneself, Socrates? I heard Philolaus, when he was living in our city, say the same thing you just said, and I have heard it from others, too, that one must not do this; but I never heard anyone say anything definite about it."[3]

Philolaus is at best a shadowy figure—even to Plato, apparently. Still more shadowy is one Lysis. If Lysis was a Tarentine at all, he must have left his native city at a young age to study Pythagoreanism at Croton. The Crotonian philosophers seem to have met in the house of Milo (who had long been dead), but in a violent reaction against Pythagoreanism in the mid-fifth century, the house was burned and everybody in it died except Lysis and a Tarentine named Archippus, also young and therefore agile enough to escape. Lysis, like Philolaus, went to Thebes, where in his old age he taught Epaminondas, destined for greatness like Aristotle's pupil Alexander. So at least runs the story in its least muddled version. Whether or not it is essentially true, the interesting thing is that later generations credited Lysis with having been a Tarentine—an indication, perhaps, of the reputation as a philosophical center that continued to invest the city. In about 34 B.C., for instance, Cornelius Nepos announced that Epaminondas had had an excellent education because "Lysis, the Pythagorean from Tarentum, taught him the tenets of his system. Even as a youth Epaminondas followed Lysis' instruction so closely that he preferred the friendship of the austere, old man to that of boys his own age."[4]

It was largely by means of Pythagoreanism that Taras made its intellectual reputation; the school must have flourished there in the fourth century. There was, for example, Kleinias, dating perhaps from the middle of the century. His devotion to the brotherhood inspired him to make the voyage from Italy to Cyrene on the north African coast so that he could give money to a man whose fortune had been ruined in some political involvement. Kleinias had never met the man but knew that he was a Phythagorean, and that was enough.[5] There was also Aristoxenus, who, like Philolaus and Lysis earlier, looked for fame in the old Greek world. He went to Corinth and eventually to Athens, where he studied under the Pythagorean teacher Xenophilus and under Aristotle, achieving such prominence that he evidently expected to succeed Aristotle himself as head of the Lyceum in 322 B.C.; but Theophrastus was desginated instead. Aristoxenus may have returned to Taras after this disappointment.

Next to Archytas, Aristoxenus was probably the most renowned philosopher trained at Taras, even if he was not responsible for all of the 453 books with which the *Lexikon* of the tenth century Byzantine scholar Suidas credits him. A few of his works are known to us by title or from fragments. He wrote a great deal on music. We have portions of his *Principles and Elements of Harmonics*, dealing with matters such as pitch, keys, intervals, and the psychological effects of music (a topic that interested him as it did Plato). We also have fragments of his *Elements of Rhythm*; and we know that he wrote treatises on melody, on listening to music, on flute players (whom he considered inferior to players on stringed instruments), and on various kinds of dance. His father at Taras had given him some of his musical education, and the Phythagorean environment must also have stimulated his interest in the subject.

But his extremely orderly method of definition, categorization, division, and subdivision probably owed more to Aristotle than to Archytas or Pythagoras himself. He seems to have lacked the excitement and vision of his Pythagorean predecessors. He did, however, compose a biography of Pythagoras among other *Lives*; and one of Archytas too (of which we have three fragments). His biography of Plato was, it would appear, more narrowly critical than favorable. Philosophically he seems to have been most attracted to questions of human morality, least to metaphysical subjects, though there are only scattered shreds and references to judge from. He had a high respect for law and order and wrote on government. For his many works which we have lost, his fellow ancients esteemed him greatly.[6]

The most influential man living in Taras toward the end of the fourth century and in the early part of the third was not a philosopher but a playwright. The comic dramatist Rhinthon had probably been born at Syracuse, but he spent his creative life at Taras, providing the citizens with phlyax farces. Thirty-eight plays are attributed to him. We know the titles of nine of them, and there are enough fragments to make it clear that he wrote in a broad Dorian dialect, as is only to be expected of a man from Syracuse with a Tarentine audience in mind. If he did grow up in Syracuse, where Epicharmus had developed the phlyax form, he could have learned his comic technique there. It seems to have consisted not so much of making myth and heroic legend look ridiculous in themselves as of parodying their treatment by serious writers such as Euripides. The frequency of Euripides' tragedies on the Tarentine stage in the fourth century—the fact that of all tragic playwrights he would have been most familiar to Tarentines—no doubt made him an especially appropriate target for parody. Eight of the nine known titles of works by

Rhinthon apparently refer to tragedies by Euripides; they include *Iphigenia at Aulis, Iphigenia in Tauris,* and *Orestes.* There may have been considerable play on words, and Euripidean phrases juxtaposed with low or gross terms. We have too little to form a judgment; we know only that Rhinthon, whatever he did, highly amused the Tarentines.[7]

In the third century, drama in the Greek world was put on by guilds modeled after the one at Athens, which had been established around the middle of the fourth century. The guilds sent out troupes to compete in dramatic festivals, which, in an age that loved theatrics, occurred at many places. A troupe usually consisted of three actors (either tragic or comic), a man to play the flute, and a trainer or manager. Members of the chorus were supplied by the city staging the festival. Although the actors perhaps never achieved the fame of contestants in the Olympics and other games, they were just as much representatives of their polis and would have been celebrated at home. One of the most notorious was a tragic actor from Taras named Dracon, who won prizes at festivals in the two great seats of the worship of Apollo, Delphi and the island of Delos.[8] Taras's successful competition in stage productions in the older Greek areas during this period indicates not only the far-spread character of Hellenistic culture but also the importance of Taras as a center for theater.

The poet Leonidas was a native of Taras if we can believe his verse. But most of his epigrams were manifestly not written in his native city. To judge from allusions in the poems, he spent his mature life in old Greece (for instance, the Dorian Peloponnesus) and Asia Minor (for instance, the Dorian island of Cos). In what is probably his most autobiographical poem, his own epitaph—if it is by him at all—he laments his long absence from his birthplace: "I lie far from Italy and from Taras my home. This is more bitter to me than death. Such is the life of wanderers, no life."[9]

We are ignorant of that life except for what he says in his poems. The picture he presents is that of a moneyless, uncelebrated, unsettled man: "Me Leonidas, doom'd to want and wander." Poverty itself would not be so bad, but to be homeless as well, always on the move, is hard to take:

> Waste not thy flesh, O man, with journeying, wandering endlessly,
>   On from land unto land, on without rest, without aim:
> Waste not thy flesh, if only a cabin ungarnish'd may shelter thee,
>   Comforted, spite of storms, by a fitful flicker of flame.[10]

It is the portrait of a bohemian—part-wistful, part-embittered, without direction or even, perhaps, motivation; and it is reminiscent of poets he must have admired, such as the outspoken, caustic Archilochus of the seventh century B.C. The picture may be an artistic fiction, a kind of persona, calculated to appeal to the Hellenistic Age; or it may be largely true. At least nothing directly contradicts it. Leonidas, in so far as we know, did not have a royal patron, did not head a school, and did not establish a reputation as a literary leader whom others consulted, although Roman poets would imitate him. His mannered, elaborate, artificial style, characterized by the compounding of words to fashion new words, does not negate the picture of a poor wanderer; a vagabond can be well educated. The large number of his poems preserved in the *Palatine Anthology*—about one hundred—is not necessarily proof that he exercised great literary influence during his lifetime, since the *Palatine Anthology* (sometimes called the *Greek Anthology*) is, at best, a haphazard collection. Still, the preservation of one hundred poems does at least suggest that he enjoyed more fame during his life than he is willing to admit, and this in turn suggests that the poor Leonidas of the epigrams may be Leonidas's own creation.

He was somewhat younger than Rhinthon—perhaps only a little, perhaps a generation or more. The question of his age revolves around a poem (6.130) which the *Palatine Anthology* attributes to him, one in which Pyrrhus dedicates to Athena some shields won in battle against Galatians employed as mercenaries by Antigonus Gonatas of Macedon. Pyrrhus defeated these mercenaries about 274. But the attribution of the epigram to Leonidas has been seriously questioned, and if the poem is not by him, then he could have lived considerably later.[11]

Most of his extant poems are epitaphs, some of them in the form of votive epigrams (or dedications of offerings to a deity), and almost all are in the elegaic couplet. Several, referring to wars against Taras's enemies the Lucanians, may have been written early, before Leonidas left Italy, but of course that is only an assumption; he could have been remembering. His subject was very often some man or woman as poor as he himself claimed to be—a farmer, a sailor, a shepherd, a carpenter, a weaver, or a whore (somewhat better off than the others). The verses are rich in the homely details of simple lives. The carpenter offers his tools to the patroness of manual arts:

> Theris, whose hands were cunning,
> Gives to Pallas, now the years
> Of craftsmanship are over,
> His stiff saw with curved handle,
> His bright axe, his plane, and his
> Revolving auger.[12]

The courtesan Kallikleia dedicates her most precious possessions to Aphrodite:

> The silver Eros the ankle bracelet
> the Lesbian purple hair-band
> crystal-skin breast girdle, bronze mirror,

and the wide wooden hair-trawling comb:
Kallikleia has got what she wanted:
Cretan Kypris, she leaves them at your columns.[13]

There is sympathy for these people, and an appreciation of the value of a job well done, even of the possible beauty of a human task. For instance, the work of old Platthis the weaver:

> As a runner runneth his course, the long course in the races,
> So ran she hers, the course of Athene, course of the Graces,
>     Pacing to and fro by the loom to the slow day's breaking,
> Or arranging carefully round her knee, her old shrunk knee,
> Yarn enough for the loom, with her old hand shaking,
> Of years four-score, dark Acheron flood she was given to see.
>     Lovely she was, lovely the things of her making.[14]

These brief pictures of everyday life have little room for sweetness, but Leonidas can achieve an idyllic pastoral beauty when he wants. So the dead shepherd says to the living:

> ... let me hear your sheep bleating
> While one of you sits on a rough rock, softly
> Playing the pipes to them; let a village man
> Pick wild flowers in early spring
> To decorate my grave; and let a shepherd
> Raise the full udder of a nursing ewe
> And squirt rich milk onto my tomb....[15]

That tone, however, is rare in him. He prefers to be harsh, even brutal—advising mice to rob somebody else's bread bin, where the takings will be better than in his own (6.302), or mentioning with no sentimental commentary the father who erected one tomb for his four daughters, all dead in childbirth (7.463). The sea for no good reason drowns a young boy and casts his body on a lonely beach where seagulls scream (7.652). A road passes over the grave of a forgotten man, and the wagon wheels and axles break the coffin open (7.478). People are impotent, presumptuous:

> Poor little life! Not even, so fugitive, fill'd with pleasure!
>     Hateful is death, but life hath a bitterer taste of tears.
> Behold the groundwork of bones! Exactly drawn to that measure,
>     Do ye exalt your brows, O men, to the cloudy spheres?[16]

Persons who hope are fools but perhaps deserve some pity. There are, however, individuals that deserve only scorn: the man who dresses in a dirty goatskin and carries a filthy oil flask so that he can qualify as a Cynic (6.298), the man with a tongue that stings like a wasp (7.408), or the old female alcoholic:

> ... On her grave behold, set plain
> For all to know her by, an Attic bowl.

Ev'n underground she still keeps moaning, not
For children or for husband left in life
Indigent, but for one thing only—that
The bowl is empty![17]

Although Leonidas was known to his own age and later ages as "of Taras" or "of Tarentum," he may be the least characteristic of those who went abroad as Tarentines. The dialect of his poems, though largely Dorian, is by no means entirely so (but the extant manuscripts may contain forms that his poems did not originally have). It would seem that he lived too late for Pythagoreanism; at any rate he does not reflect it. Beyond that, even his view of death is not typical of Taras in the third century B.C., when the attention paid to an afterlife—the yearning for it, perhaps—was still strong in the city. Death is for Leonidas simply a release from life's evils. Or, as for Robert Blair, Thomas Gray, Shelley, and other English poets of the eighteenth and early nineteenth centuries, it has the merit of reducing the proud. He celebrates the democratic action of death:

Know me for Crethon's monument; I show
His name; the man himself is dust below:
Crethon, who once did Asian kings outshine,
Crethon, the lord of flocks, the lord of kine,
Crethon, who once—enough! the admired, the grand,
How few feet now he fills of all that land![18]

Leonidas has no appreciation for the immortality of the soul—no sense of it, beyond that which he ascribes to the old woman moaning for her wine. The carvings on the *naiskoi* at Taras, the pictures on pottery, and other allusions to immortality as a desirable condition had apparently not impressed him during his formative years.

His milieu was the Hellenistic world in general. Although he avoided some of the favorite subjects of Hellenistic poetry—love, convivial drinking—in his compact votive epigrams or other epitaphs he was writing a type of verse that his contemporaries were also writing, and in his compound words he was indulging in a preciousness that they appreciated. His realistic, sometimes savage treatment of poor folk was a literary duplication of the taste for bronze and ceramic figures of slaves, dwarfs, drunken old women, and hunchbacks that flourished especially in Asia Minor and Alexandria. He was much less a Tarentine poet than an international one. The Hellenistic *koine*—the virtual uniformity that became evident in so many aspects of Greek life in the third century B.C.—had swept him up.

# Notes to Chapter 7

1. *Laws*, 8.840A, R. G. Bury, trans. Loeb, *Plato*, Vol. IX, p. 163.

2. Aelian, *De Natura Animalium*, 6.1. *On the Characteristics of Animals*, A. F. Scholfield, trans. Loeb, *Aelian*, Vol. II, pp. 11, 13. Aelian had been reading Plato. For Iccus's probable dates see Wuilleumier, p. 566. Wuilleumier supposes that Ikkos was practicing Pythagorean principles.

3. *Phaido*, 61 E, Harold North Fowler, trans. Loeb, *Plato*, Vol. I, p. 215. The "sage" mentioned in the *Gorgias* (493 A) as having taught that we are dead and the body is our tomb may also be Philolaus. See Wuilleumier's discussion, pp. 566-73. Cicero (*De Oratore*, 3.139) mentions Philolaus as a teacher of Archytas.

4. *Lives of Famous Men (de viris illustribus)*, 15.2, Gareth Schmeling, trans. (Lawrence, Kansas, 1971), p. 81. Diogenes Laertius, writing perhaps as late as the third century A.D., also identified Lysis as a Tarentine. For discussion see Wuilleumier, pp. 564-65, and John Burnet, *Early Greek Philosophy*, 4th ed. (1930; reprint ed., Cleveland and New York, 1962), pp. 91-92, 276. Erich Frank in his *Plato und die Sogenannten Pythagoreer* (1923; reprint ed., Tübingen, 1962) calls both Philolaus and Lysis products of a "literarische Fiktion, die nicht den Wert einer historischen Tatsache hat" (p. 294, n. 1). Wuilleumier opposes this view, but there may possibly be truth in it.

5. See Diodorus Siculus, 10.4.1. Loeb, *Didorus*, Vol. IV, p. 57. See also Wuilleumier, pp. 585-86.

6. See, for instance, Cicero, *Letters to Atticus*, 8.4, and Plutarch, *Moralia*, 1093C. See also Wuilleumier, pp. 587-607, and Delatte, *Essai*, pp. 207 ff. On Aristoxenus as a musical theorist see Kurt Sachs, *The Rise of Music in the Ancient World* (New York, 1943), pp. 199, 207-208, 211-12, 224, 261, and Gerald Abraham, *Concise Oxford History of Music* (London, New York, and Melbourne, 1979), pp. 31-34.

7. See T. B. L. Webster, *Greek Theatre Production*, pp. 164-65, and his *Hellenistic Poetry and Art* (New York, 1964), pp. 254-55, and especially Wuilleumier, pp. 618-21, 627, and Gigante, "Teatro Greco," pp. 87-90, 100-101, 108-109, 112.

8. See Webster, *Greek Theatre Production*, pp. 97, 143, 146, 170.

9. *Palatine Anthology* 7.715, Webster, trans., in *Hellenistic Poetry and Art*, p. 218.

10. *Palatine Anthology* 6.300 and 7.736, Edwyn Bevan, trans., in *The Poems of Leonidas of Tarentum* (Oxford, 1931), pp. 16, 14.

11. See especially A. S. F. Gow, "Leonidas of Tarentum," *Classical Quarterly*, New Series, 8 (1958), 113-23, and, following Gow, Webster, *Hellenistic Poetry and Art*, pp. 218-20. Webster, by examining possible influences on his poetry, concludes that Leonidas may have flourished as late as 230. Gigante and Lévêque, however, contend that the Pyrrhus poem is by Leonidas; see Gigante, "La Cultura a Taranto," Convegno 10, pp. 76-79, and Lévêque in "Il Dibattito," Convegno 10, p. 206. On Leonidas in general see Wuilleumier, pp. 633-56; the Introduction to Bevan's *Poems of Leonidas*; Gigante, "Cultura," pp. 80-131; and Branislaw Bilinski in "Il Dibattito," Convego 10, pp. 208-210.

12. 6.204, Kenneth Rexroth, trans., *The Greek Anthology and Other Greek Epigrams. A selection in modern verse translations,* Peter Jay, ed. (New York, 1973), p. 100.

13. 6.211, Peter Levi, trans. *Greek Anthology,* Jay, ed., p. 99.

14. 7.726, Bevan, trans., p. 70.

15, 7.657, Fleur Adcock,trans.,*Greek Anthology*, Jay, ed., p. 104.

16. 7.472, Bevan, trans., p. 2.

17. 7.455, Bevan, trans., p. 88.

18. 7.740, Bevan, trans., p. 4.

# 8

# The Coming of Pyrrhus

The last time Taras asked for help, it was for help against Rome. Whether a conflict between Taras and Rome was inevitable has been debated often. The prevalent modern view is that there was not room in Italy for both a growing Roman power and a bloc of independent Greek states, that the progress toward war was inexorable. On the other side it can be said that, at the time at least, Rome had so many other problems that the senate did not really want a Greek war.[1] Among the ancients, besides, Taras had a bad press, in so far as we can tell from what survives. Roman authors, or men writing for a Roman audience, did not mind blaming Taras rather than Rome for rendering war necessary. Dio Cassius, for instance, affirmed that the Tarentines "forced the Romans even against their will to make war upon them."[2]

Certainly Rome's troubles in other parts of Italy might have deterred it from taking on the Greeks of the South. In 285 the Gauls, pushed from their lands by a churning of peoples in central Europe, crossed the Apennines and descended on more fruitful areas to take possession or to plunder. This was part of a tremendous Gallic surge against the civilizations to the south; other Gauls, also pushed from behind, would dash themselves against Macedon, where their final defeat would not occur until 277, and still others would invade Asia Minor. The Gauls who came down into Italy were spearheaded by a tribe called the Senones. In 284 the consul Caecilius Metellus died in battle against them, and his army was virtually annihilated. Etruscans, Samnites, and Lucanians took advantage of this defeat to repudiate their treaties with Rome. The senate dispatched envoys to the Senones to negotiate a return of prisoners, but the Senones killed the envoys. Rome proceeded to hand the Senones a defeat, but in 283 another Gallic tribe, the Boii, joined forces with the Etruscans against Rome. A Roman army led by the consul Cornelius Dolabella defeated them at Lake Vadino, but the defeat was not decisive. In 282 the Boii made war again, and again Rome dealt with them. The Etruscan cities of Vulci and Volsinii, however, were not subdued until 280.

In 284 the polis of Thurii had appealed to Rome against the Lucanians, who were conforming to custom by raiding the Greeks. Beset by such serious problems of their own in 284, the Romans may not have responded with any more than a promise. Whatever help Rome gave, however, the Thurians were grateful enough to set up a statue to the plebeian tribune Caius Aelius, who had brought their request before his fellow citizens.[3] In 282, still beleaguered by the Lucanians, Thurii appealed again to Rome. It is possible to blame Thurii for not asking help from Taras instead—to point to this city's traditional jealousy of Taras, and to call the Thurians short-sighted, in 284 as well as 282, for putting a petty Greek rivalry above the greater need for the Hellenic south to stand united against the Roman menace.[4] But if Rome had afforded the Thurians any real assurance in 284, it is no wonder they asked for Roman help again. The rising republic—the only power in Italy which, by 282, had proved able to cope with barbarians—probably impressed the Thurians as a much better bet than Taras. The repeated reliance of Taras on mercenaries could not have said much for the strength of the city; and the ambitious mercenary chiefs whom Taras chose were untrustworthy anyway.

Fabricius, consul in 282, came to the relief of Thurii with Roman troops and stationed a Roman garrison there. The Tarentines were suitably offended, as both Rome and Thurii had surely expected them to be. Taras must have looked at the presence of Roman soldiers in Thurii, about eighty miles across the gulf from Taras itself, as another threat to its security and independence, a tightening of the rope. Thurii had never been friendly of course, but having impotent unfriendly Greeks in the area was preferable to having vigorous Romans.

There was an agreement between Taras and Rome, dating possibly from the period of Alexander the Molossian in the late 330s but dating more probably from the closing years of the fourth century, when Cleonymus was presumably acting in Tarentine interests.[5] A stipulation of this agreement was that Roman ships were not to sail east of the Lacinium Promontory (located just south of Croton) and consequently into the Tarentine gulf. Taras was, in other words, excluding Romans from the waters of the gulf, no matter what encroachments they might make on land.[6] The Tarentine theater, whatever its exact location may have been, overlooked the outer harbor and the expanse of gulf beyond. In the autumn of 282, while the citizens were in the theater to celebrate the Dionysia, they saw ten Roman warships offshore.[7]

The Romans could not have expected to attack Taras with only ten ships. The possibility that they had any idea of provoking a war is remote since the prevailing temper of the senate was still one of caution.

Although the Gauls had been taken care of, there were other problems. To start military operations against the Greeks before the Lucanians and their relatives the Samnites had been disposed of—plus the Bruttians in Italy's toe and, closer to home, the Etruscans of Vulci and Volsinii—would be to undertake too much at once. Perhaps the appearance of the fleet was an attempt to establish the fact that the treaty was outmoded, that Taras no longer had the power to shut Roman ships out of any body of water. It is also conceivable that the Romans had come to support the minority party in Taras, which favored Rome. They perhaps intended to cooperate with this party in bringing about a change in government, and even to set up a garrison at Taras, which, like the one at Thurii, would watch out for Roman interests. Or Appian, writing in the second century A.D., may have been right when he said the Romans were simply "on a voyage of inspection."[8] Rome now had three colonies on or near the Adriatic coast—at Hadria in Picenum, at Castrum Novum just a little north of Hadria, and at Sena Gallica in Umbria, the northernmost of the three. The fleet may have been proceeding toward one of these. Or its destination may have been Thurii in order to support the Roman operation there, although the sources do not indicate that it was heading south.

Since this was the period when Rhinthon was active at Taras, it is pleasant to think that the Tarentines were watching one of his plays, but that is pure assumption. The only sense of immediacy for the scene is provided by Roman historians such as Dio Cassius, who says that the spectators in the theater were drunk (9.39.4-5), or again Appian, who says that an unprincipled demagogue excited the audience to fury (3.7.1). These pictures may be taken for what they are worth, which is little. Drunk or not, however, and aroused or not by a demagogue, the Tarentines were violently angry at the sight of Roman ships. A naval battle took place. The Romans seem to have been caught unprepared, which suggests that they were not under instructions to provoke a war. The enraged Tarentines sank four of the ships, killed the commander of the fleet, and took a fifth ship captive. The five remaining vessels managed to get away. The Tarentines evidently murdered some of the captive Romans and sold others into slavery.[9]

It sounds as if relations between Rome and Taras had become so strained by the time of this incident that the Tarentines—or at least the prevalent party—welcomed the opportunity to attack the Roman ships. Perhaps they were experiencing pent-up frustration over the course of events in recent years. They did not stop with the sinking and dispersal of the fleet. A body of soldiers marched to Thurii, attacked and sacked it, and drove out its pro-Roman aristocrats and the Roman garrison. The Tarentines had now shown both Rome and Thurii that their own city was still formidable. They had also asked for war.

Rome, however, seems still to have been disposed toward peace, if we can believe the Rome-oriented historians on whom we have to rely. It sent envoys to Taras under the direction of the dignified Lucius Postumius and apparently under instructions to make only reasonable demands. The Tarentines crowded the theater to see the Romans. The result must have surpassed many farces.

The Romans, wearing their purple-striped togas and their gravity, stated their demands: that nonparticipants who had been taken prisoner should be released, that the pro-Roman aristocrats of Thurii should be allowed to return home, that plundered Thurian property should be restored or paid for, and that the leaders of the anti-Roman party in Taras should be turned over to Rome. Only this last stipulation could have been construed as less than mild. The envoys spoke in Greek, either out of courtesy or because they could not expect the Tarentines to know Latin. But the audience, in a part-antagonistic and part-hilarious mood, listened to catch mistakes in the Greek and jeered when the envoys committed them. There was probably the implication that these Romans were a type of barbarian, unable to use the one really civilized tongue correctly. The audience also ridiculed the Romans' clothes. Then a funny fellow named Philonides, nicknamed Half-Bottle, walked over to Postumius, turned his back on the Roman, bent over, lifted up his own robe behind, and shit on Postumius's toga. The spectators howled and clapped their hands.

But the representative of the republic did not lose his stateliness. Holding out his fouled toga, he informed the Tarentines that they would wash it clean with their blood. The Greeks sang some dirty songs. Postumius strongly suggested that the Tarentines had a poor sense of humor.[10]

He brought the toga back to Rome without having it washed, and exhibited it. Even with this evidence to look at, the senate hesitated to come out in favor of a war against Taras before the Etruscans and the barbarians had been thoroughly subdued. After many days of debate as to whether the war should be undertaken immediately or postponed indefinitely, the senate finally voted for war. The people's assembly approved the decision.[11] The consul Lucius Aemilius Barbula, who was already conducting military operations against the Samnites, was sent orders to march into Tarentine territory and carry out deterrent actions, which probably involved the burning of fields and pastures. If the Tarentines could be cowed by these tactics into agreeing to the demands already made by Postumius and his fellow envoys, hostilities would not need to proceed any further.

Instead of accepting the Roman terms, the Tarentines considered calling in Pyrrhus of Epirus. As usual, there was division. The makeup of the two political groups in Taras at this time, and their predispositions, have to be inferred. Zonaras's twelfth-century *Epitome* of Dio says, "The elderly and well-to-do were anxious for peace, but those who were youthful and who had little or nothing were for war."[12] The peace party—the more conservative group—seems to have been at base aristocratic, like the pro-Roman party at Thurii; and it seems also to have been the party traditionally opposed to hiring mercenaries. Either its members felt that a close Roman connection would benefit the city more than a chronic dependence on unpredictable, self-interested mercenary chieftains, or they believed that war with Rome was too high a price to pay for the leadership of Greek Italy. In addition to the aristocratic or "well-to-do" base of the party, other people must have been attracted to it simply out of opposition to war.

But it was probably smaller than the "democratic" or "popular" party, whose members were the people that filled the theater to laugh at and insult the Roman envoys. Zonaras's placement of the young in this party perhaps implies a liberal viewpoint, at least a willingness to try one more mercenary general, even though the record of mercenaries so far was not impressive. The party also included those who had little or nothing to lose by a war—in other words the poorer classes of citizens, the fishermen and potters and other laborers.[13] Again the epitomizer is oversimplifying; others, neither young nor particularly poor, must have been drawn to this party in the conviction that only a final showdown with Rome would improve Taras's fortunes, that temporizing was the worst policy. It is, in fact, hard to believe that this party did not include a number of the "well-to-do"—if not landed aristocrats, at least prosperous businessmen who felt that Rome was too dangerous a threat to their own financial futures and those of their children.

And there were still many Tarentines who could be swayed in either direction. Appian is probably not accurate when he says that the Tarentines "were about equally divided in opinion" as to whether to ask Pyrrhus's help.[14] But a number of uncommitted people is implied by Plutarch's story concerning the assembly which met in the theater to decide the issue. The mood of the crowd seems generally to have been in favor of Pyrrhus and war. Into the theater, however, came prancing a man named Meton, with the gestures of a drunk, a garland on his head, and a flute girl in front of him. It looked as if he had come from an all-night banquet and brought her along. She played party songs, and he hugged her. The indulgent Tarentines shouted their endorsement of this new spectacle and wanted a song from Meton himself. But Meton, who happened to be a proponent of peace, was performing a symbolic act. He told his fellow citizens soberly that if they invited a foreign king into Taras with his army, they would no longer be able to do the kind of thing he had just been illustrating; Tarentine liberties and pleasures would be curtailed. If the story is true, it assumes a sizable body of Tarentines who could still be influenced toward peace; as for those already committed to peace, most of them, Plutarch says, had been afraid to come to the meeting. But the anti-Roman authorities had Meton thrown out of the theater before he could do more damage to their side.[15]

The democratic party may have been overconfident, but at least it could count on the city's naval superiority to Rome. At the time the Roman fleet of ten ships invaded Tarentine waters to its own regret, the republic had not developed its navy, whereas Taras was of course a widely experienced and well equipped sea power.[16] As for the choice of Pyrrhus, he already shone with glory as a military chief. If he agreed to come, he would certainly shed luster on the city, and if any military leader could help Taras against so dangerous an enemy as Rome, he could. His kingdom, besides, was right across the Ionian Sea from Taras, simplifying the problem of transportation.

Polybius, in the century following these events, offered his own explanation for the choice of Pyrrhus: "It was the pride engendered by prosperity which made the Tarentines call in Pyrrhus of Epirus. For in every case where a democracy has for long enjoyed power, it naturally begins to be sick of present conditions and next looks out for a master, and having found one very soon hates him again, as the change is manifestly much for the worse."[17] A Greek writing from the Roman point of view, Polybius illustrates the unfavorable press that Taras would get for its part in the Pyrrhic wars. There is probably a modicum of truth in his comments, however. A restlessness, a dissatisfaction, almost a whimsicality is detectable in the Taras of this period— in the Tarentines assembled at the theater, for instance. But the city was no longer as prosperous as Polybius implies, nor quite as sick.

Perhaps in the summer of 281—the precise date is not determinable— Taras sent ambassadors across the Ionian Sea to Pyrrhus's capital at Ambracia, apparently a preliminary group to make the proposal and a follow-up group to secure Pyrrhus's consent and discuss terms. According to Pausanias, they talked up the riches of Italy. According to Plutarch, they brought gifts and promised the king a very large fighting force already in Italy, made up of Tarentines and barbarian enemies of Rome (Lucanians, Messapians, Samnites) and amounting to 20,000 horsemen and 350,000 foot soldiers. Either the ambassadors were exaggerating or Plutarch was.[18]

Pyrrhus had led a violent life so far. Born in 319 or 318 B.C., he was rescued as a baby from the court of his own father, king of Epirus, where an enemy faction had taken over, and after an exciting flight was brought to Glaucias, a friendly Illyrian king. At Glaucias's court he spent his childhood, reared along with his host's own children, but in 307, when Pyrrhus was about twelve, Glaucias led an army into Epirus and (Pyrrhus's father now being dead) set him on the throne of his ancestors. In Epirus he reigned as a teenage monarch until, while he was away to attend the wedding of one of Glaucias's sons, a faction led by his uncle took over, and Pyrrhus was throneless again. About seventeen by this time, 303/302, he became a soldier of fortune, a mercenary serving under his sister's hard-drinking husband, the ambitious and warlike Demetrius, Besieger of Cities. In 301 Demetrius was defeated by the monarchs of Egypt and Syria in the Battle of Ipsus, but Pyrrhus, who took to war perhaps more than to anything else, performed gallantly in the great conflict. Demetrius sent him as a hostage to the court of Ptolemy I Soter at the new and glistening Greek-style Egyptian capital, Alexandria. Not a man to let opportunities slip by, Pyrrhus established friendly relations with Ptolemy, which meant that he had to abandon Demetrius. With Ptolemy's help he regained the throne in Epirus, where rebels had killed his uncle and his uncle's children. He also married the princess Antigone, daughter of Ptolemy's wife Berenice by a former husband.[19]

In Epirus Pyrrhus reigned jointly with his second cousin Neoptolemus. But a joint reign could not endure. There were rivalries and rumors at court, culminating in Neoptolemus's murder at a dinner to which Pyrrhus had invited him. Pyrrhus proceeded to enlarge his kingdom, mainly at the expense of Macedon. At first he helped the new Macedonian king, Alexander, son of Cassander, against his brother Antipater (another example of a joint reign that did not work out), and the grateful Alexander gave him lands in return, including Ambracia, where he established his capital. Later Pyrrhus became involved in wars against his old friend, onetime employer, and brother-in-law, Demetrius, who had now succeeded in making himself Macedonian king.

It was primarily through these wars, in which he took much territory that had once belonged to Macedon, that he gained his reputation as a superb general and a dashing soldier. Plutarch tells the story of his hand-to-hand combat with the general Pantauchus, whom Demetrius had left in charge of Aetolia and who had offered Pyrrhus a challenge: "At first they hurled their spears, then, coming to close quarters, they plied their swords with might and skill. Pyrrhus got one wound, but gave Pantauchus two, one in the thigh, and one along the neck, and put him to flight and overthrew him; he did not kill him, however, for his friends hauled him away. Then the Epeirots, exalted by the victory of their king and admiring his valor, overwhelmed and cut to pieces the phalanx of the Macedonians. . . . "[20] Whether strictly true or not, this tale of glory illustrates the Homeric reputation that Pyrrhus was developing.

After the death of his wife Antigone, he had married Lanasa, daughter of Agathocles of Syracuse. (He also married the daughter of an Illyrian chief and the daughter of King Audoleon of Paeonia.) Lanasa had brought him as part of her dowry the island of Corcyra off the Epirot coast. But she deserted him and went to her island, which she invited Demetrius to share with her. It would be a while before Pyrrhus got the island back. In the meantime, however, he carried on the Macedonian wars and even succeeded in making himself king in Macedon for a time, though he had to share his extensive territories with the aged Lysimachus of Thrace, who had helped to overthrow Demetrius. Pyrrhus and Lysimachus worked together with relative amicability at first, but toward the end of 286 Pyrrhus became so distrustful that he allied himself secretly with Demetrius's son, Antigonus Gonatas. Lysimachus threw his army into Pyrrhus's territory, chasing him out. Knowing that in spite of his charisma he was helpless against Lysimachus's enormous military machine, Pyrrhus limped back home. The Macedonian army , astutely siding with a winner, elected Lysimachus king of Macedon.

Pyrrhus now sulked in Epirus—and was unable to prevent Lysimachus in 283 from invading it, plundering the tombs of its kings (Pyrrhus's ancestors), and taking Acarnania to make this area in northwestern Greece a vassal state of Macedon. The coasts and mountains of Illyria north of Epirus belonged to Pyrrhus, but he was still, when the Tarentine embassy arrived in 281, a failure in his own terms, a poor player in the game of power with his fellow warrior kings. At the age of thirty-seven or thirty-eight, young enough yet to have a future—restive, preeminently a man of action, sick of sitting at home but without much chance of winning the east—he reigned over a meager land, one which would be unable to supply him with enough troops to compete against the more potent kings who ruled the rich territories of Egypt, Syria and Mesopotamia, Thrace, or Sicily.[21] The Tarentine invitation, therefore, with its promise of Italiot Greek and barbarian troops to add to his own, came at a very opportune time, as the Tarentines must have known. Italy offered land and glory. He may even have thought of extending his conquests to Sicily, if things went well—or beyond Sicily to the Carthaginian possessions in northern Africa.[22]

There may have been another motive, for a man so conscious of military fame. In the early third century, the example of Alexander the Great still glowed as an ignis fatuus, tempting kings to launch out and do likewise. Pyrrhus's father had been first cousin to Alexander's mother, Olympias, and the rather close relationship to the god-king perhaps heightened Pyrrhus's desire to emulate him.[23] In his previous thrusts at conquest and his valor in personal combat, he seems to have looked to Alexander as a model. The admiring Macedonians whom he defeated compared him to Alexander. "The other kings, they said, represented Alexander with their purple robes, their body-guards, the inclination of their necks, and their louder tones in conversation; but Pyrrhus alone, in arms and action."[24] Before one of his victories, according to Plutarch, he had a vision of Alexander lying on a couch: " 'And how, O King,' Pyrrhus ventured to ask, 'when thou art sick, canst thou give me aid and help?' 'My name itself will give it,' said the king, and mounting a Nisaean horse he led the way."[25] If Pyrrhus could not go east like Alexander, he would go west like his other relative, his father's cousin the Molossian, and win Alexandrine victories there.

Another motivating factor, one that involves Rome as the enemy of Pyrrhus, has been suggested. Pyrrhus traced his ancestry to Achilles, greatest of Homeric heroes, whose son Neoptolemus, according to the story, had taken possession of Epirus, married a native princess named Lanassa, and sired the Epirot royal house. Pausanias says that, while the Tarentine envoys were making their request, "Pyrrhus remembered the capture of Troy, which he took to be an omen of his success in the war, as he was a descendant of Achilles making war upon a colony of Trojans."[26] According to the thesis, Pyrrhus as the new Achilles conceived of Rome as the new Troy, destined to be destroyed under his leadership as the old Troy had been obliterated by the Greeks of the heroic age. In fact, the whole legend of Rome's Trojan connection, the legend which Virgil would later popularize in the *Aeneid* with his emphasis on the Trojan fugitive Aeneas as the progenitor of the Roman nation, started as a conscious creation on Pyrrhus's part to put his venture into a heroic cast. So runs the theory at any rate.[27]

It is attractive but perhaps romantic. A belief in Rome's Trojan origins was evidently several centuries older than Pyrrhus; if he made use of the belief at all, it was not as his own creation but simply as a convenience. But the concept of Trojans as people with whom Roman enemies could be equated would probably not have occurred to Pyrrhus or to his contemporaries, trained in boyhood on an epic poem that heroized Trojans as well as Greeks. Pyrrhus, in fact, had a sister named Troas and a grandmother of the same name, and had given one of his sons the Trojan name Helenus. He claimed descent not only from Achilles but from the royal Trojan house. After the fall of Troy the mourning Andromache, widow of the Trojan hero Hector, was given to Achilles' son Neoptolemus, either as wife or concubine. When Neoptolemus died he bequeathed her to Helenus, one of the many sons of the dead King Priam of Troy, and they lived in Epirus, where Helenus sired a royal race just as

Neoptolemus had sired one. Pyrrhus's grandmother Troas claimed descent from both kingly houses and therefore from both Neoptolemus's father, Achilles, and Helenus's father, Priam. Through Troas, Pyrrhus could make the same exalted claim; and with all these Trojan connections, he could hardly have conceived of himself as heir to the epic enmity between Greeks and Trojans.

This, then, was the man who had agreed to fight for Taras—the Eagle, as his soldiers called him—a king with illustrious ancestors and illustrious relatives, monarch over semi-Greek mountain folk, rambunctious adventurer down from the hills, self-styled Homeric hero eager for glory, defeated military strategist whom Hannibal would praise as the best of generals.[28] Unlike some other Hellenistic rulers—most notably Ptolemy I Soter, founder of the great museum at Alexandria, and Antigonus Gonatas, friend of the philosopher Zeno—he was not much interested in intellectual matters. He would write books, but on military tactics, based on his own experiences. His effect on his troops, however, must have been extraordinary. Plutarch says that people even attributed supernatural qualities to him. They believed that he had the power to cure diseases of the spleen: the sick person would lie on his back on the ground, and Pyrrhus would put his right foot on the spleen and sacrifice a white cock. The big toe of that foot was divine, Plutarch says, and when Pyrrhus was cremated, it did not burn.[29]

Pyrrhus probably did not set sail for Italy with his forces until the late spring of 280. Before that—according to Plutarch, who is as usual suspect—a follower whom he valued highly had tried to dissuade him from making the expedition. This was Cineas, a Thessalian who possessed rhetorical abilities reminiscent of Demosthenes and who was the closest Pyrrhus came to an intellectual friend. Cineas's argument, put into rhetorical terms by Plutarch, was this: if you conquer southern Italy, then conquer Sicily, then go on to Carthaginian Africa and conquer it, and with all this power behind you turn to the east and win back the Macedon that you have lost, what will you really have gained? You can sit at ease in Epirus, drink and converse, and have just as much pleasure without all the trouble.[30] If Cineas ever did say this kind of thing to Pyrrhus, he had no great effect. What Pyrrhus did was to send an advance force of 3,000 men to Italy and to send Cineas too, apparently as their commander.[31] The Roman consul Aemilius was ambushed in a pass by the Tarentines and the advance force from Epirus, but since he moved his captives to the head of the line, the Tarentines and Epirots had to let up on the spears and arrows and slings so as not to hit their own friends.[32] That was the beginning of the war.

The Romans undertook the war with some psychological disadvantages. It must have been a blow to learn that Pyrrhus had accepted

Taras's invitation—that what had started as, it was hoped, nothing more than an action of intimidation, was developing into a full-scale conflict. In spite of his recent defeats, Pyrrhus's reputation remained extremely impressive, greater than that of any Roman general, though Dio is probably exaggerating when he describes the Romans as "overcome with fear, since they had heard that he was a great warrior himself and had a large and irresistible army."[33] The remark about the army is significant. In the early Hellenistic Age, less than two generations since the death of Alexander the Great and just after a series of prolonged and terrible wars fought out among his successors, a Greek army must have connoted military expertise of the first order and a high degree of ferocity.

The republic, besides, was far from united. The war party, plebeian and urban, interested in overcoming a Hellenic city that interfered with trade, was opposed by a conservative group, agriculturally oriented, who wanted to cultivate their own acres undisturbed; and many members of the senate were still unconvinced that a struggle with the Greek South at that particular moment was wise.[34]

Polybius, perhaps a little naively, gives Rome a psychological advantage that it may not really have enjoyed. The recent wars against the Gauls and Etruscans, he says, had gotten Roman soldiers used to being cut up by an enemy, so that they did not have to fear the terrible Greeks any more than they feared anybody else (2.20.8-10; see also 1.6.7). It is no doubt true, however, that in the struggles of the mid-280s the Roman troops had gotten battle experience as good as Pyrrhus's own troops had gotten in the Macedonian wars. And Rome did have a definite geographical advantage. The cities federated with Rome across the central part of the peninsula meant that Pyrrhus and Taras had to face a wide and diversified territory occupied by enemies, as Hannibal would have to do later in the century. Pyrrhus could deal with the Italian federation only by striking at various parts of this broad, Hydralike area; if Rome kept him confined in the foot of the Italian boot, he could accomplish little. Besides, if the Roman army suffered serious losses, it could be replenished on home ground. If Pyrrhus needed more Epirots, he would have to send across the Ionian Sea for them. Only more barbarians and possibly more Tarentines and other Greeks could be added in Italy.

Taras disptached ships to carry over Pyrrhus's troops and their equipment, just as it had done for Cleonymus in 303. Antiochus I—monarch of the vast Seleucid dominions since the assassination of his father Seleucus in the late summer of 281—sent money. The epitomizer Justin, who probably lived in the third century A.D., says that Ptolemy Ceraunus, ruthless son of Ptolemy I of Egypt and murderer of Seleucus, sent 5,000 foot soldiers, 4,000 horsemen, and fifty elephants, but these figures are no doubt a considerable improvement on the truth.[35] Antigonus Gonatas, son of Demetrius and claimant to the throne of Macedon, contributed transport ships to supplement the ones from Taras. All of these men, members of the second generation of heirs to Alexander's winnings, were glad to get Pyrrhus out of the way so that they could pursue their own wars without his interference. According to Plutarch ("Pyrrhus," 15.1), Pyrrhus embarked from Epirus with about 20,000 hoplites, 3,000 horsemen, 2,000 archers, 500 slingers, and twenty elephants. These numbers are surely inaccurate but must suffice in the absence of others. Whether they include the contributions from Ptolemy Ceraunus is uncertain; presumably they do. The elephants may have been the gifts of Ceraunus, if Justin is correct in saying that Ceraunus sent some, or they may have been ones that Pyrrhus himself had taken in battle against Demetrius, or they may have been a combination of both.[36]

It was probably May of 280 when Pyrrhus made the crossing.[37] Transporting so large a force across the water would not have been an easy project, especially considering the horses and the elephants. We are not given the precise route.[38] It is conceivable that he paused on the way to retake the island of Corcyra—or he may have retaken it a few years earlier.[39]

Whether or not he added the difficulties of a maritime siege to the strain of crossing, he did have to cope with a violent storm, narrated by Zonaras (8.2) and more elaborately by Plutarch ("Pyrrhus," 15-16.1). It was night, and the ships were in the middle of the Ionian Sea when the tempest struck. In its fury, according to Plutarch, vessels foundered on the rocks of the Iapygian promontory or were blown off toward Sicily and Africa. Pyrrhus himself, hero that he was, jumped into the water and swam and swam. At daybreak, weary but undaunted, he was cast onto shore in the land of the Messapians. Several of his ships beached at about the same time, with fewer than 2,000 foot soldiers, a sprinkling of cavalry, and two of the precious elephants. The friendly Messapians rushed to the rescue. Pyrrhus and his dwindled army managed to get up the Iapygian peninsula to Taras, and Cineas and the Epirot soldiers under his command came out to escort them into the city. Eventually most of the other ships limped in, so that, as it turned out, the loss was not very great. The story, though no doubt based on fact, sounds a little fabulous, as if Plutarch is trying to write in an epic mode appropriate to the royal adventurer.[40]

Pyrrhus had sent on ahead from Epirus to Taras not only Cineas but also an officer named Milon, who may have been in charge of a separate advance force of Epirots or may have commanded the men with whom

Cineas had come. These early arrivals had been posted on the wall guarding the eastern edge of the city, and they had also gotten the acropolis ready for residence by the king.[41] The emotional condition of Taras at the moment of Pyrrhus's arrival can perhaps be inferred from recent events. The consul Aemilius Barbula had of course been devastating the fields and orchards in the summer and fall of 281, trying to frighten the city but under no orders to lay siege, sparing the lands of those known to be sympathetic toward Rome (which must have exacerbated party animosity), and treating captives with sufficient leniency to show that Rome could still be merciful although its patience was running out. The effect was to strengthen the aristocratic, pro-Roman element within the polis to such an extent that a pro-Roman aristocrat named Agis was made strategus, with the power to treat with the Romans. This is an important indication of the degree to which Taras, like Rome itself, was still of two minds. The pro-Roman effort at intimidation stood a good chance of working. Then, probably in the autumn of 281, Cineas and Milon arrived with the advance Epirot troops—the orator and the officer, perhaps under instructions to influence the city by the double blow of rhetorical eloquence and military action. Agis was replaced as strategus by a man favoring Pyrrhus. Aemilius Barbula was ambushed by some Tarentines and the advance force from Epirus—the first instance in which Taras's men and Pyrrhus's men acted as one against the Romans. The consul retired to winter quarters at Venusia northwest of Taras, where Rome had established a colony 20,000 strong in 291, so that he was no longer on hand to frighten Tarentines into friendship with Rome.

Meanwhile anti-Roman Tarentines were busy diplomatically, organizing the other Greek cities—friendly Heraclea, Metapontum, even the traditionally inimical Thurii—into an informal league for resistance to Rome, and securing the support of Rome's barbarian enemies also. When Pyrrhus arrived in the spring of 280, the pro-Roman party must have been very much in the background—probably diminished in size, latent but for the moment impotent. As the anti-Roman majority watched the bulk of his seasoned troops come in soon after, and as they saw the strange and formidable elephants, enthusiasm must have mounted. Rome did not have the seapower to attack Pyrrhus's ships on the way over, but now it did nothing on land either; and this fact possibly raised Tarentine confidence even higher.[42] A large part of the city looked boldly forward to the coming conflict, an answer once and for all to the Roman threat.

We do not know the specific terms of the agreement worked out by Pyrrhus and the second batch of Tarentine envoys in Epirus, any more than we know the specific terms of the contracts between Taras and its former mercenary generals. For instance, we have no indication of the relationship, the distribution of powers, between Pyrrhus and the strategus. Taras was, however, in the asking position; it was Pyrrhus who conferred the favor. For that reason, Taras must have granted him extraordinary authority, as developments in the city soon showed.

A decision to reduce the weight of the silver stater or didrachm from about 7.77 grams to 6.60 grams was evidently made in 281, before Pyrrhus arrived, or in 280 soon after his arrival. The weight of the silver drachm was already less than half that of the traditional didrachm, but the drachm was probably designed for use by cities with which Taras traded rather than for transactions within Taras itself. The weight reduction of the didrachm, the first in over a century, served Pyrrhus's purpose even if he had not requested it or even if he was not empowered to demand it. Since more didrachms could now be turned out from a given amount of silver, more were available for the payment of his troops. The ouput of silver during the Pyrrhic wars was very large, and much of the coinage must have gone to the Epirot soldiers under Pyrrhus's command and to the barbarian allies.[43]

Whatever Pyrrhus's part in the devaluation of the coinage may have been (if he had any part in it at all), he imposed severe restraints on the daily lives of the citizens. He was, after all, a general beyond anything else, and Taras was his camp. According to Plutarch he found the citizens not at all disposed to be soldiers: ". . . seeing that the multitude were incapable, unless under strong constraint, of either saving themselves or saving others, but were inclined to let him do their fighting for them while they remained at home in the enjoyment of their baths and social festivities, he closed up the gymnasia and the public walks, where, as they strolled about, they fought out their country's battles in talk; he also put a stop to drinking-bouts, revels, and festivals, as unseasonable, called the men to arms, and was stern and inexorable in his enrolment of them for military service."[44]

Plutarch's approach to Taras as luxury ridden is very close to that of Strabo, and it is not atypical of Graeco-Romans writing about anti-Roman Greeks in the imperial period. The object is to denigrate Greeks in contrast to virtuous Romans, who built an empire while other people played. But there is no doubt some truth in the picture, even so. The closing of the gymnasia, centers of life for any Greek city, must have come as a blow to the Tarentines. Still harder to take was the closing of the theater.[45] But aside from simple disciplinarianism, Pyrrhus probably had his own reason for this harsh act. The Tarentines' beloved theater, meeting place for the citizens, was a breeding ground of discontent, where mob psychology could be practiced in an appropriately dramatic setting. If the anti-Pyrrhic undercurrent could rally anywhere, it was at the theater. Forbidding banquets and revels was also for Pyrrhus's own protection, since anti-Pyrrhic sentiments, unvoiced in the sober day, might be cried out loud at a drunken party.

Plutarch says that many young Tarentines, not attuned to living under military discipline, left the city; and Zonaras says that Pyrrhus posted guards to keep people in. Appian makes it sound even worse: "Pyrrhus . . . ordered the citizens to severe military exercise, under penalty of death if they disobeyed. Then the Tarentines, utterly worn out by exercises and tasks to which they were unaccustomed, fled the city as though it were a foreign government and took refuge in the fields. Then the king closed the gates and placed guards over them. In this way the Tarentines gained a clear perception of their own folly."[46] This sounds like an exaggeration. Of course there was much disenchantment when Pyrrhus placed Taras under a military kind of government, but whether he had the authority to impose the death penalty on disobedient young Tarentines is questionable. Leaders of the opposition may have had to escape from the city or face death, but these Roman sympathizers were, in the present state of affairs, traitors, for whom a death penalty would not have been inexcusable, and the city itself could easily have imposed it. An anecdote which presumably relates to this period portrays Pyrrhus in much less harsh a light. At a drinking party (not forbidden in this case, apparently) some unhappy young men started making seditious remarks. When they were brought before Pyrrhus for punishment, they told him that they would have said a lot more if the wine had not run out. Pyrrhus appreciated their ready wit and let them go. He was, after all, a Greek.[47]

More oppressive for many Tarentines than Pyrrhus's disciplinary measures was the quartering of his troops in the city. Even though Taras was, by Greek standards, a large place, it could not have absorbed about 25,000 foreign soldiers very comfortably. Billeted in Tarentine homes, far from their own wives and in close association with Tarentine women and boys, they must have caused trouble. There may also have been a food problem, with the extra population in the city and with the farms laid waste by the Romans. Meanwhile Pyrrhus continued to prepare for war by training the Tarentines. To lessen the possibility of mutiny, he mixed them with his own soldiers rather than create strictly Tarentine units, where disaffection could easily spread and flourish. Reluctant or eager, ready or not, they would soon fight Rome.

# Notes to Chapter 8

1. For a typical expression of the first view see Lévêque, *Pyrrhos*, pp. 245-46 (citing J. Heurgon's *Capoue Préromaine*). Tenney Frank, on the other hand, stresses the senate's hesitation to take anti-Tarentine measures and believes that "the young democratic leaders—the plebeian assembly attained sovereign powers only in 287—took matters into their own hands and overrode the senate" ("Pyrrhus," *Cambridge Ancient History*, Vol. VII, p. 641). For a more moderate view see H. H. Scullard, *A History of the Roman World 753-146 B.C.*, 4th rev. ed. (London and New York, 1980), p. 140.

2. 9.39.3, Earnest Cary, trans. Loeb, *Dio*, Vol. I, 297. On Taras's bad press see Wuilleumier, pp. 99-100.

3. The Roman response must remain a matter of guesswork; see especially the discussions in Wuilleumier, pp. 100-101, and Frank, *CAH* VII, 640-41. Frank remarks that Aelius proposed "some measure of assistance" and that the Thurians "received the moral support of Rome." These terms are as definite as any.

4. Lévêque, for instance, speaks of "les rivalités entre cités helléniques qui permirent d'abord à Rome de prendre pied dans le Sud de l'Italie" (p. 246). Wuilleumier affirms that even in 284 Thurii, "trop jalouse de Tarente pour lui demander seccours, sacrifia les intérêts helléniques en faisant appel à Rome" (p. 100).

5. Tenney Frank (*CAH* VII, 640) and Cary (*History of the Greek World*, p. 177) opt for the earlier date; most other scholars prefer the later one. Scullard attaches "perhaps" to the earlier date (*History of the Roman World*, p. 139; see also p. 482, n. 13).

6. Cary (see above) believes that the agreement also safeguarded against Roman aggression the grazing country in the Apulian hinterland that Taras acquired in the period 334-330.

7. The date is Wuilleumier's, p. 103.

8. Appian, *Roman History*, 3 ("Samnite History") 7.1, Horace White, trans. Loeb, *Appian*, Vol. I, pp. 77.

9. See, in addition to Dio and Appian, Florus, 1.13.3-5; Orosius, *Seven Books of History Against the Pagans*, 4.1; and Zonaras, *Epitome Historion*, 8.2. Zonaras, epitomizing Dio, claims that the Roman commander had assumed the Tarentines would be friendly.

10. See the accounts of the embassy in Dionysius of Halicarnassus, 19.5.1-5; Appian, 3.7.2; Florus, 1.13.5; Dio Cassius, 9.39.6-9; and Zonaras (epitomizing Dio of course), 8.2. Since the narratives agree in the main, one has to doubt all of them or none. The Roman demands, however, are given only in Appian.

11. See especially Dionysius of Halicarnassus, 19.6.1-3.

12. 8.2, Earnest Cary, trans. Loeb, *Dio*, Vol. I, p. 301.

13. Pierre Lévêque in "Il Dibattito," Convegno 10, pp. 205-206, stresses the division between rich and poor as the primary difference between the parties.

14. 3.7.2. Loeb, *Appian*, Vol. I, p. 81.

15. See Plutarch, "Pyrrhus," 13.2-5; Dio Cassius, 9.39.10; and especially Dionysius of Halicarnassus, 19.8.1-3. But the story does sound suspect, like something invented after Pyrrhus's rigorous measures against Tarentine amusements were well known.

16. See Frank, *Economic Survey,* Vol. I, p. 55, and Mustilli, "Civiltà," p. 25.

17. 8.24, W. R. Paton, trans. Loeb III, 507, 509.

18. See Pausanias, 1.12.1; Plutarch, "Pyrrhus," 13.5-6; and Lévêque, *Pyrrhos,* pp. 248-49 (on the date) and 274-75 (on the numbers). See also, on the numbers, the comments of P. A. Brunt, *Italian Manpower 225 B.C.-A.D. 14* (Oxford, 1971), pp. 59-60, n. 1. Unless otherwise noted, subsequent references to Lévêque will be to *Pyrrhos.*

19. For the early events in Pyrrhus's life we are dependent mainly on Plutarch, "Pyrrhus," 2-4; see also Pausanias, 1.11.

20. "Pyrrhus," 7.5, Bernadotte Perrin, trans. Loeb, *Lives,* Vol. IX, p. 365.

21. On this last point see Lévêque, p. 251, n. 1. G. T. Griffith suggests that his army consisted largely not of Epirots but of Graeco-Macedonians; see his *Mercenaries of the Hellenistic World* (Cambridge, England, 1935), p. 64.

22. See the speculations in Lévêque, pp. 261-64.

23. Tenney Frank describes him as "Lured into nebulous ambitions by this fatal propinquity" (*Cambridge Ancient History,* VII, 642). On Pyrrhus's genealogy, see especially Lévêque, p. 84, and the table in "Pyrrhos von Epeiros" by Dietmar Kienast, Pauly-Wissowa, *Real-Encyclopädie,* 47 (1963), col 113-14.

24. Plutarch, "Pyrrhus," 8.1, Bernadotte Perrin, trans. Loeb, *Lives,* Vol. IX, p. 367.

25. "Pyrrhus," 11.2. Loeb, *Lives,* Vol. IX, p. 375.

26. 1.12.1, W. H.S. Jones, trans. Loeb, *Pausanias,* Vol. I, p. 59.

27. The thesis is that of J. Perret, *Les Origines de la Légende Troyenne* (Paris, 1942). See the discussion and rejection of it in Lévêque, pp. 251-58. Among other scholars, Arnaldo Momigliano had argued against it earlier, in his review in the *Journal of Roman Studies,* 35 (1945), 99-104.

28. Plutarch, "Pyrrhus," 8.2. Tenney Frank's comparison of him to "some viking chieftain running amuck in a Renaissance city" (*CAH* VII, 643) is felicitous.

29. See "Pyrrhus," 3.4-5.

30. "Pyrrhus," 14.1-8. See also Dio Cassius, 9.40.5, and the discussions in Lévêque, pp. 276, 289-91.

31. See Zonaras, 8.2, and Lévêque, p. 281. Lévêque points out that Cineas as envoy would not necessarily have accompanied a military force and that Pyrrhus may have dispatched two groups to Italy.

32. This at least would be the purport of Zonaras, 8.2, which puts the event in the winter before Pyrrhus's arrival.

33. 9.13, Earnest Cary, trans. Loeb, *Dio,* Vol. I, pp. 315, 317.

34. Lévêque, pp. 308-309, discusses this Roman split and rejects, without discrediting, the theory of A. Passerini that the Roman democrats wanted expansion in the region of the Po valley rather than in the south.

35. Wuilleumier, pp. 109-10, reduces the number of horsemen to 400 and the number of elephants to five.

36. Pausanias (1.12.3) says that Pyrrhus acquired his elephants in battle against Demetrius. Lévêque, p. 296, prefers to consider them the gift of Ceraunus. Zonaras (8.2), like Plutarch, says there were twenty elephants.

37. On the date see especially Lévêque, pp. 287-88.

38. See Lévêque, p. 265, and H. H. Scullard, *The Elephant in the Greek and Roman World* (Ithaca, N.Y., 1974), pp. 102-103.

39. We are told by Pausanias (1.12.1) that he retook the island with the help of Tarentine ships. For the suggestion that 280 was the date, see Wuilleumier, p. 111. Demetrius, who had possessed Corcyra since 291/290, had been disastrously defeated in Asia in 285 and had died an alcoholic in 283, so that Pyrrhus may have been able to retake Corcyra prior to 280; Lévêque, pp. 175-76, opts for 281. If Taras sent a fleet to help him sometime before 280, he perhaps considered himself under obligation to the city, and this may have been one reason he granted the Tarentine request for aid.

40. Both Wuilleumier (pp. 111-12) and Lévêque (pp. 297-98) comment on romantic elements in the account.

41. See Zonaras, 8.2. Lévêque, p. 282, dates the advent of both Cineas and Milon to autumn 281.

42. Lévêque, p. 298, suggests that if the Pyrrhic forces landed in May, at the time when Rome began a new consular year, the change of consuls temporarily rendered Rome inactive.

43. For discussion see Evans, *"Horsemen,"* p. 139; Wuilleumier, pp. 112, 200-201; and Lévêque, pp. 300, 430-31. Lévêque, pp. 433-34, observes that a similar weight reduction occurred about the same time in other South Italiot Greek cities, and speculates that the intention was to conform to the Roman six-scruple piece—a testimony to the growing commercial influence of Rome in South Italy. But his date of 289 for the beginning of the six-scruple piece (p. 450), representing a weight reduction of the Romano-Campanian didrachm, is denied by more recent scholarship. See Michael H. Crawford, *Roman Republican Coinage* (Cambridge, England, 1974), Vol. I, pp. 37-41, arguing that the so-called Romano-Campanian didrachm did not even begin until about 280. Stazio, "Aspetti e Momenti," pp. 171-72, cites to much the same purpose Rudi Thomsen's *Early Roman Coinage* (Copenhagen, 1957-61), Vol. III, pp. 138 ff. But see also Burnett's "Coinages of Rome and Magna Graecia," which reconsiders in the light of new evidence the alternate chronology, that of R. E. Mitchell, dating the beginning of the Romano-Campanian didrachm in the late fourth century. Burnett (p. 109) calls Evans's case for 281 as the year of the weight reduction weak, since the elephant and (on gold) the fighting Athena appeared as symbols at about the same time on coins of Neapolis, which was not

in favor of Pyrrhus, and since coins struck in the name of Pyrrhus himself in Italy conformed to the Attic standard. The second of these arguments may not be relevant; Pyrrhus may have had nothing to do directly with Taras's decision to reduce the weight of its didrachm. Burnett proposes no other date, even for the Neapolitan coins with elephant symbol, and (pp. 115-16) accepts Evans's chronology for Period VII, the period of Pyrrhus..

44. "Pyrrhus," 16.2, Bernadotte Perrin, trans. Loeb, *Lives,* Vol. IX, 393.

45. See Zonaras, 8.2.

46. *Roman History,* 3.8, Horace White, trans. Loeb, *Appian,* Vol. I, p. 81.

47. For this anecdote see Plutarch, "Pyrrhus," 8.5, and his *Moralia,* 184D; Dio Cassius, 10.47; Valerius Maximus, 5.1, ext. 3; Quintilian, 6.3.10; and Zonaras, 8.6.

# 9

# The Pyrrhic Campaigns

On the first of May 280, Publius Valerius Laevinus and Tiberius Coruncanius became the new consuls at Rome. Coruncanius was assigned the Etruscan problem, which was heading toward settlement, and Laevinus was given the more difficult job of dealing with Taras and Pyrrhus. While Rome garrisoned its allied cities, Laevinus marched southeast to relieve his predecessor Aemilius Barbula, who, it will be remembered, had spent the winter in the Roman foundation of Venusia northwest of Taras. On the way, Laevinus seized a Lucanian strongpoint (according to Zonaras, 8.3) and left troops there. The Lucanians, active for many years against the Greeks and then the Romans, were now among Taras's barbarian allies, and Laevinus proceeded to ravage their fields. Of Taras's other allies, the Bruttians in Italy's toe, now reaching the zenith of their power, were probably the most vigorous. The Samnites, desolated by long wars against Rome—their land wasted, their people discouraged—promised to be of less help. The Messapians of Italy's heel—the people who had given Taras such trouble in their warlike past—were now, like the Lucanians, to be counted among the friends of the Greeks. It was they, of course, who had helped Pyrrhus when he was cast on their shores after the storm.[1]

When the Roman troops got close to Taras, probably late in June, Pyrrhus—gallant and impatient as usual, if not downright impulsive—decided to venture out against them although the city's allies had not yet come up. With his men from Epirus and his severely trained Tarentines, he camped between Heraclea and the city of Pandosia, farther inland, on the low ground near the Ionian Sea, with the river Siris separating him from Laevinus's camp. Partly to use up time in the hope that some of the allies would make their appearance, he either sent a herald to Laevinus with a certain proposal or wrote Laevinus a letter. Plutarch ("Pyrrhus," 16.3-4) opts for the herald, whereas the letter and Laevinus's reply are given by Dionysius of Halicarnassus (19.9.1-4, 19.10.1-5) and in briefer versions by Zonaras (8.3). Like other correspondence "recorded" in ancient sources, these epistles are of course fictitious, but both they and the message and answer carried by the herald in Plutarch agree in the main. Pyrrhus offers himself as an arbitrator to adjudicate the matter of Tarentine complaints and Roman offenses and thereby prevent a war; and Laevinus rejects this offer in a proud Roman manner.

Pyrrhus could not have been serious, since peace at this point would have ruined his chance to establish an empire of his own in Italy. But there is no reason to doubt that an exchange of some kind took place, especially if Pyrrhus was, as Zonaras implies, just stalling for time. More doubtful is the story in Dionysius of Halicarnassus (19.11) that Laevinus captured one of Pyrrhus's spies, showed the man the whole glory of the Roman army lined up for battle, and sent him back to Pyrrhus with the suggestion that Pyrrhus himself come and see the strength of Rome. This story was probably invented as a compliment to Rome by a Roman source now lost but used by Dionysius. Equally suspect is a story told by Plutarch, in which Pyrrhus in person did scout the Roman camp. Having seen how well ordered the Romans were, Pyrrhus is supposed to have remarked to a man accompanying him, " 'The discipline of these Barbarians is not barbarous; but the result will show us what it amounts to.' "[2]

The battle, to which Taras's friend Heraclea gave its name, was probably fought in July.[3] The opposing forces cannot be exactly calculated. If we use Plutarch's not very reliable figures, we can assume that Pyrrhus left Epirus with 25,000 men or more, plus twenty elephants. We do not know the number of losses in the storm at sea, being told only that the losses were not great. Already established at Taras were Cineas with possibly 3,000 men and Milon with possibly 3,000 more, unless they had 3,000 between them. Taras's allies had apparently still not arrived. Although Taras was a great city, its population in 280 cannot of course be ascertained, which makes it impossible to determine the number of Tarentines that Pyrrhus had trained. By adding perhaps a few thousand Tarentines to the Epirot troops, subtracting a few thousand Epirots drowned at sea and a few Tarentines who escaped from the city to avoid the stringent measures imposed by Pyrrhus, we can come up with a total of between 25,000 and 30,000, for whatever it is worth. As for Laevinus's forces, a Roman legion at the time consisted of about 10,000 men, roughly half of them citizens and half allies. But we do not know how many legions Laevinus had with him. The troops that had served under Aemilius Barbula in ravaging the Tarentine countryside the year before, and had wintered at Venusia, may have joined Laevinus or they may have returned to Rome. Laevinus had left some soldiers in Lucania on his march to Taras. If Laevinus had (with Barbula's troops) three or four legions at his disposal, he commanded somewhat under thirty or forty thousand men.[4]

The main course of the Battle of Heraclea is clear enough. The Romans, apprehensive that Taras's allies would soon start arriving, took the offensive by crossing the river Siris, which partly protected Pyrrhus's left flank. Both infantry and cavalry crossed. Pyrrhus met the Romans with 3,000 horsemen, hoping to scatter them with a strong charge. He fought with his usual valor and directed his men with his usual expertise as he sat on his horse. But his plan did not work, and his horse was killed. He now sent the main body of his troops against the legions, and there followed the confusion of fierce attacks, withdrawals, and counter-attacks, Roman legion against tight-packed Greek phalanx, short Roman sword against long Greek spear, with Pyrrhus the aggressor four times and Laevinus three. (Presumably the Tarentine troops were still amalgamated with Pyrrhus's men rather than constituted in units of their own, and fought and retreated alongside the Epirots.) Pyrrhus held his elephants in reserve until his final attack, and they were the decisive factor. The Romans were perhaps worn out by this time anyway. While they were trying to control their horses, panicked by the unfamiliar beasts, Pyrrhus charged with his Thessalian cavalry. The Romans fled.[5]

Incidents are reported which may never have occurred. According to one report, an Italian warrior chief named Oblacus threw himself heroically on Pyrrhus at some point in the swaying battle and even grabbed the king's spear, but was killed by Pyrrhus's friends. According to another, Pyrrhus changed armor and clothes with his faithful companion Megacles so that he himself would be less conspicuous—a prudent move which perhaps would not have been viewed as inglorious. Megacles, wearing the royal cloak dyed purple and embroidered with gold, was killed, and both armies thought the dead man was Pyrrhus until the king rode along the line of battle with his helmet thrown back to reveal his face and cheer his troops.

More credible are accounts of the terror inspired in the Romans and their horses by the elephants. Such beasts had never been seen in Italy before. Zonaras describes the Roman disarray:

... at the sight of the animals, which was out of all common experience, at their frightful trumpeting, and also at the clatter of arms which their riders made, seated in the towers, both the Romans themselves were panic-stricken and their horses became frenzied and bolted, either shaking off their riders or bearing them away. Disheartened at this, the Roman army was turned to flight, and in their rout some soldiers were slain by the men in the towers on the elephants' backs, and others by the beasts themselves, which destroyed many with their trunks and tusks (or teeth) and crushed and trampled under foot as many more.[6]

Plate 40.   Silver didrachm, c. 281-272 B.C. Rev.: Dolphin rider r. with bow and arrow; beneath dolphin, elephant r., ΔI. 21.5 mm.

According to Plutarch, the Roman losses were between 7,000 and 15,000 men, the Pyrrhic losses between 4,000 and 13,000. Whatever they amounted to within that wide range, even in this respect Pyrrhus seems to have come out a little ahead. The Roman remnants, however, made good their re-treat to some city in Apulia, and Pyrrhus's losses, even if they amounted to less than the Romans', were still considerable, no doubt including some of his experienced officers. The remark attributed to him by Dio Cassius, Zonaras, and Orosius, however—to the effect that another victory like Heraclea would ruin him—was probably never made.[7] Pyrrhus's character was hardly pessimistic, and his first encounter with the Romans was certainly a credit to his abilities as a general. He set up at Dodona in Epirus, where the great sanctuary to Zeus was located, a tablet commemorating the victory which, with the Epirots and the Tarentines, he had won over the Romans and their allies.

The Tarentines must also have been pleased: here was a fellow Greek who could handle the Romans. It was probably now that they embellished their city with a gilded bronze statue of Victory carrying a trophy over her shoulder and alighting on a globe. This statue, a work of Lysippus's pupil, Eutychides of Sicyon, was later taken to Rome, like so many other Greek things; and, ironically, it became a symbol of Roman triumph. Augustus, to mark the subordination of Egypt, put it in 29 B.C. in the Curia Julia, where the senate assembled; and the senate continued to burn incense in front of it until A.D. 382, when the Christian Gratian, ruler of an empire no longer victorious very often, stopped the custom by having the altar below the figure removed.[8]

About the time of Heraclea, the Tarentines struck silver didrachms whose reverses depicted the dolphin rider fitting an arrow to his bow in readiness for battle and, low down in the field, a Pyrrhic elephant as symbol (Plate 40). Possibly the city started striking such reverses before the battle, in advertisement of the great beasts that formed part of

Pyrrhus's war machine, but they may also have been struck as Taras's own commemoration of the victory, which the elephants had done so much to bring about. The reverses accompany two different obverse types—one with an armed horseman, the other with a male crowning a horse ridden by a boy athlete. The coins with one obverse type may have been struck before Pyrrhus's arrival; the others after Heraclea.

The story of Pyrrhus's campaigns and negotiations in the Greek West has been told many times and needs to be told here largely in so far as it involves Taras. After Heraclea there may have been diplomatic attempts on the part of the Tarentines to entice the inhabitants of south-central Italy away from the Roman federation—in fact to break up the federation and thereby cripple Rome.[9] These efforts ultimately failed, but other people rallied to the triumphant Greek. Croton, which in 284 and 282 had turned to Rome rather than to Taras for help, did an about-face and turned to Taras and Pyrrhus. Locri Epizephyrii, which had welcomed a Roman garrison of 200 men, dismissed it. As for Taras's barbarian allies—the Bruttians, the Lucanians, the Samnites—they now came rushing up, to receive Pyrrhus's mild rebuke for tardiness but also some share of the spoils.

The question of who got the spoils was a chronically delicate one in ancient warfare, and Dio Cassius suggests that it troubled the general enthusiasm over the Greek victory (9.25-26). The Epirots, he says, disappointed at not having taken as much plunder as they had anticipated, started plundering the territories of their friends. By "friends" he probably does not mean the Tarentines themselves or the other Greeks, although that is a possibility. If he does have the Tarentines in mind, the irritation that the citizens had felt toward Epirot troops quartered in their homes before Heraclea must have sprung to the surface again. But more likely Dio is thinking of the barbarian allies who had belatedly made their appearance. The Epirot activity at any rate worked against Tarentine efforts to disintegrate the Roman federation. Rome's Italian allies decided it would be foolish to befriend a general whose troops raided friends as well as enemies.

It was partly in the hope of winning allied cities away from Rome in the aftermath of glorious victory that Pyrrhus, with an army that now included the barbarians as well as Tarentines and his own Epirots, crossed the peninsula and came into Campania. Either while he was still at Taras or after he had set out, Rome sent an embassy headed by a former consul named Caius Fabricius Luscinus to discuss an exchange of prisoners.[10] During his consulship in 282, Fabricius had distinguished himself against the Lucanians, the Samnites, and the Bruttians; and the two other men in the party of envoys had also made their

names in war. Pyrrhus received them with due magnificence. According
to Dio, he sent a detachment of soldiers to escort them from the border
of Tarentine territory so that they would be protected against the mad
violence of the Tarentines, and he himself went out to greet them and
accompanied them into the city.

The interview between Fabricius and Pyrrhus, whether it occurred
within Taras or somewhere on the line of march in Lucania or Campania,
gave pro-Roman ancient sources the chance for a dramatic contrast,
complete with long speeches that were never made. Fabricius was
depicted as an austere and noble Roman of the old school—simple in
life-style, honest, upright, immovable. Pyrrhus came off at best as a king
devoted to luxury but capable of admiring Roman virtue, at worst as a
wily Greek. According to Dionysius of Halicarnassus, he took Fabricius
aside and attempted to bribe him but was so impressed when the
Roman refused the bribe that he gave up the prisoners without demanding any ransom. Plutarch says that the Greek money was not a
bribe but simply a sign of friendship, and he adds an elephant, revealed
when a curtain was suddenly drawn aside, as a Pyrrhic ruse to surprise
the imperturbable Roman; but it was Pyrrhus himself who was surprised by Fabricius's imperturbability. Florus says that Pyrrhus tried to
tempt Fabricius with part of his kingdom—declined of course. According to Appian, Pyrrhus volunteered to give up the prisoners without ransom as long as Rome agreed to peace, and he also offered
Fabricius money and possessions and the chance to come over to Epirus
and work for him; but the Roman general laughed. Dio Cassius presents
Pyrrhus as sorry that he had decided to help the unworthy Tarentines
when there were Romans in the world. Like Plutarch, Dio depicts
Pyrrhus as eager to be Fabricius's friend, and he has Fabricius rejecting
in noble Roman style the Greek's offer of friendship and the presents
that accompanied it. Dio's Fabricius delivered a long and moral speech
against the greed which he ascribed to Pyrrhus and, by implication, to
Greeks in general. The Pyrrhus of this scene desired peace; and Fabricius
would try to bring it about, since it was a commendable wish.[11] About
the only element in these accounts that can be assumed to be factual is
Pyrrhus's decision not to demand ransom for the prisoners.

There are basically two contrasting portraits of Pyrrhus in the ancient
sources that remain to us, and they can occur in works by the same
writer—notably the fullest writer, Plutarch. Pyrrhus is the dashing,
romantic adventurer, the bold warrior and charismatic leader, the modern
Achilles. He is also the cunning Greek prince, overambitious, overfond
of luxury, devoid of high moral standards. The inconsistency, in historians
writing primarily for Romans, is explicable. Pyrrhus has to be glorified, or
he would not be an enemy worthy of Rome. But he has to be denigrated

when he comes face to face with the Roman heritage of valor.

In his progress through Italy after Heraclea, Pyrrhus besieged the Campanian cities that he could not entice away from Rome. But Capua would not be intimidated into dropping the Roman alliance, and neither would Naples. Either Rome loomed as too immediate a menace or these Greek cities had learned that a close connection with Rome need not be disadvantageous. These cities, it will be recalled, had traded actively with Taras before Rome removed them from the area of Tarentine economic influence.[12] Tarentine merchants would have been pleased to see Pyrrhus break the Roman link, but that was not to be.

Without having accomplished his object, Pyrrhus marched north up the Via Latina toward Rome itself, threatened in the rear by a somewhat recuperated Roman army under Laevinus. Although Pyrrhus came close to Rome, he did not plan to take the walled and hastily defended city; the effort would be too costly. He intended only to demoralize it; and he still hoped to attract or frighten Rome's allies out of their alliance by so audacious a move as an advance on the capital. He may also have wished to effect a junction with the Etruscans of Vulci and Volsinii north of Rome.

At some time during this march, he sent the rhetorically accomplished Cineas to the city itself to present terms of peace to the senate. Cineas brought gifts for the senators' wives and children. Apparently Pyrrhus felt that these presents (which could be understood simply as tokens of respect or friendship, not as bribes), plus his victory at Heracela, plus his progress through the Italian countryside toward Rome itself, plus Cineas's persuasive powers, would be enough to overwhelm the senate. The peace proposal stipulated continued autonomy for Taras and the other Greek cities of South Italy and restoration of property seized from the Lucanians, Samnites, and other barbarians. As Pyrrhus's special friend, Taras was to have immunity from reparations. Rome would have to relinquish any idea of expansion in the South. Italy would be divided between Romans and Greeks in so far as spheres of influence were concerned, and Pyrrhus would be free to control the Greek part— to establish his empire there, probably with its seat at Taras.[13]

The senate seemed amenable. But the same assertion of Roman dignity and integrity that colors the narratives of Fabricius's embassy colors the accounts of Cineas's appearance before the senate. This time the noble Roman is Appius Claudius. Ancient and blind, he was, according to the story, led into the senate by his sons, and there he delivered a resounding speech that destroyed the effect of Cineas's clever rhetoric. He was sorry that he was not deaf as well as blind, since then he would not have been able to hear the senate talking in so un-Roman a manner and considering so shameful a peace. The chastened senators rejected Pyrrhus's proposals.

In other ways too Pyrrhus was not successful. Rome's allies stayed loyal to Rome, the Etruscans asked for peace, and the consul Tiberius Coruncanius, who had been dealing with them, marched to join Laevinus. Also, bad weather was coming on. Avoiding the Roman forces (which may not have been eager for an engagement anyway), Pyrrhus returned to Taras for the winter.

In the spring he marched northwest into Apulia since the Roman foundations there, Venusia and (considerably north of it) Luceria, would have to be taken if his control of southern Italy was to be secured. The consuls who had assumed office on the first of May 279, Publius Sulpicius Severrio and Publius Decius Mus, marched south to fight him—probably to relieve Venusia, which he was besieging. In July he met them north of Venusia at a place called Ausculum, where one of his greatest battles was fought.

The sources for the numbers of troops on both sides and the lineups of the two forces preliminary to the battle are Di-onysius of Halicarnassus, who wrote under Augustus, and Frontinus, who wrote his *Stratagems* toward the end of the first century A.D.[14] Dionysius says that Pyrrhus had 70,000 foot soldiers, 16,000 of whom had crossed from Epirus, plus slightly more than 8,000 mounted soldiers and nineteen elephants (one beast had presumably been lost in the storm in crossing or during the Battle of Heraclea). The Romans, according to Dionysius, had slightly more than 70,000 foot soldiers and about 8,000 mounted troops. Frontinus says there were around 40,000 men on each side. This figure, though less specific than Dionysius's detailed enumeration, is probably more accurate because it implies four legions of about 10,000 men each. What is more important is the agreement between the two authors that the Roman and Greek armies were evenly matched.

The Tarentines figure prominently in Frontinus's description of the line of battle. Pyrrhus put them in the center, Frontinus says, in accord with the verse in the *Iliad* (4.299) that the poorest troops belong at the midpoint of a battle line. In Frontinus's picture the soldiers brought from Epirus stood on the right flank with the Samnites, and the other barbarians (Bruttians, Lucanians, Sallentini) stood on the left. Behind, as re-serves, were the cavalry and the precious elephants. As for the consuls, they stationed their cavalry on the two flanks, their own foot soldiers and the auxiliaries in what must have been a broad middle, and more legionaries behind as a reserve force.

As Frontinus has it, then, the kinds of troops facing each other were notably unequal: inadequate Tarentines against seasoned legionaries in the middle, Pyrrhic foot soldiers against Roman cavalry on each end. His lineup suggests that Pyrrhus's rigorous training of the Tarentines had been a failure. But it is unlikely that Pyrrhus, in spite of his Homeric associations and the incalculable popularity of the *Iliad,* would have used a Homeric recipe for his own battle plan; and Frontinus, in attributing military inadequacy to the Tarentine troops, may have been thinking of the Tarentines of his own age rather than those almost four centuries earlier. Coins may in this instance not be a particularly dependable source. But during the Pyrrhic hegemony and before it, a frequent coin type was that showing the young Tarentine, the ephebe, equipped for war and spearing from the back of a horse; and this suggests that military exercises had been customary in Taras long before Pyrrhus's arrival, as they certainly would have been at a city so beset by barbarians and committed to defending the Greeks of South Italy. Taras's objections, when Pyrrhus tried to marshal the men into a fighting force, may constitute a gross exaggeration on the part of Rome-oriented sources, an attempt to portray Taras as just another Greek city addicted to easy living.

In any case, Dionysius's more specific account of the lineup is to be preferred. He stretches four Roman legions along the center (the Romans themselves interspersed with their Italian allies), places the Roman cavalry at each side as Frontinus does, and puts in reserve not only light infantry but chariots with spiked wheels to deal with the elephants. He has Thesprotians and Chaonians from Epirus in the middle of Pyrrhus's line, immediately to their right some barbarians (Bruttians and Lucanians) and then the Tarentine soldiers, who were therefore not far from the center. The Tarentines carried white shields, evidently silver; his bothering to mention this graphic detail implies its importance, since he mentions few others. Next to the Tarentines on the right were the Ambraciots, some Italiot mercenaries in the employ of Taras, and then a phalanx of Macedonians, protected on the right end by cavalry composed of Bruttians, Samnites with their long shields, Thessalians lent to Pyrrhus by Ptolemy Ceruanus, and more mercenaries in Tarentine employ. The horsemen guarding the left end were Ambraciots, Lucanians, various Greek mercenaries, and Tarentines. Between the left end and the Thesprotians and Chaonians in the center were the Samnite allies, then more mercenaries whom Pyrrhus had brought from Greece: Aetolians, Acarnanians, Athamanians. Pyrrhus himself sat his horse behind the line at a point from which he could watch the progress of the battle or hurry to a trouble spot, and 2,000 crack cavalry surrounded him.

Both Frontinus's account and Dionysius's imply that the Tarentines, instead of being mingled with Pyrrhus's other troops to forestall the possibility of mutiny, now constituted separate bodies of men. They may very well have, although neither account is clear enough to establish that all the components of Pyrrhus's army functioned as separate groups. If they did, his confidence in the loyalty of the Tarentines had risen since Heraclea.

Ancient narratives of the battle vary widely.[15] For instance, Dionysius, Orosius, and Zonaras describe it as if it occupied one day whereas Plutarch, more convincingly, gives it two days. Dionysius devotes much attention to the armed chariots, carts, or wagons which the Romans had devised to deal with the elephants; Plutarch does not mention them. Dionysius says that some Daunian allies of Rome sacked and burned Pyrrhus's camp, but Plutarch does not mention this either.

On what was probably the first day, the elephants could not be put to use since the fighting took place on hilly ground and in a forested area along a river that separated the two camps. There were attacks and counterattacks without much result, the men slugging it out as at Heracela. During the night Pyrrhus occupied some heights which the Romans had held earlier but from which they had descended to go to their camp for the night, never suspecting that the Greeks would climb up in the darkness.[16] The next day's battle occurred on level ground. The Macedonians serving under Pyrrhus distinguished themselves, beating the First Legion. But Taras's barbarian allies, the Lucanians and Bruttians, gave up in the face of the Roman soldiers, according to Dionysius; and the Tarentines, seeing them running, ran too. Troops, even well-trained ones, can of course cave. But Dionysius was writing for a Roman audience that would appreciate this picture of an enemy as cowardly, and he was presumably using Roman sources.[17] These facts allow us to question his report of the Tarentines' conduct, though it may very well be true.

Employing the same tactics as at Heraclea, Pyrrhus at the last moment sent in his elephants—ridden by men in towers, according to Dionysius. The 300 carts which the Romans had devised as a counterweapon were, if Dionysius's description can be relied on, extraordinarily elaborate contraptions.[18] They had transverse poles that could be swung in any direction, with tridents, spikes, or scythes attached to them to cut up the elephants; and they had grappling irons, probably for dealing with the towers on the backs of the beasts. Some had grapnels wrapped in tow and then covered with pitch, which could be set on fire to frighten the monsters. But the wagons were pulled by oxen, which could not have made them very fast, and the numerous troops that they carried made them even slower. The riders in the elephants' towers threw down spears on this solid assembly, and Pyrrhus's nimble soldiers hamstrung the oxen. The Roman device was a failure. Zonaras tells a different story: Pyrrhus attacked the other end of the Roman line with his elephants, so that the Romans could not even use their carts.

The Greek evidently won, as Plutarch says, though his victory was a dubious one: Livy was apparently not sure who had come out ahead, and neither was Dionysius. The Romans withdrew in good order, not in flight. Both sides had suffered considerable casualties.[19] Pyrrhus had not achieved his objective of freeing northern Apulia from Roman control. The most that can be said is that he was not chased and harassed by the Romans as he marched back to what may have been an embarrassed Taras.

At the beginning of May in 278 Quintus Aemilius Papus and Caius Fabricius, who had been consuls in 282, assumed office for a second time together. There are various versions of a story which, like the accounts of Fabricius's meeting with Pyrrhus after Heraclea, depict the Roman as an unwavering exemplar of stern old virtue. It seems that somebody associated with Pyrrhus—in some versions his physician— went to Fabricius with the offer to poison Pyrrhus and thereby end the war. But Fabricius, outraged by so underhanded a proposal, sent the man back to Pyrrhus with a letter exposing him. The story concerns Taras only because in some versions the grateful king showed his appreciation by releasing his prisoners without ransom, and Fabricius, not to be outdone in courtesy, responded by releasing prisoners too. In the tale related by Plutarch, these consisted of Samnites and Tarentines ("Pyrrhus," 21.1-4). But the whole story is very likely a historical fiction, another case of turning Fabricius into a symbol of old Roman incorruptibility.[20]

The sources are especially contradictory and confusing with regard to diplomatic negotiations after Ausculum. It may be that Fabricius went to Taras to talk with Pyrrhus a second time about an exchange of prisoners and terms of peace, and that Pyrrhus later sent Cineas to Rome on a second embassy to the same purpose. More likely, however, only a second embassy of Cineas occurred.[21]

Pyrrhus, presumably nursing his wounds in winter quarters at Taras late in 279 or early in 278, had reasons for wishing to conclude a peace. Even if Ausculum had not been a resounding victory for him, he had treated the Romans roughly enough to expect that they would listen to his proposals. It would, besides, be particularly good to achieve some resolution of the Italian problem because he was already thinking of other worlds to conquer. Just what his proposals were—how they differed from the proposals presented by Cineaas in the preceding year, if they differed at all—cannot be determined from the sources. Cineas was again unsuccessful—probably because a representative of Carthage was in Rome at the same time to conclude a treaty of mutual assistance.

If Rome could depend on Carthaginian help, it could carry on the war. This was very likely what prompted Carthage to propose the treaty of assistance—so that Rome would not make peace with Pyrrhus and the Greek would be kept busy in Italy and would not interfere with Carthaginian ambitions elsewhere, namely in Sicily. Appian, however, says that Rome did return the prisoners it had taken, including the Tarentines (3.11.2).

Because Pyrrhus's thoughts were turning away from Italy, he did not carry on campaigns against Rome in the spring and summer of 278. Early in 279 Ceraunus, king of Macedon by this time, had died in battle against the Celts, and after an interval of confusion the Macedonians, perhaps toward the end of 279, had sent an invitation that Pyrrhus become their king. He may or may not have decided against this before receiving a different invitation. The Syracusan tyrant Agathocles had died in 289, and the passing of that powerful empire builder, plus the internal dissensions that resulted, left Sicily open to Carthaginian aggression. Carthage already held the western part of Sicily but wanted the whole island. Perhaps in the fall of 279, before Cineas left for Rome, envoys from several Sicilian cities came to Taras to ask Pyrrhus for help against the Carthaginians, and they promised him as his reward the cities of Syracuse, Acragas, and Leontini. He put off making a decision, however, until Cineas returned from Rome. The question of how Taras and the barbarian allies would react was no doubt one reason for his hesitation. By the spring of 278 Carthage was besieging Syracuse, and the Sicilians were desperate. Pyrrhus sent the invaluable Cineas to Sicily to investigate the situation at first hand. When Cineas got back, Pyrrhus determined to accept the Sicilian invitation. Perhaps he could carry the Carthaginian war out of Sicily into northern Africa itself, and make himself king of a rich empire stretching from Africa up through Sicily and into southern Italy.

At Taras, therefore, matters must have been hanging fire in the winter of 279/278 and the following spring, as people wondered, first, whether Cineas's mission to Rome would be successful, then what their champion was going to do. He did not set sail for Sicily until the late summer or even the fall of 278 (most likely September), and he left a garrison at Taras under the command of his seasoned officer Milon and promised to be back. He also garrisoned allied cities, especially Locri Epizephyrii. But he took with him 8,000 men—no doubt few of them Tarentines— and the elephants.

The sources indicate that Taras looked on the whole thing as a desertion. As Pausanias has it, "he abandoned Tarentum and the Italiots on the coast." Plutarch is more specific: "The Tarentines were much displeased at this, and demanded that he either apply himself to the task for which he had come, namely to help them in their war with Rome, or else abandon their territory and leave them their city as he had found it. To this demand he made no very gracious reply, but ordering them to keep quiet and await his convenience, he sailed off."[22] This heated exchange between Pyrrhus and the Tarentines may reflect renewed activity by the anti-Pyrrhic faction, quiescent for a while but now taking advantage of an opportunity to complain.

Perhaps Pyrrhus aggravated the displeasure—if not of Taras itself, then of Taras's allies—by his own inaction shortly before leaving. In the winter of 278/277 Fabricius celebrated a triumph over Taras and its barbarian friends, the Samnites, Lucanians, and Bruttians.[23] He must therefore have been campaigning in southern Italy in the warm months of 278. We do not hear of Pyrrhus going out from Taras against him; perhaps Pyrrhus was too busy making preparations for the Sicilian venture or, with that venture in prospect, did not wish to risk his Epirot troops against the Romans.[24] The other possibility—that Fabricius waited until Pyrrhus had sailed from Taras in late summer or early fall with his 8,000 men and his elephants, then profited by the king's absence to descend on southern Italy and carry on a successful campaign—would also not have endeared Pyrrhus to the Tarentines or their friends.

Taras was forsaken by one of those friends either during Fabricius's campaign or as a result of it. Heraclea allied itself with Rome as a *civitas aequissimo ac foedere*—in other words under conditions very favorable to the ally, though the exact terms are unknown. The loss of Heraclea must have been a serious blow to Taras. Heraclea had, after all, been founded largely under Tarentine sponsorship, was located less than forty miles from Taras itself, and, in the past, had been attached to Taras by ties that included the speaking of Greek in the Dorian dialect. It was at Heraclea that the Tarentine-dominated league of Italiot Greek states had been centered during the great days of Tarentine hegemony. It was Heraclean types—the head of Athena, Heracles wrestling the lion—that Taras put on its diobols. Apart from the practical disadvantage of having another Roman ally so close, the psychological effect of Heraclea's defection could not have been easy for Tarentines to adjust to.

Fabricius, probably in this same period, delivered into Roman hands a city that had recently slipped out. This affair involved Taras only tangentially, but it was another instance of the weakening of Greek control in southern Italy and the tightening of Roman influence there. In 282, when the Bruttians and Lucanians were besieging Thurii and Pyrrhus had not yet been invited into Italy, the people of Rhegium on the Italian toe had asked Fabricius, consul then for the first time, to place a Roman garrison in their city. They were afraid that the barbarians would launch an attack on Rhegium, and they were also afraid that Taras would attack it—or so say Dionysius of Halicarnassus and Polybius.

Fabricius had consequently left 1,200 men at the city, Romans evidently of Campanian origin, commanded by a Campanian named Decius. But Decius soon decided to take over Rhegium for himself. When Pyrrhus landed in Italy in the spring of 280, Decius told his officers that prominent Rhegians planned to bring Pyrrhus to the city so that he could kill the Romans and govern it for his own purposes. The story was a lie, but in those early days of Pyrrhus's presence in Italy, when the Greek and Roman worlds must both have been wondering what the famous man would do, it sounded plausible. Decius's officers believed it and, at his instigation, murdered the prominent Rhegians at their feasts or in their beds.

With the Greek leaders out of the way, Decius ruled as tyrant. He and his soldiers lived splendidly off the spoils of the city. He allied Rhegium with Messana across the strait in Sicily, where fellow Campanians—the Mamertini or Sons of Mars, as they called themselves—were running things. This alliance gave him domination of the valuable passage between the Ionian/Mediterranean and the Tyrrhenian Seas. But Decius's regime was not long. In his days of power and plenty, he developed eye trouble. He sent to Messana for a physician, not knowing that the man was a Rhegian by birth and hated this interloper who had murdered his compatriots. The doctor put an ointment on Decius's eyes and returned to Messana. When Decius wiped off the ointment, he discovered that he was blind. The physician had applied a strong caustic that had burned out Decius's eyeballs.

Apparently Decius could not retain control long after this. Rome was planning to deal with the traitor anyway. In 278 some of his men, realizing that their only hope for survival was betrayal, opened the city to Fabricius—no doubt while he was campaigning against the Samnites, the Lucanians, or more likely the Bruttians, who lived nearby. Fabricius restored order. The soldiers most closely involved in the plot were taken to Rome and, as traitors, had their heads axed off in the Forum; Decius himself got away. The southernmost part of the peninsula was again in Roman hands.[25]

Pyrrhus spent over two years in Sicily. He frightened away the Carthaginian navy besieging Syracuse, was proclaimed king, coined money in gold, silver, and bronze at Syracuse, and liberated other cities from Carthaginian overlordship. But he angered many Sicilians by his favoritism toward the Epirot soldiers, his harsh treatment of Sicilian officers, and executions of prominent men. As Sicilian support for him declined, he became worried. He had informed the Carthaginians that he would consent to no terms of peace except their abandonment of the whole island and was besieging Lilybaeum, which they still held, but in the winter of 277/276 he abandoned the siege.[26] The Samnites and the

Tarentines, according to Plutarch, had sent him letters asking him to come back.

The Romans had naturally taken advantage of Pyrrhus's absence. Under the consuls for 277, Publius Cornelius Rufinus and Junius Bubulcus Brutus, they invaded and devastated Samnite territory. But they were badly defeated. Rufinus then attacked the Lucanians and Bruttians and, according to Zonaras, used a ruse to retake Croton, which had thrown off its Roman allegiance and accepted a garrison sent from Taras. But the ruse, involving pretended Roman deserters who told the Crotonians that Rufinus was on his way south when he really was not, sounds more like an overused story than the truth. Zonaras goes on to say that the Locrians now went over to the Roman side, but this is also suspect, since Locri was anti-Roman soon after.[27] Rome seems not to have attempted a siege of Taras, probably because of the strong force that Pyrrhus had left there under Milon. Taras's appeal to Pyrrhus for help may therefore have been less frantic than it sounds in Plutarch. According to him, the Tarentines and the Samnites "had been excluded from all their territories, could with difficulty maintain the war even in their cities, and begged for his assistance."[28] Plutarch's words, in fact, may actually have reference to the disheartened Samnites only.

Pyrrhus sailed back to Italy with 20,000 foot soldiers (many of whom he had recruited in Sicily), 3,000 horsemen, and the elephants. He besieged Rhegium (now under Roman occupation of course, since this was two years after Decius's debacle). But the Carthaginian navy attacked his fleet, sinking or disabling about half his ships, and some Mamertines from across the strait at Messana dealt severely with his troops on land and apparently did away with two of the elephants.

Whether or not Locri Epizephyrii had defected from the Greek side to Rome in 277, Pyrrhus appalled the city, and no doubt the whole Greek population of southern Italy, by plundering the temple of the goddess of the dead on his way back to Taras. The sanctuary of Persephone, long famous and full of gold and other precious offerings, stood just outside the walls of Locri. Pyrrhus, daring though he was, must have been very badly in need of funds to commit this act of desecration. He loaded the sacred treasures onto his ships, which sailed up the coast toward Taras while he proceeded on land. But the offended goddess sent a swift punishment: a terrific storm scattered and wrecked the ships. The king hurriedly restored to her temple as much of her wealth as was recoverable.[29]

Crippled therefore, ultimately unsuccessful in Sicily, and in need of much money, Pyrrhus returned to a Taras horrified by the sacrilege at Locri. He was a badly tarnished champion. His main virtue at this point, aside from his undeniable bravery, was probably the large supply of

Plate 41.    Gold stater, c. 281-272 B.C.
Obv.: Head of Zeus l., lau-
reate; to r., NK. 17.5 mm.
*ANS/SNG* Part I, No. 1039.
*Courtesy of the American Nu-
mismatic Society, New York*

mercenaries he brought with him from Sicily.[30] The Romans meanwhile had been wearing down the Tarentines and their allies; in the
warm months of 276 the two consuls for that year had camped again in
the area, no doubt ravaging fields and spreading discouragement; one
of them, Quintus Fabius Maximus Gurges, was accorded a triumph
over the Samnites, Lucanians, and Bruttians. For the Tarentines the war
had by this time begun to look like a continuous condition, destined to
drag on without startling achievement and without glory.

Pyrrhus passed the winter of 276/275 in Taras, where the citizens now
had to play host to his thousands of Sicilians. If Pyrrhus was still short
on funds, these Sicilians may have been disgruntled and therefore
unpleasant guests. But they surely included Syracusans—Dorians like
the Tarentines themselves, speaking the same dialect, and in that respect
more endurable than mountain men from Epirus. How the mercenaries were paid during this period is difficult to estimate; although a
great deal of coinage was struck at Taras during the Pyrrhic hegemony,
we cannot precisely tell how much pertains to 276/275. Pyrrhus's
presence—the fire of his character, his indestructible faith in the future—
may have inspired the Tarentines, the mercenaries, and the allies with
new confidence, whether money was plentiful or not. We gather from
Plutarch ("Pyrrhus," 24.4) that, before he resumed the war, Pyrrhus had
been able to add to his own forces the finest of Tarentine soldiers.

The consuls who took office at the beginning of May 275 were
Manius Curius Dentatus, who marched against the Samnites, and
Cornelius Lentulus Caudinus, who marched against the Lucanians.
There had been an epidemic in Rome, and even worse, the statue of
Jupiter had been toppled from the Capitol in a terrible storm, sug-
gesting disaster to the state. The Roman armies must therefore have set
out in some gloom. Pyrrhus sent part of his own army into Lucania
against Lentulus but proceeded with most of his troops against Curius

Plate 42.  Rev. of No. 41. Eagle r. on thunderbolt; at r., two amphorae and TAPANTI-NΩN. *Courtesy of the American Numismatic Society, New York.*

Dentatus, who was in Samnite territory between Apulia and Campania near the town of Malventum. Some gloom perhaps hung over Pyrrhus's troops too, if men feared that Persephone had not yet completed her revenge.

The Battle of Malventum (Beneventum), Pyrrhus's last great fight in Italy, took place in the late spring or early summer of 275.[31] The numbers of men on the Greek side and the Roman side are not calculable, but Pyrrhus's army was probably larger than Curius's. Whether fear of Persephone bothered him we do not know. Dionysius (20.10.1-2) argues that all the advantages were with him and that only Persephone's anger caused his defeat, and remarks that Pyrrhus himself in his memoirs admitted to an apprehension of the goddess. But Dionysius also says (20.12.1-2) that on the eve of the battle Pyrrhus had an unfavorable dream in which most of his teeth fell out, and this sounds like the kind of literary embroidery that too often decorates accounts of battles. It makes Pyrrhus's anxiety concerning Persephone less credible although Dionysius would probably not have cited the memoirs unless the passage about Persephone occurred there.

Plutarch, who does not attribute Pyrrhus's defeat to the intervention of the goddess, suggests that one important factor may have been a lack of enthusiasm on the part of the Samnites, discouraged by years of unsuccessful war against Rome and resentful of Pyrrhus's Sicilian expedition ("Pyrrhus," 25.1). Pyrrhus evidently attempted a night attack against the Roman camp on an eminence, but it was abortive. At dawn Curius attacked the Greeks and their allies and even took some elephants, less terrifying now than they had been earlier. Pyrrhus counterattacked with more elephants and drove him back to his camp. But the Roman forces rallied and these elephants, Pyrrhus's greatest strength in the past, now contributed to his defeat. When the Romans hurled their heavy javelins into them, the great beasts turned tail and ran amok

Plate 43.  Silver didrachm, c. 281-272
B.C. Obv.: Horseman lanc-
ing r., equipped with shield
and two extra lances. Be-
neath horse, ΦINTY. 20
mm.

among Pyrrhus's own troops, causing chaos. Pyrrhus retreated.[32] The
role of the Tarentines in this battle is nowhere indicated.

The retreat was orderly, without Roman pursuit. Pyrrhus came back
to what was no doubt a dispirited Taras. Among the Romans the Greek
name of the battle site, whose first syllable, "Mal," suggested misfortune
to a Latin ear, was changed to Beneventum, "Well arrived" or even
perhaps "Turned out well."

Pyrrhus was finished in Italy; there were neither men nor funds to
support further campaigns. In the autumn of 275 he sailed from Taras
back to Epirus with about 8,000 foot soldiers and 500 horsemen,
according to Plutarch ("Pyrrhus," 26.2). There is a tradition that he
departed surreptitiously at night.[33] But Plutarch says nothing of this,
and in view of the number of troops that went with him a secret
departure would hardly have been possible. Taras may even have
provided ships for transport. Pyrrhus promised the Tarentines that he
would return some day. Although he never did come back, he left some
troops in the citadel under the command of his reliable general, Milon,
and his own son Helenus—an indication that whereas he did not intend
to see Italy again if something better offered, he was reluctant to give up
his Italian option entirely.

Pyrrhus's failure in Italy can be attributed to the fact that he had
attached himself to a doomed cause, that of Greek independence in the
face of Rome. It can also be blamed on the inadequacy of his allies—the
Samnites going disheartened into battle at Malventum, the unmanly
Tarentines.[34] We do not know enough about Taras's performance at this
period, however, to lay much of the blame on the city. Taras may have
called on Pyrrhus as the easiest way out of a hard problem. But it is too
tempting to use the city as an example of the degeneracy of Italiot
Greeks in the third century. The stories of Tarentine indignation at
Pyrrhus's initial efforts to impose martial austerity on the city must be in

Plate 44.   Silver didrachm, c. 281-272
B.C. Rev.: dolphin rider l.
with spears, shield, and
Nike; waves beneath. To l.
of dolphin, ΓΥ. 19.5 mm.

considerable degree true, yet they may refer mainly to the faction that
had resisted Pyrrhus's advent from the beginning; and in spite of this
indignation Tarentines evidently did their share in all of Pyrrhus's
Italian campaigns. The only suggestions that they did not fight well
concern the Battle of Ausculum. Frontinus, it may be recalled, states
that Pyrrhus stationed the Tarentines in the center of his battle line at
Ausculum because of the Homeric prescription that the weakest troops
belong in the middle; and Dionysius says that during the battle the
Tarentines fled. But both these statements are highly suspect, and even
if they do have a factual basis, they do not add up to a reliable picture of
Tarentine valor throughout the Pyrrhic period. The Tarentines may
have been weak, but we do not know. Pyrrhus's Epirots, in the long run,
did no better.

Pyrrhus's departure did not mean that the war was over for Taras,
though Rome seems not to have paid a great deal of attention to the city
for the next couple of years. The factions within the city increased in
acrimony; it was apparently a case of disappointed people turning on
one another. Perhaps early in 273 Pyrrhus recalled his son Helenus to
help him in an expedition in the Peloponnesus, leaving only Milon in
charge of the Epirot garrison. The pro-Roman party, led by a certain
Nikon, attacked Milon but could not drive him out, established themselves in a fort of their own somewhere in Tarentine territory, and
(according to Zonaras) made a separate pact with Rome.
   In 272 the Romans mounted an all-out campaign against the city.
While the consul Carvilius Maximus harassed the Samnites again, his
fellow consul Papirius Cursor appeared with his army outside Taras's
walls. At the same time a Carthaginian fleet may have anchored in the
harbor—either at the Tarentines' request, to help them against Rome,
or in conformity to the Carthaginian/Roman treaty of several years

Plate 45.   Silver didrachm. Rev. of
No. 43. Dolphin rider 1.
with Nike and spear; un-
der dolphin, prow 1. To 1.
of dolphin, ΓΟΑΥ.

before, to help Rome against Taras. If such a fleet ever existed, it sailed away without doing anything. Frontinus says that Milon now betrayed this unmanageable city by going to Papirius, bringing back generous promises which he claimed Papirius had made, and, after he had lulled the citizens into a false sense of security, handing over their state. All we really know is that he did surrender Taras to Rome.[35]

The elephant used as symbol on some of the silver didrachms struck during this period has already been mentioned as a reference to Pyrrhus. In other ways too the coinage minted during the Pyrrhic hegemony reflected the presence of the great man. There were gold staters with favorite Epirot types on both obverse and reverse: on the obverse the head of Zeus (but laureate rather than crowned with oak leaves as on money struck in Epirus), on the reverse Zeus's eagle spreading his wings (Plates 41-42). Some of these coins bore as symbol beside the eagle on the reverse a fighting Athena similar to the figure that Pyrrhus used on coins which he himself struck in Sicily. Among the reverse symbols on these staters, however, the Tarentines included twin amphorae 'as an allusion not to Pyrrhus but probably to their own important cult of the Dioscuri, whose stars sometimes surmounted the amphorae. Gold drachms had the head of Heracles on the obverse, perhaps with reference to Heraclea before its defection, and Taras himself in a biga on the reverse. After Pyrrhus, no more gold coins were ever struck at the city. The active Tarentine mint also produced a few bronze pieces, weighing about 20 grams. Like the gold staters, these bronzes bore the laureate head of Zeus on the obverse. Nike, bringer of victory, carried Zeus's thunderbolt on the reverse.[36]

The propagandistic function of coinage was not a Roman discovery, though the Romans developed and sophisticated it. We cannot say to what degree a Tarentine of the Pyrrhic period would have read certain

Plate 46. Silver didrachm, c. 281-272 B.C. Helmeted horseman with shield and two spears, l. Behind, ΙΩ. Under horse, Ϝ Ι and ΑΠΟΛΛΩ in two lines. 20 mm.

coins as specific references to a victory over Rome, but it is conceivable that magistrates in charge of the coinage hoped that he would see them in that light. Many of the reduced-weight silver didrachms, at any rate, appear to carry allusions to the war. The horseman on the obverse of some of these abundant coins wore a helmet, held a shield and spears, and struck downward with another spear in a manner reminiscent of earlier issues of military significance·(Plate 43). On the reverse the dolphin rider sometimes reached out his hand to support a little Nike who crowned him with success; or he himself was equipped for war with the weapon of his father, a trident held upright, and often with a shield as well; or he aimed the trident aslant (perhaps at an enemy rather than a fish) as the horseman did with his spear; or he held two spears and a shield with one hand and a little Nike with the other, still crowning him (Plate 44); or he had, besides the Nike, a cornucopia, possibly in allusion to the fruits of victory; or he carried a horned helmet and had the stars of the Dioscuri on both sides of him.

In addition to the elephant there were, on didrachms evidently struck early in the Pyrrhic period, reverse symbols possibly pointing to Pyrrhus. A thunderbolt, as the weapon of Zeus, may have designated Epirus; and a prow perhaps suggested the ships that had carried the Epirot army to Italy (Plate 45). But obverse symbols too appeared occasionally on these silver coins, and they certainly did not have reference to the general: the twin amphorae again, or a little silenus apparently shitting, or the top of an Ionic column. On some late pieces there was, under the dolphin on the reverse, a cantharus.

On the obverse of didrachms probably struck toward the end of the period, the horseman carried a shield that hid him from head to waist, and it is tempting to see in this version of the armed horseman an emphasis on protection rather than aggression (Plate 46). Other obverse types had nothing to do with the war: the horseman as a boy, for

Plate 47.    Silver didrachm. Obv. of No. 44. Dioskouroi riding l. Between their heads, monogram.

Plate 48.    Silver didrachm, c. 281-272 B.C. Obv.: Boy on standing horse l.; nude male r. crowning horse. Beneath hórse, ΑΡΙΣΤΙΠ in three lines. 19.5 mm.

instance, crowning his mount and perhaps being crowned in turn by a flying Nike, not for any military action but because he had been successful in the equestrian games (it was on some of these coins that twin amphorae appeared under the horse). Another obverse showed the Dioscuri, mantled, riding together to the left (Plate 47)—a revival of a type struck about 344-334 or, on Jenkins's chronology, perhaps ten or fifteen years later. Whereas some of the reverses with the dolphin rider equipped with bow and arrow above the Pyrrhic elephant were paired with an equally military obverse (the armed horseman lancing down), others were paired with an agonistic type irrelevant to the war: a boy on a stationary horse which a standing male figure was crowning (Plate 48). This was another revival of a type from 344-334 or shortly after, and so was the dolphin rider with bow and arrow, except that in the earlier type he held three arrows. The obverses of a few didrachms had a young rider leaping from a cantering horse, an illustration of the kind of race still customary at Taras.

Plate 49.    Silver didrachm. Rev. of
No. 46. Dolphin rider with
bunch of grapes and dis-
taff. Behind, ANΘ. 20 mm.

On a nonmiliatry reverse the dolphin rider carried in his left hand the much-used Tarentine symbol, the distaff of the woolen industry, and held in the right hand a bunch of grapes (Plate 49). This dolphin rider, far from being the lean, athletic figure that appeared on the military reverses, was a boy of plump proportions—probably, as on some earlier coins, Iacchos the son of Hades/Dionysus and Persephone. Occasionally this fattish youth bore, instead of the bunch of grapes, an *akrostolion*, the ornament on the stern of a ship.[37]

The didrachms of the years 281-272 include, then, a wide variety of types, some of them repeated from earlier periods but many of them new. The nonmilitary types, with their references to the city's games and its cults, suggest an emphasis on the old, traditional ways during this time of crisis; and some of them, like some of the military types with no Pyrrhic allusions, may date from after Pyrrhus's departure. In this decade or less, the mint turned out a very large amount of coinage but did what is by no means always done in periods of mass production of coins: it retained imagination and quality of design. The beauty and inventiveness of these pieces struck in years of unusual stress testify to the Tarentines' extraordinary devotion to art.

# Notes to Chapter 9

1. For a discussion of Taras's barbarian friends see Lévêque, pp. 304-307.

2. "Pyrrhus," 16.5, Bernadotte Perrin, trans. Loeb, *Lives*, Vol. IX, p. 395. The former story occurs in Zonaras, Eutropius, and Frontinus (*Stratagems*), as well as in Dionysius. See the discussion of both in Lévêque, pp. 323-24.

3. See Wuilleumier, p. 114, and Lévêque, p. 328. On the credibility of the sources, and the identity of those used by Dionysius and Plutarch, see Frank in *CAH* VII, 644; Wuilleumier, p. 114; and Lévêque, pp. 65, 322-23.

4. See the estimates in Wuilleumier, pp. 114-15, and Lévêque, pp. 321-22. Cary (*History of the Greek World*, p. 177) estimates that Taras never put more than 15,000 of its own citizens into the field at one time, but he is not speaking with particular reference to the Pyrrhic period, for which the number is probably far too large. N. G. L. Hammond in the *Oxford Classical Dictionary*, s.v. "Pyrrhus," states that Pyrrhus's army at Heraclea numbered 25,000 men; the estimate of 25-30,000 is Wuilleumier's.

5. The fullest accounts of the battle are those in Plutarch, "Pyrrhus," 16.5-10, 17.1-5, and Zonaras, 8.3. See also Dionysius of Halicarnassus, 19.12; Dio Cassius, 9.18-19; Florus, *Epitome*, 1.13; Frontinus, *Stratagems*, 2.4.13; Pausanias, 1.12.2-4; Eutropius, 2.11; and Orosius, 4.1. Orosius is useless.

6. 8.3, Earnest Cary, trans. Loeb, *Dio*, Vol. I, p. 325. Most scholars have questioned the "towers on the elephants' backs." Although Scullard questions them too, he is inclined to give Zonaras the benefit of the doubt; see *Elephant*, pp. 104-105.

7. In addition to Dio, Zonaras, and Orosius as cited in n. 5, see for similar remarks, *De Viris Illustribus (Deeds of Famous Men)*, 35, and Florus, *Epitome*, 1.13.18. Plutarch, "Pyrrhus" 21.9, places a similar remark after Ausculum.

8. See Dio Cassius, 51.22.1-2, and Lévêque, pp. 332-33. The statue continued to be a rallying point for Rome's pagan aristocracy until 408, when it was destroyed.

9. On this point see Homo, *Primitive Italy*, pp. 206-207.

10. Livy (20.59.7), Dio Cassius (9.29), and Zonaras (8.4) say that the envoys were sent to Tarentum. Lévêque (p. 368) prefers to consider the embassy and the march concurrent. The chronology of the latter half of 280 and 279 is disputable. I have in general followed Lévêque as most sensible. See his admirable discussion, pp. 360-70.

11. See Dionysius of Halicarnassus, 19.13-18; Plutarch, "Pyrrhus," 20.1-5; Florus, *Epitome*, 1.21; Appian, *Roman History*, 3.10.3-5; Dio Cassius, 9.33-38; and, following Dio, Zonaras, 8.4. Livy (Libri XIII Periocha), Florus (1.13.15), Eutropius (2.12), and *De Viris Illustribus* (35) also mention that Pyrrhus restored the prisoners without ransom.

12. Another theory, not provable, should be mentioned here: that the so-called Campano-Tarentine didrachms, struck at Taras on the Campanian standard for trade with Naples and probably other Campanian cities, are actually pre-

Pyrrhic in date and therefore indicate that Taras was carrying on extensive trade relations with Campania in defiance of the Romans. For discussion see Stazio, "Aspetti e Momenti," pp. 178-79.

13. These would seem to be the terms of Pyrrhus's proposal as reported by Appian (3.10.1), which Lévêque (pp. 349-50) views as the most accurate. The fullest accounts of Cineas's embassy are found in Appian, 3.10.1-2; Plutarch, "Pyrrhus," 18.1-6, 19.1-5; and Zonaras, 8.4. See also Cicero, *De Senectute*, 6.15-16; Livy, Libri XIII Periocha; Florus, *Epitome*, 1.13.20; Eutropius, 2.12-13; and Ammianus Marcellinus, 16.10.5. The reports by Plutarch, Appian, and Zonaras mention Taras specifically.

14. See Dionysius, 20.1, and Frontinus, 2.3.21. On the reliability of these sources and others see Wuilleumier, pp. 120-23; Lévêque, pp. 55-58, 70-77, 377-80, 390-94; and Scullard, *Elephant*, p. 107. These scholars agree that with regard to the line of battle (though perhaps not in other respects) Dionysius is preferable to Frontinus. Griffith (*Mercenaries*, pp. 61-62) relies on Dionysius to establish the largely mercenary makeup of Pyrrhus's army. The date of July for the battle is that of Lévêque, p. 399.

15. The principal accounts are those of Plutarch, "Pyrrhus," 21.5-10; Dionysius, 20.2-3; and Zonaras, 8.5. See also Orosius, 4.1; Livy, Libri XIII Periocha; Florus, *Epitome*, 1.13.9-10; and Eutropius, 2.13.

16. This is Lévêque's interpretation, pp. 385-86.

17. See Lévêque, pp. 55-58; and on sources for Pyrrhus in general, see his excellent "Introduction: Les Sources," pp. 15-77.

18. Lévêque, considering them imaginary, likens them to something that Hieronymus Bosch might have dreamed up (pp. 388-89), while Scullard (*Elephant*, pp. 107-109) argues for their authenticity.

19. The numbers vary so widely in the various sources that they are not worth citing. See the discussions in Wuilleumier, p. 123, and Lévêque, pp. 394-95.

20. Wuilleumier, p. 129, says that the story "mérite peu de créance." Lévêque, pp. 405-406, rejects it out of hand.

21. See Wuilleumier's excellent discussion (pp. 125-30) of ancient sources and scholarship prior to 1939 regarding whether there were one or two meetings between Fabricius and Pyrrhus, one or two embassies of Cineas to Rome. Wuilleumier concludes that Rome had sent Fabricius to see Pyrrhus in the winter of 280/279 to negotiate an exchange of prisoners, and that Pyrrhus sent Cineas to Rome after Ausculum on his unsuccessful mission to the senate, already recounted. Frank (*CAH* VII, 648) believes that Fabricius conferred with Pyrrhus a second time in the winter of 279/278 (in other words before his second consulship) and that Pyrrhus then sent Cineas to Rome to ratify the terms of peace. According to Lévêque, pp. 368-69, there was no second conference between Fabricius and Pyrrhus, but after Ausculum Cineas did go to Rome a second time. See Scullard, *History*, p. 483, n. 17, for other scholarly discussions of the problem. Only the distorted report of Justin claims definitely that Fabricius visited Pyrrhus in 279/278.

22. Plutarch, "Pyrrhus," 22.3, Bernadotte Perrin, trans. Loeb, *Lives,* Vol. IX, p. 419. Pausanias, 1.12.5, W. H. S. Jones, trans. Loeb, *Pausanias,* Vol. I, p. 61. Lévêque, a little too defensive concerning Pyrrhus, tries to show that Tarentine displeasure was greatly exaggerated by some anti-Pyrrhic source used by Plutarch and that it would not have been justified anyway, since he could strengthen the Greek position in Italy not by continuing the war against Rome, which would not give up, but by establishing a strong Greek empire (pp. 420-22). It is implausible to hold that a state will not react unfavorably when a friend leaves it for a fresh venture.

23. See Frank in *CAH* VII, 650; Wuilleumier, pp. 131-32; and Lévêque, p. 510.

24. See—vague though he is on the matter—Dio Cassius, 10.45.

25. See the accounts of the affair in Dionysius, 20.4.1-8, 20.5.1-5; Appian, 3.9.1-3; Dio Cassius, 9.7-12; and Polybius, 1.7.6-13. Polybius says there were 4,000 soldiers under Decius. Several years later the garrison at Rhegium again proved disloyal. See Toynbee, *Hannibal's Legacy,* Vol. I, pp. 101-102, for the conjecture that the massacre of prominent Rhegians had been ordered by Fabricius himself to forestall a plot on the part of those Rhegians to turn the city over to Pyrrhus. The idea is interesting but hardly provable.

26. The date is Lévêque's, pp. 506-507.

27. See Zonaras, 8.6. Lévêque, pp. 497, 511-513, classes both claims as fictions.

28. "Pyrrhus," 23.5, Perrin, trans., Loeb, *Lives,* Vol. IX, pp. 423, 425.

29. See Livy, 29.8.9-11, 29.18.3-6; Dionysius, 20.9.1-3; Appian, 3.12.1-2; and Dio Cassius, 10.48. If Rufinus had in fact restored Croton to Roman control in 277, Pyrrhus may now have taken it back, driving out some Campanians from Rhegium who had occupied it in the meantime; see Frank in *CAH* VII, 654.

30. See Griffith, *Mercenaries,* pp. 62-63, arguing that these troops were mercenaries enlisted in the name Taras, not Sicilian allies of Pyrrhus himself.

31. The site is not clear from the sources; most likely it was near Mal(Bene)ventum, as Plutarch says, rather than in Lucania, as Orosius and Florus say. See Lévêque, pp. 517-19, on the site and against the hypothesis of Wuilleumier, pp. 134-35, that there were actually two battles, one fought by Pyrrhus against Curius near Malventum, the other fought by the force that Pyrrhus had dispatched against the consul Cornelius Lentulus.

32. The most reliable account of the battle is that in Plutarch, "Pyrrhus," 25. See also Dionysius, 20.12.3; Frontinus, *Stratagems,* 4.1.14; Florus, *Epitome,* 1.13.11-12; Aelian, *De Natura Animalium,* 1.38 (probably referring to this battle); Eutropius, 2.14; Orosius, 4.2; and Zonaras, 8.6. Orosius says that the Romans used fire darts against the elephants, but he may be thinking of Ausculum. Dionysius mentions a wounded baby elephant that caused confusion, and Florus and Zonaras describe the little calf's mother as causing more confusion by her maternal agitation. Lévêque (pp. 522-24, 526-28) rejects the story of the baby elephant as fiction and says that Roman sources place too much importance on Pyrrhus's elephants anyway; but Scullard, who should know more about ele-

phants, argues persuasively against both these positions (*Elephant*, pp. 111-13).

33. See Pausanias, 13.1; Justin, 25.3; and Polyaenus, 6.6.1.

34. Lévêque attributes to the Tarentines "l'agonie morale d'un monde, jadis plein de dynamisme et brillant d'un éclat incomparable, et qui maintenant s'abandonnait à son destin" (p. 538). His otherwise superb scholarship may perhaps suffer from a tendency to regard Pyrrhus as the hero that he claimed to be and to excuse him, when excuses are not, strictly speaking, justified.

35. The main sources for these events are Zonaras, 8.6; Livy, 24.9.8 and Libri XIV Periocha; and Frontinus, *Stratagems*, 3.3.1. Frank (*CAH* VII, 656) concludes that the Carthaginian fleet had come to help Rome in accord with the treaty. Toynbee (*Hannibal's Legacy*, Vol. I, p. 549) seems to be of the same opinion. Scullard thinks it probable that the Carthaginians were merely reconnoitering (*History*, p. 164; on the scholarship see p. 488, n. 8). Wuilleumier argues persuasively that there was no Carthaginian fleet (pp. 137-39). See also Homo (*Primitive Italy*, pp. 215-16), who depicts Milon as confronted with the interesting problem of whether to give the city to Carthage or to Rome.

36. There were also smaller gold coins, with various types. For discussion see Evans, "*Horsemen*," pp. 139-40; Wuilleumier, pp. 388-89; Lévêque, pp. 431-33; and (on the amphorae) Cook, *Zeus*, Vol. II, pp. 1064-65 (Appendix H). Fractions of gold staters at Taras were usually struck on a duodecimal system, but fourths and eighths were now issued for the only time in Tarentine history, perhaps for the convenience of the mercenaries, since these subdivisions conformed to the Attic system in use throughout the Eastern part of the Greek world. Although Pyrrhus struck most of his own Western coinage in Sicily, he did strike a little in Italy, probably at Locri; see Lévêque, pp. 422, 427-29. See Ravel, *Collection . . . Vlasto*, nos. 28-61, for gold coins attributed to the Pyrrhic hegemony at Taras. For bronze coins with head of Zeus/Nike holding thunderbolt, see nos. 1798-1801. On nos. 1802-06 Nike crowns a trophy.

37. For these and other didrachms of the Pyrrhic hegemony see Ravel, nos. 710-818; also the discussion in Evans, pp. 136-63.

# 10

# Roman Interlude

The terms of peace were not hard on Taras. According to Zonaras (8.6), the wall protecting the eastern side of the city was taken down and Taras had to pay tribute and to give its weapons and ships over to Rome, but after the trouble it had caused, these stipulations were surely not severe. Taras became an ally of Rome, and to enforce the alliance a Roman garrison was stationed in the citadel, but the presence of this garrison could not have been as onerous as the presence of Pyrrhus and his thousands of men. The city retained its autonomy, as is shown by the fact that it continued to strike its own coins. Although it could not make war on its own and was under the obligation of helping Rome in time of war, in most respects it carried on as before, manufacturing and trading, fishing and farming, determining its own internal policies. The pro-Roman element in its population may even have benefited from the new arrangement, but that is only a guess. In contrast to the other Greek cities of southern Italy, it did not suffer a marked decline in population; at the outbreak of the Hannibalic War in 218 it probably ranked third in population among the cities of Italy.[1]

What Taras had lost was not freedom of action so much as influence and power. It was no longer the chief of the Greek cities in southern Italy; there was no chief. The very concept of a Greek West was fading. It would last longer in Sicily than in Italy, but even in Sicily it would be over by the end of the century. The cities that had Hellenized southern Italy would in time be Romanized, though people of Greek descent would continue to live there and, some of them, to speak the Greek language. Meanwhile those cities, like their fallen leader, were at liberty in most ways but under the ultimate domination of the superpower. Locri, like Taras, would have to furnish ships to Rome; and during the Second Punic War (218-201) if not before, Locri along with Metapontum and Thurii would be garrisoned by Rome. Heraclea of course had gone over to Rome of its own accord. The Campanian soldiers serving Rome at Rhegium tried a second revolt about 271/270 but, like their predecessors, had their heads cut off for it.

The barbarians no longer offered any great impediment to Roman unification of Italy either, though some of them—for instance, the Bruttians—would make another effort late in the century, when Hannibal was marching through the peninsula. In 269/268 the Samnites, having fought so long and suffered so much, were finally rendered tractable; in 268 Rome planted a Latin colony in Samnite territory at what was now called Beneventum. The Lucanians also submitted, and the consuls for 266 subdued the Messapians and Sallentini.

Rome's war against Pyrrhus had done more for Rome than simply to remove the major obstacle to peninsular advance. As the Romans fought Pyrrhus, they had observed the military tactics of the Greeks— how to move a large army efficiently, where to place diverse bodies of men most advantageously for a battle, when to throw a new contingent into the fight. Rome had never come up against a great Greek power before; it would not forget the lessons Pyrrhus with his Epirots and Tarentines had taught it.[2]

No doubt many Romans of the third century B.C. stubbornly resisted the influence of Greek culture as their ancestors had done, but, partly through contact with Taras and the other conquered cities of the Greek South, some Romans now began to appreciate the beauty and sophistication of things Greek. Evidently not much in the way of spoils was taken from Taras by Papirius's army in 272; the pictures and statues, gold and purple mentioned by Florus (*Epitome* 1.13.27) as figuring in the triumph of that year probably belonged to the later triumph, in 209. But by one means or another a work made at Taras must occasionally have gotten to Rome. Romans who traveled to Taras on matters of business, besides, could see a great Greek city in all its splendor, even the statues by Lysippus. The Tarentine Livius Andronicus, captured in the war as a child and brought to Rome, translated the *Odyssey* and Greek tragedies and New Comedies into Latin and went on to write plays modeled after the Greek plays he knew. The republic inevitably became more cultivated from being touched by Taras[3].

If Dio Cassius and Zonaras can be believed, when Rome went to war against Carthage in 264, it used as an excuse the claim that the Punic fleet which appeared off Taras in 272 had come to help the Tarentines in violation of the Roman/Carthaginian treaty.[4] It should be remembered, however, that we do not really know why the Carthaginian ships appeared at this time, if they appeared at all.

Polybius, stressing the Romans' inexperience at shipbuilding and navigation at the beginning of the war, says that Rome borrowed fifty-oared vessels and triremes from several Greek cities, Taras among them.[5] But the involvement of Taras in the First Punic War (264-41) is unclear and may not have amounted to much. Like the other maritime Greek cities, Taras was allied to Rome as what is often termed a *socius navalis*. This presumably meant that its contribution in time of war amounted to ships and crews to man them, rather than to soldiers for Rome's land forces. Whether Taras had to contribute to the land army as well is not known, though there is some evidence that it did.[6]

If the Tarentines did have to furnish some land troops—or if Rome simply allowed certain Tarentines to serve in allied detachments on their own volition, as may conceivably have been the case—their treatment by Rome would not have been especially kind. Taras itself would have been responsible for the maintenance of these troops—with the exception of food for the men and horses, supplied by Rome. High-ranking officers would have been Roman; a Tarentine could never be promoted beyond subaltern rank. The Romans would have taken the major part of the booty and land allotments consequent on a campaign.[7] As for the crews that Taras provided to man the ships, these would have consisted of *proletarii*, unqualified for military service on land.[8] The conditions of service for such men aboard a Roman ship may be assumed to have been less than felicitous.

The Tarentines as allies but noncitizens were exempt from the *tributum*, a capital tax levied on the real and personal property of Romans in time of need, which was usually time of war. There were, however, local taxes which a citizen of Taras had to pay to the local treasury for the city's own expenses and which had nothing to do with Rome. In addition, Taras would have had to pay dues in kind to Rome. These were imposed on allied cities on occasions such as the advent of a Roman magistrate on circuit, who, along with his considerable entourage, was housed and fed at local expense. How Taras handled these taxes is unknown, but presumably it in turn had to tax its citizens for payments in kind, and apparently the visiting magistrates could be exorbitant in their expectations. Finally, there were customs duties, paid in specie. But, Roman taxation aside, a Tarentine lived his daily life under the regulations of Taras. He still voted for the city's officials according to Tarentine practice; he married, owned property, bought and sold as prescribed by Tarentine law. He belonged, first of all, to an autonomous polis.[9]

In the mid-240s Rome established a colony at the Messapian port of Brentesion on the Adriatic, from then on Brundisium. One purpose of the colony must have been to enable Rome to keep an eye on the Greeks of South Italy. At about the same time, the Appian Way was extended to Brundisium. From Beneventum the road now stretched southeastward through Venusia to Taras itself, then northeastward across the Italian heel through the town of Uria to Brundisium[10] Taras was bound up

Plate 50.   Campano-Tarentine didrachm, c. 272-235 B.C.
Obv.: Female head l.
(Parthemope? Satyra?). 20
mm.

Plate 51.   Rev. of no. 50. Boy rider
crowning stationary horse r.
Behind boy, dolphin; be-
low horse, lion. 20 mm.

securely in the Roman network. Roman officials or troops could travel
easily to this place which the Romans were calling Tarentum.

At some time in the third century, probably soon after the Pyrrhic
Wars and on into the middle of the century or beyond, Taras struck in
considerable quantity so-called Campano-Tarentine didrachms. These
were obviously meant for trade with the Campanian area, especially
with Naples. They conformed to the Campanian weight standard,
lower than the pre-Pyrrhic standard at Taras but higher than the Tarentine
reduced standard. On the obverse, instead of the horseman, was a
female head (Plate 50). Although it resembled the head of the siren
Parthenope, which had occupied the obverse of Neapolitan coins for
many years and with which Neapolitans could have associated it, for
Tarentines the head probably represented Satyra, lover of Poseidon and
mother of the eponymous hero Taras. A Tarentine boy athlete appeared
on the reverse, crowning his horse; and under the horse was a symbol
such as a dolphin, a lion, a tripod, the top of an Ionic column, an anchor,

Plate 52. Silver didrachm, c. 272-235 B.C. Obv.: Boy crowning stationary horse r.; beneath horse, bearded mask facing. On l., monogram. Under raised foreleg of horse, KYNON in two lines (Ravel/ Vlasto No. 859 has KI rather than KY). 19.5 mm.

Plate 53. Silver didrachm, c. 272-235 B.C. Obv.: Boy on stationary horse r.; Nike flying up behind. To r., EYN; beneath horse, ΔAMOKPI-TOΣ. 19.5 mm.

or a cornucopia—or in some cases there were two symbols[11] (Plate 51). If this coinage was struck soon after the Pyrrhic Wars, it illustrates the lenient treatment of Taras by Rome, which evidently allowed the city to maintain special trade relations with Campania. It also testifies to the continued commercial prosperity of Taras into the middle of the century.

Not only the Campano-Tarentine didrachms but didrachms with typical Tarentine types were struck in some quantity in the post-Pyrrhic period. They suggest, like the issues for Campania, that Tarentine commercial activity was still significant. They also suggest that, finally, a decline in artistic standards had set in with regard to coins as with regard to limestone sculpture, which, it may be recalled, petered out around the middle of the century. The flans tended to be smaller than those of coins of the Pyrrhic hegemony, and the types were less imaginatively designed and less carefully engraved. This is not to say, however, that the didrachms were devoid of artistic merit; it is just that in comparison with previous issues they suffer. Toward the end, however, there seems to have been an attempt to make the money more beautiful again.

Plate 54. Silver didrachm, c. 272-235 B.C. Obv.: Horseman r. in helmet and lorica, with lance and shield. Under horse, Ⱶ HPAKΛHTOΣ in two lines. 17.5 mm.

Plate 55. Silver didrachm, c. 272-235 B.C. Obv.: Horseman l. wearing helmet and thorax and holding shield behind, on stationary horse. Beneath horse, APIΣTΩN. 19 mm.

Evans considered the attempt so remarkable that he placed the post-Pyrrhic didrachms in two groups. His Period VIII extends from about 272 to 235, and his Period IX extends from about 235 to 228.[12]

Many of the didrachms of Period VIII had on the obverse the pacific type of the boy equestrian crowning his horse—executed usually, but not always, in a cursory fashion. On a few of these a bearded mask appeared as a symbol beneath the horse—possibly with reference to drama, which, in so far as we know, was still a favorite amusement of the city (Plate 52). On some of the obverses a little Nike flew up from behind to crown the rider for success in the games (Plate 53). Rarer types were that of the Dioscuri, caped and wearing their peaked helmets, riding to the left, and that of a horseman shown almost facing, holding a patera and crowned by a flying Nike—like the Dioscuri, an ambitious design for the period.

More surprising for a conquered city committed to peace was a revival of the horseman lancing downward. Other obverses showed, sometimes on a stationary horse and sometimes on a prancing one, a

Plate 56. Silver didrachm, c. 235 B.C. or later. Obv.: Horseman facing, wearing tunic, thorax, shoulder pieces, and mantle, on horse r.; Nike crowning horseman. On l., monogram. Below horse, ΚΑΛΛΙΚΡΑΤΗΣ. 17 mm.

Plate 57. Silver didrachm, c. 272-235 B.C. Rev. of No. 52. Dolphin rider l. holding kantharos.

rider wearing a helmet and cuirass and equipped with a lance and shield (Plate 54). On still others a rider, again cuirassed, held a javelin in his upraised right hand; or, helmeted, he held a shield behind him (Plate 55)—a pose reminiscent of an obverse struck during the Age of Archytas, except that on the earlier coin the rider wore no armor and was definitely an ephebe competing in the games.

All these post-Pyrrhic riders are usually interpreted not as athletes but as warriors. To designate them competitors in equestrian religious games rather than soldiers would require more specific knowledge of Tarentine games than we have. It is possible that they represent participants in military exercises, aspects of a cavalryman's training, and that they are consequently both agonistic and military at the same time, though not idealizations of the Tarentine on campaign.[13] But a question remains unanswered: why should mounted soldiers—men performing military exercizes even if not actually at war—appear at all on the money of a city committed to peace?

In Hellenistic times the Tarentine cavalry was famous. Somehow—

Plate 58.  Silver didrachm. Rev. of No. 55. Dolphin rider 1. holding hippocamp and trident. Behind figure, ΙΩΝ.

Plate 59.  Silver didrachm. Rev. of No. 54. Androgynous dolphin rider 1., holding flower and cornucopiae. Behind, E and thymiaterion (incense altar).

we do not know just how—the term "Tarentine" even came to be applied to a certain kind of light cavalry, apparently mercenary in most cases, whether it came from Taras or not. The term presumably denoted a definite style of fighting used by such cavalry, or perhaps two styles: one in which the horseman threw a short spear from far off, without ever coming into physical contact with the enemy, and the other, the more common style, in which the horseman, generally equipped with three spears, threw one or two of them from a distance and then attacked at close quarters with the third.[14] We do not even know for sure whether these techniques were favored by the city's own cavalry in Hellenistic times or before, though the application of the term "Tarentine" to them certainly implies that they were. Extant sources say nothing about the practices of Tarentine horsemen in Pyrrhus's army. The second technique may, however, be illustrated by the didrachms from the Pyrrhic period and earlier on which the horseman carries three spears and a shield (Plates 27, 29, 43). In the post-Pyrrhic period it is not at all unlikely that horsemen from Taras hired out as mercenaries. We

Plate 60.  Silver didrachm, 235 B.C.
or later. Rev. of No. 56.
Dolphin rider 1. holding
Nike and trident. Behind
rider, NE.

Plate 61.  Silver didrachm, c. 272-235
B.C. Rev.: Dolphin rider 1.
with chlamys, brandishing
trident; owl behind. 19
mm.

have no proof that they did, but in an age of mercenary armies, it would be surprising if such notorious cavalrymen did not. If the military horsemen on post-Pyrrhic coins represent men at army exercises, therefore—or if they are idealizations of men in battle—they may, like the distaff, be another advertisement of a Tarentine product.

During Evans's Period IX, from about 235 to 228, when more artistic effort is noticeable in the dies, some of the obverses continued the pacific type of the naked young athlete crowning his victorious horse. On others he carried a torch on a swift-galloping steed (an illustration of another equestrian game?) or, dressed in a short tunic, leaned back precariously on his springing mount and clung with one hand to its mane. Or the rider, perhaps one of the Dioscuri, in a tunic and with a chlamys billowing out behind, held a scabbarded sword under his left arm. There were still military types too. In one the horseman, wearing a lorica, hurled a short javelin, perhaps performing the first "Tarentine" mode of warfare. In another—the most ambitious type of all, perhaps, and one of the most realistic depictions of a warrior on Greek coinage—

the horseman, though unhelmeted, wore tunic, thorax, shoulder pieces, and mantle, rode to the right on a heavier horse than usual with his face turned toward the onlooker, and held out his right hand to receive a little Nike (Plate 56). These military obverses may, again, have been advertisements of a commodity in which the city excelled.

On the reverses of coins of Periods VIII and IX, the figure on the dolphin, who could look decidedly androgynous, carried various attributes—a cantharus, a trident, a cornucopia, a hippocamp, sometimes a Nike (Plates 57-60). Occasionally he brandished his trident (Plate 61). Reverse symbols included, once more, the twin amphorae.[15]

Evans assumed that the Tarentine mint ceased functioning about 228, to resume production only in the Hannibalic period. The Hannibalic coins were struck on a reduced weight standard and in a far poorer style, and this, to Evans, indicated a break when no didrachms were struck at all. Another argument he used for the temporary closing of the Tarentine mint involved Rome. A Roman campaign in Illyria in 229 resulted in the establishment of protectorates over the ports of Dyrrhachium (Epidamnus) and Apollonia on the Adriatic Sea and the much-transferred island of Corcyra. One of Rome's objects, Evans said, was to extend to these areas the use of its newly adopted silver coin, which we call the *victoriatus* because of the Victory setting up a trophy on the reverse. Rome evidently did not want Taras interfering with its new currency and therefore, around 228, cracked down on the Tarentine mint, showing less leniency than it had in the past toward its Greek ally.[16]

Evans's view was the prevailing one for a long time after his *"Horsemen"* was published in 1889. Recently, however, the inception of both the *victoriatus* and the *denarius* has been dated to about 211.[17] The new dating has gained general acceptance; and in consequence, the assignment of a cessation of Tarentine coinage to 228 has lost its major support. There may still have been a break, but on the other hand Tarentine coinage may have continued right through to the Hannibalic period.[18] What used to be considered an indication of an increased severity in Rome's treatment of Taras, the shutting down of the mint that had been operating for almost three centuries, may not have occurred.

There are, however, other suggestions of heightened Roman harshness toward Taras. The extension of the Appian Way to Brundisium perhaps subjected the Tarentines to tighter supervision. To the 4,200 Roman foot soldiers and 200 horsemen who according to Polybius (2.24.13) were garrisoned in the city in 225, Rome may have added a contingent of allied troops of comparable size, drawn perhaps from Umbria and the Etruscan area. There is at any rate no reason to think that, simply because Polybius does not mention it, an allied contingent was not attached to the legion at Taras as to other legions.[19] These additional foreigners quartered in the city would have been an irritation. Possibly, then, more and more Tarentines chafed under the Roman alliance as they remembered that they were Greeks and that their city had once been glorious.

# Notes to Chapter 10

1. Most scholars comment on the generous terms of the peace, though Homo (*Primitive Italy,* pp. 216-17) considers them burdensome. On the population, see Toynbee, *Hannibal's Legacy,* Vol. I, pp. 102, 490. Since Taras was a conquered enemy, the treaty would have been a *foedus iniquum,* somewhat less permissive than a *foedus aequum.* Our knowledge of both kinds of treaties is not extensive. See the excellent discussion in E. Badian, *Foreign Clientelae (264-70 B.C.)* (Oxford, 1958), pp. 25-28.

2. This at least is the view of Lévêque, p. 52, though in his Pyrrhic partisanship he perhaps exaggerates Rome's debt to Pyrrhus's military experience a little.

3. Wuilleumier, pp. 677-79, speculates regarding Tarentine influence after 249 on the *Ludi Tarentini,* rites at Rome which, as a result of that influence, celebrated such deities as Dis and Proserpina.

4. See Dio Cassius, 11.43.1, and Zonaras, 8.8

5. 1.20.9-14. But see also Moretti ("Problemi," pp. 55-56), who casts doubt on this claim. Wuilleumier, on the other hand, stresses Taras's participation in the war (p. 143).

6. See Badian's discussion (*Foreign Clientelae,* pp. 28-30) of the opposed views (1) that the Greek allied cities had to furnish ships and crews only and (2) that their military obligations were no different from those of other allies. The theory that they did not contribute to Rome's land forces is based on the fact that mention of these cities is omitted from the tabulation of Roman and allied troops in 225 given by Polybius (2.24). The theory that they did contribute to Rome's land forces is based partly on Livy's mention of five young Tarentines who, he says, had been captured by the Carthaginians in the Second Punic War while fighting for Rome (24.13.1; for the implication that Neapolitans also had to serve in Rome's land forces see 23.1.5-9). Badian feels that the denial of any difference existing between the military requirements of a Greek ally and another ally is a case of going too far. Brunt (*Italian Manpower,* p. 50) believes that the Greek cities had to furnish some land troops and explains the omission of these allies from Polybius's list on the ground that in 225 Rome would not have considered their potential contributions very important—not a thoroughly convincing argument. The reason why Polybius does not mention the Greek cities remains a puzzle.

7. See the discussion in Homo, *Primitive Italy,* pp. 232-35.

8. See Toynbee, Vol. I, p. 493.

9. See the excellent discussion of taxation and the rights and limitations of a noncitizen in Homo, pp. 235-41.

10. See Strabo, 6.3.7.

11. See discussions in Evans, pp. 131-32, 170-76; Wuilleumier, pp. 143-44, 386; Stazio, "Aspetti e Momenti," pp. 178-79; and Burnett, "Coinages of Rome and Magna Graecia", p. 96. The coins are pictured in Ravel, *Collection . . . Vlasto,* nos. 991-1043.

12. See *"Horsemen,"* pp. 168-69. Evans (pp. 169-70) assumes from the abundance of the coinage that Taras was flourishing during Period VIII. The year 235 as a dividing date between the two periods is of course only approximate. Burnett, compressing Evans's chronology at both ends, redates Evans's Period VIII to 270-50 and Period IX to 250-40 (see "Coinages of Rome and Magna Graecia," pp. 115-16).

13. See Wuilleumier, p. 188.

14. See Wuilleumier, pp. 187-88, for the best discussion of these techniques, and Aelian, *Tactics,* chaps. 2 and 4, for the clearest ancient description of them. On ancient references to mounted "Tarentines" (apparently not from Taras) in battle, see Wuilleumier's discussion, pp. 666-68, and, among the sources themselves, particularly Polybius, 4.77.5-7, 11.12-4-7, 11.13.1-8, and Livy, 37.40.12-

15. See Ravel, nos. 938-70, and discussion in Evans, pp. 183-96. Evans (pp. 185-86) seems to relate the military as well as nonmilitary equestrian types to a presumed revival, about 235, of "some religious celebration of an agonistic character."

16. See Evans, pp. 191-93.

17. See Crawford, *Roman Republican Coinage,* Vol. I, pp. 7-10, 28-35.

18. Burnett, however, ends Evans's Period IX about 240; see above, n. 12.

19. Toynbee (*Hannibal's Legacy,* Vol. I, pp. 481-82) argues strongly for this point.

# 11

# State Suicide: The Hannibalic Connection

Hannibal descended from the Alps onto the plains of northern Italy late in 218. He hoped to do what Pyrrhus had hoped to do after Heraclea: to break up the federation of states allied to Rome. His chance came in 216 with the great defeat of the Romans at Cannae. There were defections after that: peoples nursing old grudges against the republic, startled and delighted by the crushing of Roman power at Cannae, fell away to what they thought would be the winning side. Among these peoples were Taras's friends from Pyrrhic days, the Bruttians and the Samnites. Three centuries later the poet Silius Italicus would say about this period of disloyalty to Rome: "It was like a horrible plague that spread infection all over the country."[1]

But Silius Italicus was using a certain amount of poetic license. The swing away from Rome, though serious, was less decisive than Hannibal had expected. The Etruscans, for instance, stayed loyal. The Gauls were hesitant to break away, although they eventually did declare for Hannibal and, in November, cut up two legions. The Samnites could do little, with strong Roman settlements in their territory at Venusia and Beneventum. Some of the Apulians had revolted, but Rome had settlements at Luceria and Canusium to intimidate them. Among the Greek cities in Campania, Naples and Cumae and Nola stayed in the Roman federation; so did the Samnite foundation of Puteoli. Capua, however, defected.

Rome was of course particularly worried about the Greek cities of the Southeast. In 215 it reinforced the garrison at Taras with more troops.[2] It also dispatched twenty-five ships to guard the coast of the heel between Taras on the western shore and Brundisium on the eastern or Adriatic shore.[3] Locri, Croton, and Caulonia (all in Bruttium, the southernmost part of the peninsula) did allow Carthaginian forces to take them. This meant that Carthage controlled most of the extreme South. But Rhegium on the strait of Messana did not defect.

Livy says that in Croton, once so rich and influential, only about 2,000 citizens remained at this time (23.30.6-7). The diminished place did not put up much resistance. Bruttians fighting for Carthage had preceded the Carthaginian general Hanno to Croton. According to Livy, in the citadel the aristocrats "were at the time maintaining themselves, besieged even by their own plebs as well as by the Bruttians," and when delegates came from Locri, which had already voted to go over to Carthage, the Crotonians agreed to evacuate their city and move to Locri to live.[4] The division of the Crotonians into aristocrats favoring Rome and plebs opposed to Rome (and besieging their own aristocrats) is reminiscent of the social split in the Greek cities at the time of Pyrrhus. In depleted, depopulated Croton as in the other Hellenic cities of the Southeast, the split seems to have become a traditional thing.

But the situation was in fact not quite that simple, at least in Locri. Livy insists that "the Greek cities . . . were all the more ready to remain in alliance with Rome because they saw that the Bruttii, whom they both hated and feared, had gone over to the side of the Carthaginians." He consequently has to explain the vote of the Locrian assembly to surrender to Carthage on the ground that many Locrians had already left their city and were virtual hostages in the hands of the Carthaginians, plus the fact that "all the fickle preferred political change and a new alliance.[5]

Hannibal wintered in Apulia in 215/214. In the spring of 214 Roman soldiers stationed at Beneventum defeated troops coming up from the south under Hanno's command—largely Bruttians and Lucanians. Hannibal marched toward Taras and Heraclea.

Taras now assumed an importance that it had not had in more than half a century. It was still not only a city of great size (unlike the other Greek cities of southeastern Italy) but a great port. With the port of Brundisium securely in Roman hands, the occupation of Taras by Carthaginian troops would have been very advantageous to Hannibal. For example, when Philip V of Macedon sent envoys to Hannibal to discuss the matter of a treaty of assistance between Macedon and Carthage, they would have landed at Taras as passengers from Greece had been doing for hundreds of years, if Taras had not been full of Roman soldiers. As it was, the Macedonians had to disembark way to the south, near the Lacinium Promontory in Bruttium.

On their way back they were captured at sea by the Romans. Worried that Macedon would now send help to Hannibal, Rome doubled the fleet guarding the coast. The second twenty-five ships, according to Livy, plus the five ships which had carried the Macedonian prisoners to Rome, sailed from Ostia to Taras (23.38.8-10). The Greek ally was as important to Rome as it could be to Hannibal.

The mood of the city at this critical time can hardly be estimated. For its mood at the time of Pyrrhus's arrival, there are facts to go on: the recent activities of the pro-Roman and anti-Roman parties, the coming of Cineas and Milon. But about the city's feelings near the beginning of the Second Punic War, there is less information. If Taras did contribute ships to Rome, it also contributed proletarian crews to man those ships. Whether or not it was also required to contribute men to fight on land, there were (or had been) Tarentine soldiers in Rome's land armies. Livy, for instance, mentions five young Tarentine aristocrats who had been taken captive by the Carthaginians, some at Cannae and the others at Lake Trasimenus, and who were later freed by Hannibal (24.13.1). Within the city, therefore, lived families more or less committed to the military success of Rome. We know this, but we cannot be sure of much more.

The pro-Roman faction at Taras had in any case not died out after Pyrrhus, any more than it had at Croton. Several decades of prosperity for Taras as a Roman ally may in fact have strengthened it. But as succeeding events make clear, many Tarentines, like perhaps the majority of people in the cities to the south which had gone over to Hannibal, were extremely discontented with Rome. As Carthaginian troops approached, they looked eagerly for a chance to break the Roman alliance forever.

Either the five young Tarentines had been fighting unwillingly on the Roman side, or they had had a change of heart because of Hannibal's generosity in returning captured allies of Rome to their homes. They had now been delegated by Taras—at least by its anti-Roman faction— to ask Hannibal to approach within view of the city. They assured him that as soon as his army was seen, Taras would go over to him. The anti-Roman party was in control inside the city: "... the common people were in the power of the younger men, the Tarentine state in the hands of the common people."[6] It sounds like a repetition of the Pyrrhic situation: an anti-Roman majority composed of nonaristocratic citizens and dominated by the young. And this may have been the case.

Or the whole story may be an invention by Livy to discredit Taras in the eyes of a Roman reading public. He has the five Tarentines come to Hannibal at Lake Avernus near Cumae in Campania, which would imply that Hannibal had withdrawn that far from the Tarentine area— an implication not easily supportable.[7] This hardly credible aspect of the story makes the rest of the story difficult to accept as an indication of Tarentine feeling; but it is all we have except for the reaction of the city when Hannibal did come near. The proportion of anti-Roman to pro-Roman citizens is absolutely incalculable. So is the extent to which the anti-Roman party was composed of the young, if it was.

Hannibal had been devastating the countryside in customary fashion but, according to Livy, stopped his depredations in the vicinity of the city in order to give the impression that he was kindly. He camped a short distance to the east of Taras, whose walls, torn down as one of the terms of 272, had been built up again. Marcus Livius, in charge of the garrison of 4,200 Roman foot soldiers and 200 Roman cavalry inside, and perhaps a body of allies as well, posted guards on the walls and at the gates. And nothing happened. The citizens showed no sign of breaking away from Rome. Perhaps even the most anti-Roman were intimidated by the legionaries in their midst; perhaps the majority felt that the chance of freedom was not worth the risk. Hannibal apparently believed that he could not do much without help from inside. After waiting around a few days he withdrew.[8]

Cold weather was coming on, and his campaigning was over for the year. He ravaged the fields of grain near Heraclea and Metapontum, took several thousand horses in Apulia, and, not having had an especially good season, retired for the winter to Salapia on the Apulian coast.

In the latter part of 213 or fairly early in 212, however, he marched on Taras again.[9] This time he intended to take the city whether the citizens helped him or not. And this time Rome played into his hands. At Rome were a number of hostages from Taras and Thurii, kept under loose guard in the somewhat ironically named Atrium of Liberty to ensure the loyalty of their states to the republic. But a Tarentine called Phileas who happened to be residing in Rome—more or less to represent Tarentine interests, according to Livy—persuaded them to make a break for freedom. He bribed two temple wardens, and the hostages consequently escaped from the Atrium of Liberty at night. The next day they were captured and brought back to Rome. The Romans scourged them with rods and then, feeling that this was not enough punishment, threw them to death from the Tarpeian Rock.[10] Taras and Thurii, shocked and infuriated when the news reached them, had been given a good reason for being anti-Roman. While the families of the hostages were mourning, the pro-Roman element must have been hard pressed to justify the conduct of Rome toward its allies.

At Taras thirteen young citizens conspired to let Hannibal in. Significantly, they were aristocrats (according to Livy), like the five young men who may or may not have communicated with Hannibal at Lake Avernus. One might expect a treasonable plot to have come from the democratic element, if this was in fact still the anti-Roman party. Perhaps loyalties were by this time not really a matter of class; possibly an anti-Roman spirit was beginning to sweep over the republic's traditional friends. The dead hostages themselves had been aristocrats; their punishment would have turned other aristocrats (their relatives, for instance) against Rome. It may have been, however, that there was already a split within the upper class, its older members in general staying loyal to Rome while its younger, more excitable members swung in the direction of rebellion.[11]

The conspirators—who were in fact relatives or friends of the hostages—went out of Taras one night in the fall of 213, saying that they were going hunting. Hannibal was within three days' march of the city. When they got near his camp, eleven of them hid in the woods, but the two leaders proceeded to the camp itself, where they were naturally made prisoner. They asked to be taken to Hannibal, and they told him about the temper of the Tarentines and about their plot. The delighted general praised them and arranged it so that they and their companions might have Carthaginian cattle to take back to Taras. This would make it look as if they had been out of the city to forage the cattle. Livy and Polybius do not explain why they did not simply retain their guise as hunters.[12]

One of the two leaders of the conspirators, Philemenus, had in fact a reputation as a hunter, and he used this reputation to advantage in the next few weeks. He and his friends would leave the city at night by a postern gate as if they were a hunting party, and in the interest of realism they would bring back game, sometimes actually killed by themselves, sometimes provided by Hannibal—game which they presented with their compliments to the Roman commander or to the guard at the gate. The guard became so used to their comings and goings that all Philemenus had to do was to whistle, and the gate would be opened. During the second meeting with Hannibal, the terms of the proposed takeover were discussed: Taras would be set free, the Carthaginians would exact no tribute and would impose no burden on the citizens (such as a garrison), but Hannibal's soldiers would be allowed to plunder the houses where Romans lived. The later meetings presumably finalized plans for the delivery of the city.[13]

The main sources concerning the entry itself are still Polybius and Livy, and their stories agree in almost all respects. When Hannibal decided it was time to act, he picked about 10,000 men from his army—both infantry and cavalry—ordering them to take provisions for four days. The march (according to Polybius) was timed so that they would arrive at Taras when the Roman commander, Marcus Livius, had been at a banquet and would consequently not be at his most alert. Ahead of the army went about eighty Numidian horsemen to capture or otherwise dispose of farmers who had seen the column and might blab. Hannibal did not tell his soldiers where they were going.

Reports that the Numidians were overrunning the countryside filtered into the city. But Livius's banquet, held at a building sacred to the Muses close to the marketplace, had started in the afternoon and was well under way. Livius, content and intoxicated, decided that the next morning he would send out half his cavalry to look into the matter. (Livy records this decision but omits the whole matter of the banquet, probably so as not to make an ancestor look any worse than was absolutely necessary.) At night, when the drinkers were breaking up, some of the conspirators joined them, pretending to have run across them by accident and to be drunk themselves. They hilariously saw Livius safely home and then roamed through the city, watching for any indication that the plot was known—watching especially the streets leading to the market for anything out of the ordinary. Some were posted near Livius's house to keep that under surveillance. Nothing out of the ordinary occurred.

Hannibal approached the Temenid Gate in the wall on the city's eastern edge. A distance outside the gate stood a tomb, perhaps only a hill or perhaps a building on a hill, which some people knew as the Tomb of Hyacinthus and others as the Tomb of Apollo Hyacinthus, according to Polybius; and his uncertainty indicates the difficulty in keeping the two deities separate in Hellenistic times if not before. Here, as had been planned, Hannibal had a fire lighted. Inside the city— among the *naiskoi* in the great eastern cemetery—the conspirators were waiting for this signal, headed by Philemenus's chief confederate, Nikon. They lighted an answering fire. Both fires were extinguished, and it was time for the next phase of the plan.

The conspirators proceeded to the Temenid Gate, sprang on the guards, and killed them. They opened the gate, and Hannibal with some of his troops came through.

Philemenus had not been inside the city with the others but outside with Hannibal. On the principle that two chances are better than one, he now went to the postern gate and gave his familiar whistle, as if he was returning from hunting. He and the three men with him carried a stretcher on which lay a tremendous boar. The guard, expecting a slice or so as usual, opened the gate. While the sentry was admiring the magnificent animal, one of Philemenus's companions sent a hunting spear through him. Outside stood about a thousand Libyan soldiers. Thirty of them rushed in, killed the guards at what seems to have been an adjacent gate, and let in the rest. No doubt conducted by Philemenus, they proceeded through the dark streets to the marketplace where the bronze statue of Zeus by Lysippus stood. There they joined Hannibal and the main body of troops.[14]

Hannibal sent 2,000 Celts through Taras, divided into three units, each of which was guided by two Tarentines. They were to hunt up Romans and kill them. The Tarentine guides yelled to their fellow citizens, telling them to stay put, and they would be all right. Most Tarentines had of course been asleep. As they woke up to the unusual noise in the streets—the shouts of Hannibal's men, the ring of arms, the screams of dying Romans—they could only guess what was happening. Some of them interpreted the commotion as caused by the Romans themselves on a raid of Tarentine houses. They heard Roman trumpets sound the call to arms in the theater; but the sound was not quite right because the trumpets were actually being blown by Hannibal's men, and as the well-trained Roman soldiers rushed to answer the call, Celts and Carthaginians pounced on them in the shadowy streets and slaughtered them.

As for Livius the Roman commander, he too had waked up—still drunk according to Polybius, or possibly already experiencing a hangover—and he had realized more quickly than some of the Tarentines that the Carthaginians were inside the walls. Attended by servants, he had made his way to a gate that gave access to the harbor and, in a small boat, had crossed the Mare Piccolo to the citadel, still in Roman possession. Romans who had escaped massacre joined him there.

It was now day, and Tarentines coming out of their houses could see dead Romans in the streets. The conspirators and Hannibal's heralds went through Taras announcing that Carthage had freed the city and summoning the citizens to a meeting in the marketplace. Many of the pro-Roman inhabitants had already gone to the citadel, where they would hole up with the remnant of the Roman troops. When the other Tarentines had crowded into the agora, Hannibal made a speech. He reminded them that he had been kind enough to return to their homes the Tarentines taken prisoner while serving with the Romans, and he animadverted against arrogant Roman control. Polybius says that the Tarentines cheered every sentence. He instructed them to identify their dwelling places by writing their names on the doors (according to Livy) or just by writing "Tarentine" (according to Polybius). These residences would not be touched. Carthaginian troops would plunder the others, as part of the bargain with Philemenus. Any Roman sympathizer who identified as Tarentine a house where a Roman lived would be killed. (In addition to the soldiers, there must have been quite a number of Roman civilians in Taras at the time.) The loot was considerable.[15]

Although the city was now Hannibal's, its citadel remained in Roman hands. A fortified rock with cliffs protecting it on the side that faced the water and a wide moat and wall protecting it on the side that faced the city, it was for the time being impregnable. Hannibal realized this and, after a few preliminary attempts at siege—attacking with movable towers and catapults, the Romans responding with their own engines, shooting stones down on Hannibal's machines and catching his grappling hooks in slip knots—he gave up the idea of taking it over, at least for a while. But it stood as a powerful threat to his own security and the security of Taras. According to Appian there were about 5,000 Romans inside, plus the Tarentines who were Roman sympathizers and had fled there.[16] Half the Roman garrison stationed at Metapontum was transferred to the citadel, and Roman ships ran the Carthaginian blockade and got into the harbor with loads of grain from Etruria so that those inside were in no danger of immediate starvation.[17] The Roman soldiers could sally out at any time they chose, to harass the Carthaginians and the citizenry, and no doubt many Tarentines felt that their joy in their new freedom had been premature. There was an even worse problem. Situated in the western part of the peninsula, the citadel dominated the inner harbor (the Mare Piccolo) and controlled the bridge or bridges at its mouth. This meant that the whole Tarentine fleet was shut up in the harbor. In a very real sense the Tarentines, not the Romans, were prisoners.

Since Hannibal could not take the citadel in the near future, he did the next best thing: he rendered it as ineffectual as possible. Under fire from the Romans and with the help of his Tarentine friends, he constructed, parallel to the wall of the citadel, counterworks that eventually consisted of a palisade, a trench, a wall of dirt dug up for the trench, and a second palisade on top of this earth wall. Apparently he also had another wall built, extending from a street called Savior to an avenue called Broad Street, giving the city closer protection.[18] These defenses, in which the Tarentines must have participated with a newborn enthusiasm, sealed off the city from Roman attacks. With the imagination of a military genius, Hannibal also contrived to transfer the Tarentine navy from the harbor in the Mare Piccolo to the harbor in the Mare Grande, from which it could operate freely. A main thoroughfare bisected the city, leading from one port to the other. It was wide enough to accommodate ships. Hannibal had it paved and had flat wagons constructed. The Tarentines gathered tackle together to pull the ships out of the water, then put the ships on the wagons, and with mules to pull the wagons, transported the entire fleet via the thoroughfare to the outer harbor.[19] It took only a few days to accomplish this feat of military engineering. The Tarentines could laugh at the Romans. With Hannibal to lead them, they would once again be free.

Meanwhile—in 212, apparently—the takeover of Taras had an effect on Roman allies remaining in southern Italy. Thurii—remembering Rome's treatment of the escaped hostages, some of whom had been Thurians—went over to Hannibal. Metapontum, with half its garrison now at the Tarentine citadel, also defected to Carthage. Heraclea, quick to break alliances, now looked to Hannibal also. A leading Lucanian who had been fighting for Rome changed sides too, no doubt bringing his followers with him. He tricked the Roman proconsul, Sempronius Gracchus, into death at the hands of Numidians hiding in ambush.[20]

The future of Rome in southern Italy looked doubtful.

In other areas Rome was doing better. For instance, the Carthaginian general Bomilcar, in charge of a fleet of 130 ships and a supply convoy meant to relieve Syracuse from Roman siege, sailed away from Sicily when the Roman fleet approached. With his fighting men, Bomilcar docked at Taras. Having quartered Greek and Illyrian soldiers in the past, then Romans, the city was now host to an enormous number of Punic troops. Whether some were put up in town or all remained on their ships, they were to prove increasingly inconvenient, simply because they had to be fed.

From the city of Capua in Campania, which had defected to Hannibal in 216, messengers came to Hannibal requesting Carthaginian help against the forces of the two Roman consuls. Capua was already close to starvation. According to Livy, the envoys made the point that not even Taras was worth more to Hannibal than their own fair city. Hannibal ordered Hanno to march into Campania to ensure a supply of grain, and he dispatched 2,000 horsemen to help the Capuans. Messengers from Capua came to him again, and, anxious though he was by this time to take the Tarentine citadel, he apparently agreed that retaining this western city with an Etruscan and Samnite past was very important. He marched into Campania with select cavalry and foot soldiers, leaving his baggage and heavy-armed troops in the land of the Bruttians in the Italian toe, and leaving Bomilcar the Carthaginian in charge at Taras.[21] He even threatened Rome. But he was unable to raise the Roman siege; in 211 Capua capitulated. So did Syracuse. Even though Hannibal won a considerable victory over the Romans at Herdoniae in Apulia in 210, Tarentine hopes for a Carthaginian triumph and the ultimate independence of the city must have dropped by this time. The Carthaginians had been in the city between two and three years now and the war seemed no closer to an end. Rhegium across from Sicily was still in Roman control, and Hannibal proved unable to take it.

Bomilcar's presence at Taras, besides, was increasingly irritating. The crowds of men on his ship were supposed to make it safe for food to be brought into the city and to prevent supplies from reaching the citadel, but actually they ate more grain than they could see safely into Taras. According to Polybius, Bomilcar finally was "compelled to sail off at the earnest request of the inhabitants."[22]

A quick-witted man could use such unsettled times to his own advantage. One who tried was named Heraclides—son of lower-class citizens, formerly a male prostitute. Because he was intelligent, skilled especially at architectural engineering, he was put in charge of some repairs being made to the walls; and in this capacity he was given the keys to a gate. It apparently occurred to him that he could make a profit by betraying the city to the Romans. At least this was what his fellow citizens suspected, and they expelled him. Their suspicions may have been unfounded—simply a case of the nervousness, almost hysteria, within the city—but Heraclides' later history suggests that he could not be trusted. He went to the Roman camp, but the Romans discovered him transmitting secret messages to Taras and to Hannibal, and they sent him packing too.[23]

Grain was the important thing. Although the Tarentines inside the city were better off in this respect than the Romans and their Tarentine friends in the citadel, the situation seems to have been developing into a case of mutual starvation. Much of the grain for Taras now had to come from Bruttium, and the Bruttians were running out of it.[24] Parties of Tarentines roamed the countryside for grain; as 4,000 of them wandered around through territory which must already have been pretty effectually devastated, Livius sent 2,500 armed men out of the citadel to cut them down in the fields.[25]

From the rich granaries of Sicily a large supply of food was ordered by Rome for the men in the citadel. (This was evidently in 210, shortly before the slaughter of the 4,000 Tarentines in the fields.) A fleet of about twenty ships—two triremes, three quinqueremes, and approximately fifteen vessels from allied cities such as Elea and Posidonia—joined the grain ships at Rhegium and convoyed them up the coast, evidently toward a point where the grain could be unloaded without fear of running into the Carthaginian navy blockading Taras itself. From this point the grain would have been carried overland to the citadel. But about fifteen miles from Taras a Tarentine fleet met the Romans. Livy stresses the ferocity, the desperateness of the battle—the Tarentines fighting to preserve their new freedom by starving the citadel into surrender, the Romans fighting to preserve the integrity of the citadel in the face of what Rome viewed as Tarentine treachery.

It was as personal a struggle as possible. When the ships had rammed each other with their beaks, the commanders would throw out the grappling irons with their heavy chains, and when the vessels were fastened together, the men would leap from one to the other, using their swords as if in a battle on land. Ships were stuck so tight to one another that a missile rarely fell between two of them into the water. The Tarentine fleet was commanded by a man named Democrates, but in charge of the foremost vessel was Nikon, second to Philemenus in the gang of conspirators that had let Hannibal in. Nobody hated Romans more passionately than he did. His vessel and the ship of the Roman commander, Decimus Quinctius, were stuck tight together. The Roman was shouting orders and urging his soldiers on. From his own ship Nikon hurled a spear. It was a direct hit; Quinctius toppled into the water, a dead hero. Nikon crossed to the enemy ship, followed by his men. The Romans, leaderless now, retreated to the stern. A Tarentine trireme loomed up behind. Caught in the middle, the Roman ship was captured. This was the turn in the battle. The other Roman ships scattered in all directions. The Tarentines chased them, and some of the Roman ships were sunk. Others made for shore, where the Romans found themselves exposed to the tender treatment of Thurians and Metapontines. As for the vessels carrying the grain, the Tarentines got a few of them, but most of them sailed away, so that neither the Romans nor the Tarentines were fed.[26] For Taras, however, the victory was still a great one. The enthusiastic assembly and people voted to institute an annual festival commemorating it. But the festival would not be annual for long. In 209 Rome undertook to recapture the city.[27]

From the Roman standpoint it was high time for this. Even for the sake of national pride, the garrison had to be rescued. More practically, Hannibal had to be deprived of his main port in Italy; until then an end to this long war would not be in sight. If Taras fell to the Romans, besides, the rest of Greek Italy would be likelier to fall. Taras, though no longer a leader of Italiot Greeks in the old sense, was the key to the preservation of their integrity.

The consuls for 209 were Quintus Fulvius Flaccus and the elderly Quintus Fabius Maximus. The plan was for Fulvius to campaign in Lucania and Bruttium, keeping Hannibal occupied there, while Fabius, having picked up two legions from Sicily at Brundisium, marched toward Taras. The proconsul Marcellus campaigned against the Carthaginians in Apulia. From the fleet off Sicily the commander Laevinus sent thirty ships to cooperate with Fabius's land army. An emergency supply of gold was voted to finance the operations of 209—4,000 pounds of gold bars, money from the Sacred Treasury, most of which came from a 5 percent tax on the manumission of slaves. About 500 pounds of gold went to each of the two consuls and proconsuls. An extra 100 pounds went to Fabius, who was to have it conveyed to the citadel. The rest of the gold would be spent on clothes for the army in Spain.

Fabius encamped his legions at the entrance to the inner harbor, where he was in communication with Livius in the citadel. He fitted the Roman ships with artillery, with ballistae and catapults, with stones, with ladders for eventually storming the walls. Hannibal, still in Bruttium, sent a corps of Bruttians under an officer named Carthalo to help the Punic soldiers stationed in the city. Bomilcar returned with his fleet to defend Taras, though he soon sailed off to Corcyra instead to help Philip of Macedon in his contemplated war against the pro-Roman Greeks of the Aetolian League. What the Tarentines had expected and surely dreaded—all the horror of a siege—was now beginning.[28]

But the Tarentines did not have to endure as much as they had anticipated. The commander of the Bruttian contingent, in charge of a stretch of the wall, was in love with a beautiful Tarentine girl whose brother happened to be serving with the Romans—an example of the divided loyalties in this city at the point of collapse. There is no record of whether the Bruttian had met the girl recently, since coming to the city to fight for Hannibal, or whether he had somehow known her earlier. But his passion put an end to the siege. Fabius contrived to have the lady's brother enter Taras in the guise of a deserter from the Romans. Once inside, the brother soon persuaded the love-struck Bruttian to betray the Greeks.

The plan was simple. The Romans made a big, noisy attack in the western sector with naval forces as well as land troops, attracting the defenders to the spot by yelling and blowing their trumpets. But this was only a diversion. The Bruttian had told Fabius the point in the eastern wall at which the city could really be entered.

The greatest uproar came from the citadel, and the Tarentine Democrates—the same man who had defeated the Roman fleet the year before—hurried in that direction with his troops. Meanwhile Fabius and some of his men went with ladders to the appointed place in the eastern wall. The regular guards had been removed, according to Livy, and the Bruttians on duty helped the Romans climb in. Fabius's men proceeded to open a nearby gate so that more Romans could enter. They marched to the agora. For the second time in a few years, Taras had been surprised.[29]

There was a battle in the marketplace, but the Tarentines (according to Livy, at any rate) did not put up much resistance. A number of them probably thought that even a return to Rome was preferable to this precarious Carthaginian occupation. Democrates died; so did the conspirator Nikon, who had sent the Roman commander overboard in the sea battle in 210. As for the chief conspirator, Philemenus, he had dashed from the marketplace on horseback; but though his horse was sighted later, Philemenus was never found. A rumor arose that he had committed suicide by leaping into an open well. He certainly might have done so; it was better than waiting for death at the hands of the Romans. Many Carthaginians and Tarentines fell in the general melee; and Livy says that the Romans killed Bruttians, either because they despised these traditional enemies of Rome or because the fact that Bruttians serving under Hannibal had let the Romans in was humiliating and should be suppressed.[30]

The sack of the city followed. Taras was still rich, and the Romans took a great deal of gold and silver—coins, statues, jewelry—as well as paintings and statues in bronze. Loot from Capua and Syracuse had been carried to Rome only a couple of years earlier. The Tarentine spoils of 209, piled on the spoils of 211, contributed to temper strict Roman virtue with an appreciation of art. Roman soldiers even carted off the seated Heracles by Lysippus, but they could not manage Lysippus's immense bronze statue of Zeus, which remained to overlook the marketplace. The seated Heracles eventually decorated the Capitol at Rome, but many deities aside from Lysippus's Zeus stayed at Taras. A famous remark about them is attributed to Fabius: when a clerk inquired what was to be done with the large statues of warrior deities (perhaps Zeus, Athena, Ares, and Poseidon, though they are not named), the general is supposed to have replied, "Let the Tarentines keep their angry gods." As for the citizens themselves, 30,000 were taken away as slaves.[31]

Serving in Fabius's army was Cato, later called the Elder, in his middle twenties at the time. There is a tradition that he was put up at the home of an aged Tarentine called Nearchus, a latter-day Pythagorean. Nearchus was an aristocrat and an inflexible pro-Roman. It would be interesting to know how he had managed to get along during the years of Carthaginian occupation; no mention is made of his having lived in the citadel. According to the tradition, he instructed the young Cato that carnal pleasure, gratification of sensual passion, submission to lust, is the fault of youth, from which old age is fortunately free. This speech was not original with Nearchus; it had been repeated to him as the words of Archytas himself. It seems to have confirmed the already sober Cato in his natural bent toward restraint.[32] The story may not be true, but this account of a conversation between an ancient Greek philosopher—the last of the race at Taras—and an eager, moral young Roman provides an attractive alternative to the year's record of spoliation and blood.

Whether or not there had been a break in the production of coinage late in the Roman alliance, Taras struck coins during the Carthaginian occupation. There were a few half-staters, not with the Athena head/owl types of former drachms but with types familiar from didrachms: a young horseman crowning his mount on the obverse and the dolphin rider with various attributes on the reverse. Most of the coins, however, were didrachms. They had the old familiar types. On the obverse the boy athlete crowned his horse, a naked rider aimed a spear, or a horseman was shown in helmet and cuirass (Plate 62). On the reverse the dolphin rider held various attributes (trident and *akrostolion*, cornucopia, cantharus) (Plate 63). Sometimes he stretched a chlamys-draped left arm out in front and aimed the trident in his right hand; sometimes he received a little Nike carrying the premature wreath of victory.

Plate 62.    Silver didrachm, c. 212-209 B.C. Obv.: Horseman r. in helmet and cuirass, carrying palm branch. Under horse, ΣΩΚΑΝΝΑΣ. 18.5 mm. *ANS/SNG* Part I. No. 1272. *Courtesy of the American Numismatic Society, New York.*

Plate 63.    Silver stater, c. 212-209 B.C. Rev.: dolphin rider holding kantharos and trident; behind, eagle. *ANS/ SNG* Part I, No. 1271. 18 mm. *Courtesy of the American Numismatic Society, New York.*

But except for their types, these coins had little in common with previous Tarentine issues. The execution was hardly reminiscent of earlier attempts to produce money of artistic distinction. Although the diameter was not reduced, the weight standard was, and very sharply. For the didrachms it now varied from 3.9 to 3.5 grams, between two and three grams below the weight of didrachms from the Pyrrhic period on, which had weighed about 6.6 grams. It has, in fact, even been suggested that these coins were not didrachms but drachms. Their weight, however, is still a little too heavy for this, and the fact that their types were ones traditionally associated with the didrachm rules against their being drachms. Perhaps, as during the age of Pyrrhus, the weight reduction of the didrachm was a necessary measure to wring out of a given amount of silver more money for the troops. Or perhaps the new didrachms were meant to be used interchangeably with Carthaginian drachms, which weighed slightly over 3.8 grams.

    Another difference involved the names appearing on the obverse, presumably those of magistrates responsible for the coinage. They did not include signatures occurring in the previous period—another indication, according to Evans, that there had been a cessation of mint activity about 228. But they did include foreign-sounding names such as Serambos and Sokannas (Plate 62). Evans speculated that these non-Hellenic signatures may have belonged to Messapians or other indigenous peoples serving with Hannibal against the Romans—or, more probably, to Carthaginians administering the nominally liberated city. It is at any rate sad that this degenerate coinage, the last ever issued in the great Greek foundation, should have borne names that were not even Greek.[33]

# Notes to Chapter 11

1. *Punica,* XX, 12-13, J. D. Duff, trans. Loeb, *Silius,* Vol. II, pp. 101, 103.

2. See Brunt, *Italian Manpower,* pp. 649-51. It is not clear whether this reinforcement was a legion or, if so, whether it was a "legio classica." Brunt suspects that the reinforcement was simply amalgamated with the garrison already in place.

3. See Polybius, 2.24.13, 3.75.4, and Livy, 23.32.16-17. Wuilleumier (p. 146, n. 6) speculates that some of the ships were Tarentine.

4. Livy, 24.3.9-15, Frank Gardner Moore, trans. Loeb, *Livy,* Vol. VI, pp. 183, 185.

5. 24.1.1 and 7. Loeb, *Livy,* Vol. VI, p. 175. See Tonybee, *Hannibal's Legacy,* Vol. I, p. 266, n. 3, for certain qualifications of the generalization that Rome worked with the moneyed faction in the South Italian cities. See also Badian, *Foreign Clientelae,* pp. 147-48.

6. 24.13.3, Moore, trans. Loeb, *Livy,* Vol. VI, p. 215.

7. Wuilleumier (pp. 147-48) dismisses the story on that ground. Toynbee, however, (*Hannibal's Legacy,* Vol. I, pp. 490-94), uses it as evidence that Taras supplied land troops as well as crews for ships.

8. See Livy, 24.20.9-15.

9. Livy, though unsure on the matter, is inclined to put Hannibal's second approach to Taras in the consular year beginning March 15, 212 (since 222 the consuls assumed office on March 15). Although scholars such as Evans accepted 212 (the year from which Evans dates the resumption of Tarentine coinage), more recent scholarship has tended to prefer 213. Wuilleumier, for instance, dates the capture of Taras to autumn 213, remarking that Livy's hesitation "doit s'expliquer par la conversion des olympiades en anées consulaires" (p. 150). But J. F. Lazenby points out that Livy and Polybius (8.34.13) say that Hannibal returned to winter quarters after taking the city, and since he often did not permanently leave winter quarters until May and the new consuls did not leave Rome until April 26, "it is possible that the fall of Tarentum should be dated to between March 15th and the end of April" in the new consular year 212/211. See his *Hannibal's War: A Military History of the Second Punic War* (Warminster, England, 1978), p. 110. Later he refers definitely to "Tarentum—captured by Hannibal early in 212" (p. 161).

10. See Livy, 25.7.10-13.

11. Wuilleumier, p. 184, implies this. Evans (*"Horsemen,"* pp. 205-206) suggests that younger aristocrats were at this time tending to side with the popular party and uses the thirteen conspirators as examples. Lazenby goes further: whereas at Croton the upper classes were loyal to Rome, at Locri, Arpi, and Taras "the position was apparently reversed, with the commons favouring Rome" (*Hannibal's War,* p. 88). It is, however, perhaps not necessary to read into the Carthaginian sympathies of the five young aristocrats or the aristocratic conspirators of 213/212 an implication that nonaristocrats were Romanizers. The class division was surely not a party division to that degree, at least at Taras.

12. See Livy, 25.8.1-6, and Polybius, 8.24(26).4-13.

13. See Polybius, 8.25(27), and Livy, 25.8.7-10.

14. See Polybius, 8.25(27).11, 8.26(28)-29(31), and Livy, 25.8.11-13, 25.9.1-15. Considerably condensed accounts are given in Frontinus *Stratagems,* 3.3.6, and Appian, *Roman History,* 7.6.32. Both Frontinus and Appian call the principal conspirator not Philemenus but Cononeus. On the relevant topography see Wuilleumier, pp. 242-43; Martin, "L'Architecture," pp. 322-23, 326-27; Lo Porto, "Topografia," pp. 378-79; and Carter, *Sculpture,* p. 13.

15. See Polybius, 8.30(32).-31(33), and Livy, 25.9.16-17, 25.10; see also Wuilleumier, pp. 239-40, and Lo Porto, "Topografia," pp. 372-73.

16. See *Roman History,* 7.6.33.

17. See Livy, 25.11.10, 25.15.4-5; Polybius, 8.34(36).1; and Appian as above.

18. See Polybius, 8.32(34)-33(35); Livy, 25.11; Lo Porto, "Topografia," pp. 369-71; and Coulson, "Taras," *Princeton Encyclopedia,* p. 879.

19. See Polybius, 8.34(36); Livy, 25.11.11-20; and Appian, *Roman History,* 7.6.34.

20. See Livy, 25.15.6-17, and Appian, 7.6.35. Appian (7.6.34) has a story about the capture of some Thurians trying to bring grain into the citadel, the negotiations for ransom consequent on this, Hannibal's release of all the prisoners, and the effect that his generosity had at Thurii when they returned home.

21. See Livy, 25.13.1-4, 25.15.1-3, 25.15.18-20, 25.22.14-16, 26.5.1-3, and Zonaras, 9.5.

22. 9.9.11, W. R. Paton, trans. Loeb, *Polybius,* Vol. IV, p. 25.

23. See Polybius, 13.4.4-7.

24. See Zonaras, 9.6, and Brunt, *Italian Manpower,* p. 273.

25. See Livy, 26.39.20-23.

26. See Livy, 26.39. Pais (*Ancient Italy,* pp. 87-88) speculates that the battle was fought off Satyrion/Satyrium, about fifteen miles south of Taras, where the Romans could have unloaded the grain ships without interference.

27. See Wuilleumier, p. 159.

28. See Livy, 27.3.8-9, 27.7.7-10, 27.7.14-17, 27.8.19, 27.10.11-13, 27.12.1-6, 27.15.4-8. See also Plutarch, *Lives,* "Marcellus," 25.1-3, and Wuilleumier, pp. 160-61. Brunt, p. 667, figures that the fleet stationed at Sicily at the time had numbered considerably fewer than 100 ships before the thirty were sent to Taras.

29. See Livy, 27.15.9-20; Polybius, 10.1; Appian, *Roman History,* 7.8.49-50; Polyaenus, *Stratagems,* 8.14.3; Plutarch, *Lives,* "Fabius Maximus," 21.1-4, 22.1-3; Silius Italicus, *Punica,* XV, 320-33; Zonaras, 9.8; and Wuilleumier, pp. 161-62. Polyaenus calls the Bruttian Abrentius.

30. See Livy, 27.16.1-6; Plutarch, "Fabius Maximus," 22.5; and Orosius, 4.18.

31. See Livy, 27.16.7-9; Eutropius, 3.16; Plutarch, "Fabius Maximus," 22.5-6, and "Marcellus," 21.1-5; Pliny the Elder, *Natural History,* 34.39-41; and *De Viris Illustribus,* 43. Livy's figure of 83,000 pounds of gold is usually corrected to 3,080. Cicero (*In Verrem,* 2.4.59.135) mentions statues of a satyr and of Europa and the Bull among treasures remaining at Taras. It is unclear whether the 30,000 were already slaves (as Livy implies) or were sold into slavery (as Plutarch says). Frank admits the possibility that they were slaves to begin with (*Economic Survey,* Vol. I, pp. 99-100). See also Wuilleumier, pp. 162-63.

32. See Cicero, *De Senectute,* 12.39-41. Plutarch gives a shorter version of the speech in "Marcus Cato," 2.3. For discussion see Wuilleumier, pp. 608, 682, and Gigante, "La Cultura," p. 70.

33. For the coins see Ravel, nos. 971-90. For discussion see Evans, pp. 196-211; Wuilleumier, pp. 153, 201, 205; and M. P. Vlasto, "On a Recent Find of Coins Struck During the Hannibalic Occupation at Tarentum," *Numismatic Chronicle,* Series IV, Vol. 9 (1909), especially pp. 257-60. Evans's attempt (pp. 199-201) to relate these coins of reduced weight to the "double Victoriatus" which he thought had been struck by the Illyrian cities since about 228 is of course invalidated by the recent finding that the victoriatus itself was not struck until 211. His arguments (p. 197) for classifying the coins as didrachms seem valid, though the American Numismatic Society, *Sylloge Nummorum Graecorum,* Part I, *Etruria-Calabria* (New York, 1969) prefers to call them drachms (Plate 34).

# 12

# Afterlife: Tarentum

It is time to call the city by the name which the Romans were already using.

Over a long period of time Tarentum would lapse into a quiet unimportance, but the early years under Rome were difficult both because of its position as a defeated enemy of the republic and because of its geographical location in the still-disputed territory where Roman and Carthaginian armies marched and fought. The Tarentines—no doubt those who had favored Rome from the beginning—sent envoys to the senate immediately after the takeover of 209 to ask for lenient treatment: freedom and the preservation of the city's ancient laws, according to Livy, who does not make clear what the envoys meant by "freedom." When Fabius returned to the capital, the senate discussed what to do with Tarentum and decided that for the time being a garrison should be stationed there and that Tarentines should not be allowed to leave the city. Their condition was probably harsher than under former military occupations: they were political prisoners, and Tarentum was their prison. What else was to be done with them would not be determined until later, when there was no military crisis and the senate had more time for considering the problem.[1]

In 208 the commander Quintus Claudius Flamen established his headquarters at Tarentum. The thirty Roman ships that had been sent there for the siege were returned to Laevinus's fleet off Sicily, to participate in ravaging the North African coast if that was feasible. The consul Titus Quinctius Crispinus—envious of the fame which Fabius had gained in taking Tarentum, if we can believe Livy—besieged the still-independent city of Locri to win fame for himself; but the attempt failed. Later he and the other consul, Marcellus, decided to renew the siege of Locri, and in addition to procuring ships from Sicily to attack the city by water, they ordered part of the garrison at Tarentum to march there and attack the city by land. But Hannibal learned of this from some Thurians and hid horsemen and foot soldiers along the way. This force fell on the unsuspecting Romans, killed about 2,000 of them, and captured another 1,500.[2] No doubt there were Tarentines who, when they saw the survivors come straggling back, privately rejoiced. Other news that must have cheered the same Tarentines came soon after: the consul Crispinus had been very seriously wounded in an engagement with Hannibal's Numidians and the consul Marcellus had been killed.[3] By the end of the year Crispinus too had died—perhaps at Tarentum, though Livy is not certain of this[4].

In 207 the city was obliquely involved in the war. Some messengers from Hannibal's brother Hasdrubal, who had successfully threaded their way down the Italian peninsula through enemy territory from Cisalpine Gaul, were captured nearby. They carried a letter from Hasdrubal to Hannibal and had almost made it to Hannibal's headquarters at Metapontum when they were apprehended. Brought before the propraetor Quintus Claudius Flamen, who again commanded the two Roman legions at Tarentum, they were threatened with torture, confessed, and gave up the letter.[5] As long as Hannibal stayed in southern Italy, there was a possibility that he would try to retake Tarentum, and the garrison there was maintained, though in 206 its commander, still Claudius Flamen, lent much of it to the consul Lucius Veturius Philo for campaigning in Bruttium.[6]

By the time the Hannibalic Wars ended in 202/201, southern Italy was a wreck. The Roman and Carthaginian armies that had marched through it and fought in it year after year had succeeded in devastating the once-fruitful fields, robbing and ruining the cities, eating up the livestock, and enslaving or killing multitudes.[7] Tarentum, as has been mentioned earlier, was unusual among the Italiot Greek cities for not having shrunken drastically by the beginning of the conflict. But after 209 its population too was much diminished—by the 30,000 inhabitants taken from it as slaves, by those who had died in battles between town and citadel or who had starved to death when foraging did not go well, by those who had emigrated for political reasons. Before 213, citizens to whom Rome was obnoxious had moved to the Greek mainland or the Greek East; and after Hannibal entered the city, Roman sympathizers had also gone to those parts of the Mediterranean world, some of them evidently banished by Hannibal himself. In 208 the senate instructed one Lucius Manlius to attend the Olympics (if he could do so safely) and tell banished Tarentines who might be watching the games that if they came back home, their property would be restored to them.[8] But the number of refugees and exiles that actually did come back during the final years of the war, or even after it had ended, was probably small. A limping economy could not have attracted many.

We do not have a great deal of information about the terms which the senate imposed when it had the leisure to decide what to do with the refractory city. Apparently Tarentines could still live by their ancient laws and customs, as they had requested. But Livy puts into the mouth of a subject of Antiochus III of Syria a speech presumably delivered in 191, reproaching the Romans for their treatment of the Western Greek cities, Tarentum included. Such cities, the Eastern Greek says, have to pay tribute to Rome and provide ships as well. The Roman Sulpicius replies that the exactions are in accord with the original Roman treaties with those allies, and in fact they do not sound different from the regulations of 272.[9] Also as in 272, Tarentum after 209 had to tear down its protective walls, no longer necessary. It could not coin its own money anymore, but the use of the new Roman silver coins, the denarius and the victoriatus, may not have constituted a hardship after the slim didrachms of 212-209. The one harsh aspect of the post-Hannibalic arrangement seems to have been the confiscation of much of Tarentum's land by Rome. The republic turned this territory into an *ager publicus*, to be distributed as the republic saw fit.[10] Not many Romans would have desired land in the devastated Italian South, but the censors rented lots to the few who did, and who had the money to invest in depleted fields. As a result, the raising of livestock gradually revived—in the Tarentine region, the raising of sheep especially. The Roman ranchers on what had formerly been Tarentine property did not do much to restore the city itself, but at least the countryside was showing signs of productivity again.[11]

From the little information we have, then, the city in, say, 190 B.C. can be reconstructed as a place too big for its population, where Greek-speaking people walked among despoiled buildings reflecting a past grandeur, worshiped according to the old rites in temples unnecessarily large, and carried on whatever business they could in a marketplace robbed of magnificence. Under such conditions aggressive activity did not flourish.

This was the depth of a demographic decline which had started in earlier times, in the troubles with mercenary chieftains during the late fourth and early third centuries. Long before 209 the city had, in one way or another, been relinquishing distinction. For instance, although Taras had sent perhaps more than its quota of famous athletes to the Greek games in the Archaic and Classical periods, there is no mention of a successful Tarentine athlete during the Hellenistic Age.[12] It will be recalled that limestone sculpture for the *naiskoi* ceased around the middle of the third century. The production of painted pottery dwindled to nothing in the course of the century.[13]

It is a dismal picture but one that is not entirely unrelieved. Some trade to distant places still occurred.[14] And although the pottery industry waned, the manufacture of terra-cotta figures did not. The city, for instance, made many representations of a childlike Eros in the second century—also of comic actors and acrobats, female acrobats particularly, as well as tragic masks. Deities continued to be produced in the second and first centuries in favorite Hellenistic poses: Aphrodite carrying Eros, Aphrodite taking off a sandal. Statuettes of Nike were still made, less the divine bringer of victory now than just a seminude female with wings. Tarentine corpolasts also catered to the Hellenistic taste for grotesques—deformed bodies, deformed heads—and for animals such as rams, bulls, dolphins, lions, and griffins. The manufacture of clay figures at Tarentum flourished so much that it extended its influence over workshops in various parts of Apulia.[15] The vigor of the coroplastic industry at Tarentum in the second and first centuries B.C. is a significant indication of the city's ability to keep going and even, to a limited degree, revive.[16]

Meanwhile people of Tarentine origin, either self-exiled or exiled because of their politics, contributed occasionally to the city's reputation in foreign places, as Tarentines had done in earlier times. Tarentines skilled in horsemanship surely helped train the cavalries of the states in the Eastern Greek world or at least served in those cavalries, though we have no specifics concerning them since references to "Tarentines" denoted a manner of fighting rather than a place of origin.[17] In the early second century a former Tarentine named Heraclides, together with two partners, managed a bank on the merchant isle of Delos, where, in contrast to his native city, business was booming.[18]

And there was the other Heraclides, the architectural engineer who, during the Carthaginian occupation, had been expelled from the city on the suspicion that he planned to betray it to the Romans. He found his way to the court of Macedon, where, in the closing years of the third century and the beginning of the second, he exercised his talents for trickery and intrigue. Diodorus Siculus implies that, by malicious insinuations, he was responsible for the deaths of five courtiers of Philip V whom the king had regarded highly until then. Polyaenus says that Heraclides went to Rhodes, which was allied with Rome, in the guise of an enemy of King Philip but secretly on commission from the king; and when he had secured the Rhodians' confidence, he set fire to their docks and burned their ships. In 200 B.C. Philip put him in command of a fleet to combat the Romans off the coast of Thrace. In other words Heraclides had achieved the position of king's favorite. But like many other favorites, he incurred the animosity of those less fortunate or less opportunistic. Philip, afraid that this reaction on the part of the Macedonians would lead to trouble, catered to the will of his people by accusing Heraclides of crimes and shutting him up in prison in 199.[19]

It appears, then, that Heraclides represented the worst aspects of the degenerate Hellene. Diodorus Siculus comments: "A native of Tarentum, Heraclides was a man of surpassing wickedness, who had transformed Philip from a virtuous king into a harsh and godless tyrant, and had thereby incurred the deep hatred of all Macedonians and Greeks."[20] But so drastic an effect on the king stretches credibility. It is noteworthy that our picture of Heraclides comes solely from pro-Roman sources, whereas except for his expulsion from Tarentum as a suspected traitor at the beginning of his career, Heraclides himself seems to have been consistently anti-Roman. And even his expulsion may have been a ruse. It may be recalled that, when he was expelled, Heraclides went to the Roman camp, and that then he started corresponding clandestinely with Tarentum and with Hannibal. Perhaps, with the connivance of leading Tarentines, he had gone to the Roman camp merely on the pretense of being a traitor to Tarentum, just as he later went to Rhodes on the pretense of being an enemy of Philip. Undoubtedly he was devious, obsequious, and adept at worming his way into the confidence of kings. but in some small degree, as he comes down to us, he may be the victim of Roman propaganda, which was committed to putting the sons of his native city in as bad a light as possible.

In 186 B.C. Rome was rocked by the Bacchic scandal. The mother and stepfather of a young man whom they wanted to get out of their way suggested that he join the Greek-oriented cult of Bacchus. He told his mistress, who knew something about the secret practices of this cult and was horrified. The man eventually went to the consul Postumius, and his mistress was brought before the consul and disclosed what she knew. An inquiry was held. As aspects of the cult came to light—things such as drunkenness, lechery, homosexuality, total abandonment to irrationality, and even (according to Livy) human sacrifice—the world of Roman officialdom reacted. There were investigations, and when suspects could be found, there were trials. The investigations were not confined to Rome, since other parts of Italy also practiced the cult. The senate, which of course could not do away with the cult entirely because Bacchus or Dionysus had a place among the Roman gods, went as far as it could. It issued a decree limiting the number of participants in a Bacchic rite to five and forbidding the cult to have priests (though it could apparently have priestesses) or a treasury.[21] Notable throughout the episode is a Roman fear of foreign ways, especially Greek ways, as instruments of corruption. The Bacchic celebrations—" 'vile and alien rites,' " as Livy makes Postumius call them—had no counterpart in Roman tradition.[22] Roman religion, with the gravity of a legal contract and with its close relationship to the majesty of the state, stood appalled at the frenzy, the secrecy, and the sensuality of the Greeks.

It is possible that the cult had spread over Italy from the southern part of the peninsula, especially Tarentum, where the worship of Dionysus was still extremely important in the third century B.C. The 30,000 slaves taken at Tarentum in 209 had been dispersed to various parts of Italy—to the country districts of Apulia where entrepreneurs were beginning to operate ranches, to Etruria which Livy associates with the cult, to Rome. They may have carried their religious practices with them as the only tenable remnants of their former lives, and in the succeeding years they may have gained converts. But if this is true, the Tarentine cult had changed. At least Livy does not mention that it was in any way concerned with an afterlife, which the worship of Dionysus/Hades at Taras had stressed so strongly. Perhaps Livy's view of the cult was so prejudiced that he ignored its most praiseworthy aspect; or possibly the cult had suffered a decline in the course of its spread. But it may not have come from the Tarentine area at all. It could have reached Italy from Greece or even from Asia Minor, where versions of Dionysiac religion were also important.[23]

In any case some highly suspect form of the adoration of Bacchus or Dionysus persisted in the Tarentine region. In 185/184 the praetor Lucius Postumius, in charge at Tarentum, came down heavily on adherents of the cult, some of whom had fled to the area from other parts of Italy, perhaps in the hope that they could hide out there among coreligionists. But the whole matter is mixed up with a rebellion of shepherds—slaves, probably—that occurred at the same time. Livy speaks of them in the same breath: "And Lucius Postumius the praetor, to whom the province of Tarentum had fallen, broke up large conspiracies of shepherds and diligently prosecuted what was left of the Bacchanalian investigation."[24] Whether the shepherds' "conspiracies" were related to the Bacchic cult is unclear. They could have been, since the cult apparently drew much of its membership from the lower classes, whose resentment of the suppression of their faith could have produced covert meetings if not actual violence.[25] Or the unrest among the herdsmen may simply reflect the troubled economy still true of the area fifteen years after the end of the Hannibalic Wars and especially severe on the lower classes in spite of the gradual revival of animal husbandry. Rome viewed the uprising as one of dangerous magnitude: Lucius Postumius sentenced about 7,000 herdsmen, and many of them were executed. But these harsh measures did not stamp out contumacy. In 181 the praetor Lucius Duronius had to deal with Bacchanalian cultists in Apulia north of Tarentum, where they had been carrying on their rites for the past year or more.[26]

After the Bacchanalian affair Tarentum nearly drops out of mention. In 181, according to Livy, reports came to Rome from Tarentum and Brundisium concerning Istrian pirates from across the Adriatic who were harassing the South Italian coasts, and for the next several years Rome was vexed with this chronic problem of piracy.[27] There is a trace of literary activity. The aged and feeble tragedian Pacuvius, nephew of the poet Ennius, had retired from Rome to Tarentum. Sometime before his death about 130, the amibtious young author Accius visited him in order to read him his tragedy entitled *Atreus*. The ensuing conversation— or the story concerning it—is reported by Aulus Gellius in his *Attic Nights* almost three centuries later. The old man did not like Accius's play a great deal: it had plenty of dignity, he said, but it was unpolished. Not at all discouraged, Accius told him that fruits which are bitter at first grow sweet as they mature but fruits which start off soft and delicious just decay.[28]

In 123/122 B.C. the tribune Caius Gracchus established a Roman colony at Tarentum. It was called Neptunia and the two cities, the new Roman foundation and the ancient Spartan one, would continue to exist side by side until 89 B.C., when Italiot Greeks were granted Roman citizenship and Neptunia was amalgamated with Tarentum[29] There is no evidence by which to calculate the effect that their new neighbors had on the Greek citizens before the amalgamation; but since a process of Romanization was now gradually taking place, we can assume that Neptunia helped it along, even though there must have been conservative Tarentine Greeks who still avoided Romans as much as possible and though, until 89 B.C., the administration of the Greek city continued to be Greek.

The question of the continuity of Hellenic tradition at Tarentum between 209 and 89 has been argued back and forth. Obviously the Greek spirit, or whatever it might be called, was fading fast. Even the exiles and voluntary émigrés, while they may have kept Tarentum's name alive in foreign places, deprived the city itself of talent. Roman landholders in the Tarentine countryside, Roman magistrates and soldiers and possibly businessmen to be seen in the city, Roman travelers in town to make use of the port—in general the proximity and pressure of Roman life—had a cumulative effect. The granting of Roman citizenship in 89 B.C. is a convenient date for the end of Tarentum as a Hellenic entity, but actually of course it only capped the inevitable. Naturally, Greek elements remained even after that date. In late republican and into imperial times, the Dorian dialect would still have been heard in the streets, along with Latin. But the scarcity of inscriptions in Greek from Tarentum in the late republic and early empire, as compared with inscriptions in Latin, testifies to the Romanization of the city, and so does the frequency of Roman names among members of its governing class.[30] As for the terra-cotta industry which had represented Greek interests for so long, late in the first century B.C. and early in the first century A.D. it took on native Italic characteristics and then died out. Among the final terra-cotta figures are those of gladiators.[31]

Rome tried to forestall further decay at Tarentum by means of the constitution drawn up for the city sometime after 89 B.C. We possess fragments of this document, the Lex Municipii Tarentini. One provision in it discouraged upper-class residents—decurions or members of the local senate—from moving away by stipulating that these men should own within Tarentum or its territory a house roofed with not fewer than 1,500 tiles or be subject to an annual fine. A fine would also be imposed for unroofing, dismantling, or demolishing a house without permission, unless the owner intended to restore it.[32]

Cicero wrote letters to Atticus from Tarentum in 58 and 51 B.C.[33] In 37 B.C. the city acquired a momentary importance when Mark Antony and Octavian met there and agreed to renew the triumvirate for five years. The place was by this time, however, a tranquil backwater, so that Horace a few years later could write: "Small things befit small folk; my own delight to-day is not queenly Rome, but quiet Tibur or peaceful Tarentum."[34] Although its harbor still functioned, the harbor at Brundisium was far busier. The production of wine and wool in the surrounding country helped to give Roman Tarentum a certain prosperity but not enough to crowd its streets again. Strabo, while praising its beautiful gymnasium and its broad marketplace where the colossal bronze statue of Zeus still stood, noted that only the part of the city near the mouth of the harbor—in other words close to the acropolis—was inhabited (6.3.1). Enough people lived in this area so that Tarentum had a sizable population, but the atmosphere must have been one of departed life. If the great stretches of cemetery on the eastern side were untended— and they probably were—the effect was extraordinarily mournful.

Nero, concerned over the depopulation of the area, tried to settle veterans at Tarentum in A.D. 60. That did not help, however. Many of the veterans stole away to the provinces where they had served, lands which they knew and which offered more of a future than southern Italy. Those who did stay, already used to bachelorhood from their years in the army, did not marry and raise families to swell the population.[35]

Many of the people, both in the city itself and in the adjacent country, must have been slaves.[36] In the country, on the ranches and smaller farms, the male slaves tended to the sheep or the fruits and vegetables, and the women did the housework, the spinning, and the weaving. There may have been factories or workshops, perhaps in the city itself, for the production of especially fine textiles and for the dyeing of cloths with the Tarentine purple-red. Most of the rich probably lived on villas and came to Tarentum only when necessary. In the course of the first century A.D. the woolen industry may have stepped up somewhat, but the increase in activity would have affected the country more than the city.[37] The principal evidence we have for the recovery of some importance by Tarentum in imperial times is the construction of new buildings there—a brick amphitheater and three baths, plus an aqueduct.[38] Here was the final Romanization.

Literary references to the Tarentine region in the first century B.C. and on into early imperial times often had to do with what grew there, as one might expect. Horace mentioned its horses, sheep, honeybees, olives, and grapes. Virgil remarked that the soil was poor but all right for herbs and for flowers such as lilies, poppies, roses, and hyacinths. It was also suited for plane trees and elms and for fruit trees: the apple, the lime, the pear, the plum. Like Horace, Virgil mentioned the area's honeybees and of course its sheep, as well as cattle and goats. Pliny the Elder spoke of its sweet figs and its excellent wool and singled out Tarentine pines, myrtle, and cypress, and a variety of pear called Tarentine or Greek—also almonds, which apparently had been unknown there until sometime after Hannibal.[39] These occasional notices add up to a rather pleasant picture of the Tarentine countryside—fields and gardens, pastures and orchards, quiet places under the sun of southern Italy.

There are, once in a while, later references. Aelian, who lived in the latter part of the second century A.D. and the early part of the third, has a quaint story about a good woman of Tarentum who was so sad at the death of her husband that she could not stand the house where they had been happy and went to live among the tombs. A fledgling stork, trying to fly but inept, fell to the ground and broke a leg. The woman picked up the little stork, wrapped the wound and plastered it, fed the bird and gave it water. When it was well again and had grown its quills, she let it fly away. But the stork did not forget. By the next spring the woman had apparently moved to other quarters. As she was lying outside in the sun, the bird flew overhead, checked its course, and dropped a stone in her lap. She took the stone inside, and that night it glowed with a strange radiance, illuminating the whole interior.[40] Aelian does not say whether it possessed properties aside from simple luminescence. The story is, of course, one that could take place almost anywhere. Its Tarentine setting is interesting, however, for the matter of living among the tombs. They had no doubt been abandoned and offered free lodging.

Aelian makes another reference to Tarentum, one which suggests that the city had acquired an unenviable reputation. He is telling about things that young men can use to remove hair—for instance, the flesh of a torpedo fish or a jellyfish "dissolved in vinegar and rubbed on the cheeks." Such recipes lead him to exclaim: "What have those contrivers of evil from Tarentum and Etruria to say to this, men who after experimenting with pitch have discovered that artifice whereby they differentiate men and turn them into women?"[41]

The *Ephesian Tale* written by Xenophon of Ephesus in the second or third century A.D. also presents Tarentum as a not especially admirable place. This is one of the Greek romances so popular in late antiquity. Like others of its genre, it throbs with thrilling, improbable adventures and has a hero and heroine who stay virtuous and beautiful through everything. The novel is set in imperial times; the Egypt in which much of the plot unwinds has a Roman governor. At one point in her misadventures the heroine, Anthia, is sold to the keeper of a whorehouse in Tarentum. Chastely inclined readers will find comfort in the fact that she avoids intercourse with the house's patrons by pretending to be an epileptic. It may be significant, however, that although Xenophon could have selected almost any other port as the location of this sojourn in a whorehouse, he chose Tarentum.

If he knew what he was talking about, the marketplace was still functioning in imperial times: the brothel keeper, tired of Anthia's fits, brings her there to put her up for sale. The picture of poor Anthia standing in the market on exhibit—presumably the same market where Hannibal had addressed the Tarentines in 213 or 212 B.C.—may serve as a final glimpse of life in the classical city.

# Notes to Chapter 12

1. See Livy, 27.21.8, 27.25.2.

2. See Livy, 27.22.1-3, 9; 27.25.11-13; 27.26.1-6.

3. See Livy, 27.26.7-14, 27.27; Polybius, 10.32; and Appian, *Roman History*, 7.8.50.

4. See Livy, 27.29.1-6, 27.33.6.

5. See Livy, 27.36.10-14, 27.43.1-3.

6. See Livy, 28.10.15, 28.11.12.

7. See Frank's excellent description of the condition of southern Italy, *CAH* VIII, 334-35.

8. See Livy, 27.35.3-4.

9. See Livy, 35.16.3-10.

10. See Livy, 44.16.7 for an instance of such distribution. See also Wuilleumier, pp. 167-68, and Brunt, *Italian Manpower*, p. 279. Moretti ("Problemi," p. 57) comments that in the light of this confiscation of Tarentine land, the Roman promise to restore their possessions to Tarentines exiled by Hannibal did not amount to much. Moretti (pp. 59-60) sees in the construction of roads that avoided Tarentum a continuation of an unfriendly policy toward the city on the part of Rome.

11. See Frank's discussion in *CAH* VIII, 335-36.

12. See Moretti, "Problemi," p. 60.

13. See the discussion of artistic decadence by Filippo Coarelli in "Il Dibattito," Convegno 10, p. 201.

14. See Frank, *CAH* VIII, 349.

15. See Higgins, "Tarentine Terracottas," pp. 276-80, and *Greek Terracottas*, pp. 126-27, and Wuilleumier, pp. 420-23, 621-22.

16. Langlotz ("La Scultura," pp. 240-41) stresses the artistic revival at Tarentum in the second and first centuries.

17. For an example of such generic usage of the term see Livy, 35.28.8, 35.29.1-2.

18. See Wuilleumier, p. 168.

19. See Diodorus Siculus, 28.2; Polyaenus, *Stratagems*, 5.17.2; Polybius, 13.4.1-3, 13.5.1-6; and Livy, 31.16.2-3, 31.33.2, 31.46.8, 32.5.7.

20. 28.9, Francis R. Walton, trans. Loeb, *Diodorus*, Vol. XI, pp. 235, 237.

21. See Livy, 39.8-19. See also the commentary in Nilsson, *Dionysiac Mysteries*, pp. 13-19. Livy probably exaggerates the nefarious nature of the cult.

22. 39.15. 3, Evan T. Sage, trans. Loeb, *Livy*, Vol. XI, p. 259.

23. This is the view of Nilsson, pp. 121-22. For the more traditional view connecting the cult with Tarentum see Frank in *CAH* VIII, 351-52, and

Wuilleumier, pp. 496-97.

24. 39.41.6, Sage, trans. Loeb, *Livy*, Vol. XI, p. 353. See also 39.29.8-9.

25. Wuilleumier (p. 498, following Dieterich) explains Livy's term "pastorum coniurationes" as mystic language for Dionysiac cultists, language which Livy himself did not understand.

26. See Livy, 40.19.9-11.

27. See Livy, 40.18.4, 41.1.1-4.

28. See *Attic Nights,* 13.2.1-6.

29. See Plutarch, *Lives,* "Caius Gracchus," 8.3, 9.1-2; Pliny, *Natural History,* 3.99; *De Viris Illustribus,* 65; and Velleius Paterculus, 1.15. For commentary see Frank, *Economic Survey,* Vol. I, p. 245; Toynbee, *Hannibal's Legacy,* Vol. I, p. 407; Brunt, *Italian Manpower,* pp. 359-61; Coulson, "Taras," *Princeton Encyclopedia,* p. 879; and E. G. Hardy, *Roman Laws and Charters* (Oxford, 1912; reprint ed., New York, 1975), pp. 102-103.

30. See Moretti, "Problemi," pp. 63-65. We know of a learned Tarentine Greek of the early first century B.C., the distinguished physician Heraclides, but he may have practiced at Alexandria. See Wuilleumier, p. 609.

31. See Higgins, "Tarentine Terracottas," p. 280, and *Greek Terracottas,* p. 127. But there must still have been some "Greek" artistic activity in the city. Robertson *(History of Greek Art,* Vol. I, p. 439) mentions a Pompeian landscape featuring Andromeda and Perseus as a Tarentine creation.

32. Lex Municipii Tarentini, caps. 3 and 4. For this document see Frank Frost Abbott and Chester Allan Johnson, *Municipal Administration in the Roman Empire* (Princeton, 1926; reprint ed., New York, 1968), Part II, Municipal Document No. 20, pp. 282-84, and the translation and commentary in Hardy, *Roman Laws and Charters,* pp. 102-109.

33. See *Letters to Atticus,* 3.6, 5.6-7.

34. *Epistles,* Book I, 7.45, H. Rushton Fairclough, trans. Loeb, p. 299.

35. See Tacitus, *Annals,* 14.27.

36. Brunt calculates that the number of free adult males in Bruttium, Lucania, Apulia, and Calabria combined may not have been more than 100,000. See *Italian Manpower,* pp. 127, 370.

37. See Frank, *Economic Survey,* Vol. V, pp. 184, 202, and Brunt, pp. 362-64.

38. See Lo Porto, "Topografia," pp. 382-83.

39. See Horace, *Satires,* Book I, 6.58-59, and *Odes,* Book II, 6; Virgil, *Georgics,* 2.195-98, 4.125-46; and Pliny, *Natural History,* 8.190, 15.35, 15.55, 15.61, 15.71, 15.90, 15.122, 16.142, and 17.62. Virgil's reference in the fourth *Georgic* to the Spartan Oebalus's citadel is an allusion to Tarentum. Wuilleumier, pp. 213-17, and Frank, *Economic Survey,* Vol. V, pp. 147, 162, 164-65, discuss these and other references to the products of the area.

40. See *De Natura Animalium,* 8.22.

41. *De Natura Animalium*, 13.27, A. F. Scholfield, trans. Loeb, *Aelian*, Vol. III, p. 129.

# BIBLIOGRAPHY

## I. Sources

Aelian (Claudius Aelianus). *On the Characteristics of Animals.* Translated by A. F. Scholfield. 3 vols. Loeb Classical Library, 1959-1971.

———. *Varia Historia.* Translated by Abraham Fleming as *A Registre of Hystories,* 1576. Selections reprinted in *Library of the World's Great Literature,* Charles Dudley Warner, ed. Vol. I (New York, 1896), pp. 172-77.

Aelian (Aelianus Tacticus). *The Tacticks of Aelian.* Translated by "J. B." London, 1616; reprint ed. Amsterdam and New York, 1968.

Appian. *Roman History.* Translated by Horace White. 4 vols. Loeb Classical Library, 1912.1913.

Archytas. Fragments (*Ethical Erudition, The Good and Happy Man, On Disciplines*). In Iamblichus, below.

Aristotle. *Politics.* Translated by H. Rackham. Loeb Classical Library, 1932.

Augustine, Saint. *The City of God Against the Pagans.* Book III. Translated by George E. McCracken. Loeb Classical Library, Vol. I, 1957.

Cicero. *De Amicitia.* In *De Senectute, De Amicitia, De Divinatione.* Translated by William Armistead Falconer. Loeb Classical Library, 1923.

———. *De Officiis.* Translated by Walter Miller. Loeb Classical Library, 1913.

———. *De Oratore.* Translated by E. W. Sutton. Completed, with an Introduction, by H. Rackham. 2 vols. Loeb Classical Library, 1942.

———. *De Re Publica.* In *De Re Publica, De Legibus.* Translated by Clinton Walker Keyes. Loeb Classical Library, 1928.

———. *De Senectute.* In *De Senectute, De Amicitia, De Divinatione.* Translated by William Armistead Falconer. Loeb Classical Library, 1923.

———. *Letters to Atticus.* Translated by E. O. Winstedt. 3 vols. Loeb Classical Library, 1912-1918.

———. *The Verrine Orations.* Translated by L. H. G. Greenwood. 2 vols. Loeb Classical Library, 1928-1935.

Cornelius Nepos. *Lives of Famous Men (de viris illustribus).* Translated, together with an Introduction, by Gareth Schmeling. Lawrence, Kansas, 1971.

*Deeds of Famous Men (De Viris Illustribus).* A Bilingual Edition translated and edited by Walter K. Sherwin, Jr. Norman, Oklahoma, 1973.

Dio Cassius (Cassius Dio Cocceianus). *Roman History.* Translated by Earnest Cary. 9 vols. Loeb Classical Library, 1914.

Diodorus of Sicily (Diodorus Siculus). Translated by C. H. Oldfather (Vols. I-VI), Charles L. Sherman (Vol. VII), C. Bradford Welles (Vol. VIII), Russel M. Geer (Vols. IX-X), Francis R. Walton (Vols. XI-XII). Loeb Classical Library, 1933-1967.

Diogenes Laertius. *Lives of Eminent Philosophers.* Translated by R. D. Hicks. 2 vols. Loeb Classical Library, 1925.

Dionysius of Halicarnassus. *The Roman Antiquities.* Translated by Earnest Cary. 7 vols. Loeb Classical Library, 1937-1950.

Eutropius. *Breviarium ab Urbe Condita.* J. C. Hazzard, ed. New York, Cincinnati, and Chicago, 1898.

Florus, Lucius Annaeus. *Epitome of Roman History.* Translated by Edward Seymour Forster. Loeb Classical Library, 1929.

Frontinus. *The Stratagems.* In *The Stratagems and the Aqueducts of Rome.* Translated by Charles E. Bennett. Edited by Mary B. McElwain. Loeb Classical Library, 1925.

Gellius, Aulus. *The Attic Nights.* Translated by John C. Rolfe. 3 vols. Loeb Classical Library, 1928-1948.

*The Greek Anthology and Other Ancient Greek Epigrams. A Selection in modern verse translations.* Edited by Peter Jay. New York, 1973.

Herodotus. Translated by A.D. Godley. 4 vols. Loeb Classical Library, 1920-1925.

Horace. *The Odes and Epodes.* Translated by C. E. Bennett. Loeb Classical Library, 1914.

———— *Satires, Epistles and Ars Poetica.* Translated by H. Rushton Fairclough. Loeb Classical Library, 1926.

*Iamblichus' Life of Pythagoras, or Pythagoric Life. Accompanied by Fragments of the Ethical Writings of Certain Pythagoreans in the Doric Dialect.* Translated by Thomas Taylor. London, 1818; reprint ed., London, 1965.

Justinus, Marcus Junianus. *Justini Historiarum Philippicarum ex Trogo Pompeio Libri XLIV. Textum Wetzelianum.* Paris, 1823.

Leonidas. *The Poems of Leonidas of Tarentum.* Translated by Edwyn Bevan. Oxford, 1931.

———— See *Greek Anthology.*

*Livy.* 14 vols. Vols. IV-V, translated by B. O. Foster; VI-VIII, by Frank Gardner Moore; IX-XI, by Evan T. Sage; XII, by Evan T. Sage and Alfred C. Schlesinger; · XIII, by Alfred C. Schlesinger. Loeb Classical Library, 1926-1943.

Orosius, Paulus. *Seven Books of History Against the Pagans.* Translated, with Introduction and Notes, by Irving Woodworth Raymond. New York, 1936.

Pausanias. *Description of Greece.* Translated by W. H. S. Jones and (Vol. II) H. A. Ormond. 5 vols. Loeb Classical Library, 1918-1935.

Plato. *Epistles.* Translated by R. G. Bury. 2 vols. Loeb Classical Library, 1942.

———— *Laws.* Translated by R. G. Bury. 2 vols. Loeb Classical Library, 1926.

———— *Phaedo.* Translated by Harold North Fowler. Loeb Classical Library, 1914.

———— *The Republic.* Translated by Paul Shorey. 2 vols. Loeb Classical Library, 1935-1937.

Pliny the Elder (Caius Plinius Secundus). *Natural History.* 10 vols. Vols I-V and IX, translated by H. Rackham; VI-VIII, by W. H. S. Jones; X, by D. E. Eichholz. Loeb Classical Library, 1938-1963.

Plutarch. *The Greek Questions of Plutarch.* Translated, with a Commentary, by W. R. Halliday. Oxford, 1928; reprint ed. New York, 1975.

———— *Lives.* Translated by Bernadotte Perrin. 11 vols. Loeb Classical Library, 1914-1921.

———— *Quaestiones Conviviales.* Vols. VIII-IX. Translated by Paul A. Clement and Herbert B. Hoffleit (Vol. VIII), and (Vol. IX) E. L. Miner, Jr., F. H. Sandbach, and W. C. Helmbold. Loeb Classical Library, 1961-1969.

Polyaenus. *Polyaenus's Stratagems of War. Translated from the original Greek, by R.*

*Shepherd, F. R. S.* London, 1793; reprint ed., Chicago, 1974.

Polybius. *The Histories* Translated by W. R. Paton. 6 vols. Loeb Classical Library, 1922-1927.

———— *The Histories of Polybius translated from the text of F. Hultsch by Evelyn S. Shuckburgh, with a new introduction by F. W. Walbank* 2 vols. Bloomington, Ind., 1962.

Seneca. *De Tranquillitate Animi* In *Moral Essays* Translated by John W. Basore. Loeb Classical Library, 1932.

Silius Italicus. *Punica* Translated by J. D. Duff. 2 vols. Loeb Classical Library, 1949.

Strabo. *Geography.* Translated by Horace Leonard Jones. 8 vols. Loeb Classical Library, 1917-1932.

Suetonius. *De Viris Illustribus (The Lives of Illustrious Men).* Translated by J. C. Rolfe. Loeb Classical Library, 1914.

Tacitus. *The Annals* Translated by John Jackson. Loeb Classical Library, 1937.

Thucydides. *History of the Peloponnesian War.* Translated by Charles Forster Smith. 4 vols. Loeb Classical Library, 1919-1923.

Vergil. *Georgics* Translated by H. Rushton Fairclough. Rev. ed. 2 vols. Loeb Classical Library, 1974.

Xenophon. *An Ephesian Tale.* In *Three Greek Romances* Translated and with an Introduction by Moses Hadas. Garden City, N.Y., 1953.

Zonaras, Johannes. *Epitome Historiarum, cum C. Ducangii suisque annotationibus edidit L. Dindorfius.* 6 vols. Leipzig, 1868-1876.

———— *Epitome Historion.* Translated by Earnest Cary. In Dio Cassius, *Roman History* (see above).

## II. Modern Scholarship

Works listed below may occasionally mention Tarentine coinage. Otherwise, see Section III for the coinage.

Abbott, Frank Frost, and Allan Chester Johnson. *Municipal Administration in the Roman Empire* Princeton, 1926; reprint ed. New York, 1968.

Abraham, Gerald. *The Concise Oxford History of Music* London, New York, and Melbourne, 1979.

Adcock, F. E. "The Conquest of Central Italy," *Cambridge Ancient History,* Vol. VII. Cambridge, England, 1954; reprint ed. 1975.

Arias, Paolo Enrico. "Rapporti e Contrasti dalla Fine del VI a.C. al Dominio Romano," in *Atti del terzo convegno di studi sulla Magna Grecia* (Naples, 1964), pp. 231-57.

*Atti del . . . convegno di studi sulla Magna Grecia* See under *Studi.*

Badian, E. *Foreign Clientelae (264-70 B.C.).* Oxford, 1958.

Bald, Irene F. "Seven Recently Discovered Sculptures from Cyrene, Eastern Lybia," *Expedition,* vol. 18, no. 2 (Winter 1976), 17-19.

Belli, Carlo. *Il Tesoro di Taras (Museo Nazionale di Taranto.) Fotografie di Ciro De*

*Vicentis.* Milan/Rome, 1970.

Beloch, K. J. *Greichische Geschichte.* 2nd ed. Tome IV, 1 and 2. Berlin and Leipzig, 1925-1927.

_____ *Römische Geschichte bis zum Beginn der punischen Kriege.* Berlin, 1926.

Bérard, Jean. *La Colonisation Grecque de l'Italie Méridionale et de la Sicile dans l'Antiquité: L'Histoire et la Légende.* 2nd ed. Paris, 1957.

Bevan, Edwyn Robert. *The House of Seleucus.* 2 vols. London, 1902; reprint ed. New York, 1966.

Bieber, Margarete. *The History of the Greek and Roman Theater.* 2nd ed., rev. and enl. Princeton, 1961.

_____ *The Sculpture of the Hellenistic Age.* Rev. ed. New York, 1961.

Boardman, John. *The Greeks Overseas: The Archaeology of Their Early Colonies and Trade.* 2nd ed. Harmondsworth, Middlesex, 1973.

Brunt, P. A. *Italian Manpower 225 B.C.-A.D. 14.* Oxford, 1971.

Burnet, John. *Early Greek Philosophy.* 4th ed., 1930; reprint ed. Cleveland and New York, 1962.

Bury, J. B. "Dionysius of Syracuse," *Cambridge Ancient History,* Vol. VI. Cambridge, England, 1933; reprint ed. 1975.

Cambitoglou, Alexander. "Groups of Apulian Red-Figured Vases Decorated with Heads of Women or of Nike," *Journal of Hellenic Studies,* vol. 74 (1954), 111-21.

_____ and A. D. Trendall. *Apulian Red-figured Vase-painters of the Plain Style.* Archaeological Institute of America, 1961.

Carratelli, Giovanni Pugliese. "Per la Storia di Taranto," in *Atti del decimo convegno di studi sulla Magna Grecia* (Naples, 1971), p. 133-46.

Carter, Joseph Coleman. "Relief Sculptures from the Necropolis of Taranto," *American Journal of Archaeology,* vol. 74 (1970), 125-37.

_____ *The Sculpture of Taras.* Transactions of the American Philosophical Society, New Series, Vol. 65, Part 7. Philadelphia, 1975.

Cary, M. "Agathocles." *Cambridge Ancient History,* Vol. VII. Cambridge, England, 1954; reprint ed., 1975.

_____ *A History of the Greek World from 323 to 146 B.C.* Rev. ed., 1951; reprint ed., London, 1972.

Chesterman, James. *Classical Terracotta Figures.* With a Foreword by R. A. Higgins. Woodstock, N.Y., 1975.

Ciaceri, Emanuele. *Storia della Magna Grecia.* 3 vols. Milan, 1924-1932.

Colburn, Oliver C. "A Return to Sybaris," *Expedition,* vol. 18, no. 2 (Winter 1976), pp. 2-13.

Convegno di studi sulla Magna Grecia. See under *Studi.*

Conway, R. S. "Italy in the Etruscan Age," *Cambridge Ancient History,* Vol. IV. Cambridge, England, 1934; reprint ed., 1974.

Cook, Arthur Bernard. *Zeus: A Study in Ancient Religion.* 3 vols. Cambridge, England, 1914-1940.

Cook, R. M. *Greek Painted Pottery.* Reprinted with corrections, London, 1966.

*Corpus Vasorum Antiquorum.* Italia: Fasciolo XVIII; Taranto, Museo Nazionale, Fasciolo II. Italia: Fasciolo XXXV; Taranto, Museo Nazionale, Fasciolo III. Istituto Poligrafico delle Stato, 1942-1962.

Coulson, W. D. E. "Taras," in *The Princeton Encyclopedia of Classical Sites* (1976).

Delatte, A. *Essai sur la Politique Pythagoricienne.* Liége and Paris, 1922.

"Il Dibattito," in *Atti del decimo convegno di studi sulla Magna Grecia* (Naples, 1971). Comments by the following:
  Branislaw Bilĩnski, pp. 207-10.
  Filippo Coarelli, pp. 200-203.
  Emil Condurachi, pp. 210-12.
  Ettore Lepore, pp. 194-99.
  Pierre Lévêque, pp. 203-207.
  Claude Mossé, pp. 188-91.

Franciscis, Alfonso de. "Il Problema Artistico," in *Atti del terzo convegno di studi sulla Magna Grecia* (Naples, 1964), pp. 197-207.

Frank, Erich. *Plato und die Sogenannten Pythagoreer: Ein Kapitel aus der Geschichte des Greichischen Geistes.* Halle an der Saale, 1923; reprint ed., Tübingen, 1962.

Frank, Tenney. *An Economic Survey of Ancient Rome.* 5 vols. Baltimore, 1933-40.

—— "Italy." *Cambridge Ancient History,* Vol. VIII. Cambridge, England, 1954; reprint ed., 1975.

—— "Pyrrhus." *Cambridge Ancient History,* Vol. VII. Cambridge, England, 1954; reprint ed., 1975.

Gais, Ruth Michael. "Some Problems of River-God Iconography," *American Journal of Archaeology,* vol. 82 (1978), 355-70.

Gigante, Marcello. "La Cultura a Taranto," in *Atti del decimo convegno di studi sulla Magna Grecia* (Naples, 1971), pp. 67-131.

—— "Teatro Greco in Magna Grecia," in *Atti del sesto convegno di studi sulla Magna Grecia* (Naples, 1967), pp. 83-146.

Gow, A. S. F. "Leonidas of Tarentum," *Classical Quarterly,* New Series, vol. 8 (1958), pp. 113-23.

Griffith, G. T. *The Mercenaries of the Hellenistic World.* Cambridge, England, 1935; reprint ed., New York, 1977.

Hackforth, R. "Sicily," *Cambridge Ancient History,* Vol. V. Cambridge, England, 1935; reprint ed., 1973.

Hallward, B. L. "The Roman Defensive," *Cambridge Ancient History,* Vol. VIII. Cambridge, England, 1954; reprint ed., 1975.

Hamburger, O. *Untersuchungen über den pyrrhischen Kreig.* Diss. Würzburg, 1927.

Hardy, E. G. *Roman Laws and Charters Translated with Introduction and Notes.* Oxford, 1912; reprint ed., New York, 1975.

Harris, H. A. *Sport in Greece and Rome.* Ithaca, N.Y., 1972.

Herdejürgen, Helga. *Die tarentinischen Terrakotten des 6. bis 4. Jahrhunderts v. Chr. im Antikenmuseum Basel.* Mainz, 1971.

Higgins, R. A. *Greek Terracotta Figures.* London, 1969.

—— *Greek Terracottas.* London, 1967.

—— *Jewellery from Classical Lands.* Oxford, 1965; reprint ed., 1969.

—— "Tarantine Terracottas," in *Atti del decimo convegno di studi sulla Magna Grecia* (Naples, 1971), pp. 267-82.

Homo, Léon. *Primitive Italy and the Beginnings of Roman Imperialism.* Translated by V. Gordon Childe. New York, 1926.

Huxley, G.L. *Early Sparta.* Cambridge, Mass., 1962.

Jacquemod, M. "Sulle direttive politische di Pirre in Italia," *AEvum* (1932), pp. 445-72.

Johnson, Franklin P. *Lysippus.* New York, 1968.

Jones, A. H. M. *Sparta.* Cambridge, Mass., 1967.

Judeich, W. "König Pyrrhos Römische Politik," *Klio* (1926), pp. 1-18.

Klumbach, Hans. *Tarentiner Grabkunst.* Reutlingen, 1937.

Kurtz, Donna C., and John Boardman. *Greek Burial Customs.* Ithaca, N.Y., 1971.

Lamb, Winifred. *Greek and Roman Bronzes.* London, 1929.

Langlotz, Ernst. *Die Kunst der Westgreichen in Sizilien und Unteritalien.* Aufnahmen von Max Hirmer. Munich, 1963.

_____ "La Scultura," in *Atti del decimo convegno di studi sulla Magna Grecia* (Naples, 1971), pp. 217-47.

Lazenby, J. F. *Hannibal's War: A Military History of the Second Punic War.* Warminster, England, 1978.

*Letteratura e Arte Figurata nella Magna Grecia.* Taranto, 1966.

Lévêque, Pierre. *Pyrrhos.* Paris, 1957.

Lo Porto, Felice Gino. "Topografia Antica di Taranto," in *Atti del decimo convegno di studi sulla Magna Grecia* (Naples, 1971), pp. 343-83.

Marshall, F.H. *Catalogue of the Jewellery, Greek, Etruscan, and Roman, in the Departments of Antiquities, British Museum.* London, 1911.

Martin, Roland. "L'Architecture de Tarente", in *Atti del decimo convegno di studi sulla Magna Grecia* (Naples, 1971), pp. 311-41.

Mayo, Margaret Ellen, and Kenneth Hamma. *The Art of South Italy: Vases from Magna Graecia.* Richmond, Va., 1982.

Metzger, Henri. "L'Imagerie de Grande Grèce et les Textes Littéraires à l'Époque Classique," in *Atti del sesto convegno di studi sulla Magna Grecia* (Naples, 1967), pp. 157-81.

Michell, H. *Sparta.* Cambridge, England, 1952; reprint ed., 1964.

Momigliano, Arnaldo. Review of *Les Origines de la Légende Troyenne de Rome (281-31)* by Jacques Perret. *Journal of Roman Studies,* vol. 35 (1945), 99-104.

Moretti, Luigi. "Problemi di Storia Tarantina," in *Atti del decimo convegno di studi sulla Magna Grecia* (Naples, 1971), pp. 21-65.

Mustilli, D. "Civiltà della Magna Grecia," in *Atti del terzo convegno di studi sulla Magna Grecia* (Naples, 1964), pp. 5-47.

Myres, John L. "The Colonial Expansion of Greece," *Cambridge Ancient History,* Vol. III. Cambridge, England, 1929; reprint ed., 1970.

*The New Century Classical Handbook.* Edited by Catherine B. Avery. New York, 1962.

Niebuhr, B. G. *Römische Geschichte.* Berlin, 1853.

Niese, B. *Geschichte der Greichischen und Makedonischen Staaten seit der Schlacht bei Chaeronea.* Vols. I-II. Gotha, 1893-1899.

_____ "Zur Geschichte des pyrrischen Krieges," *Hermes* (1895), pp. 481-507.

Nilsson, Martin P. *The Dionysiac Mysteries of the Hellenistic and Roman Age.* Lund,

Sweden, 1957; reprint ed., New York, 1975.

*The Oxford Classical Dictionary.* Edited by M. Cary, J. D. Denniston, J. Wight Duff, A. D. Nock, W. D. Ross, H. H. Scullard. With the assistance of H. J. Rose, H. P. Harvey, A. Souter. Oxford, 1949; reprint ed., 1968.

Pais, Ettore. *Ancient Italy: Historical and Geographical Investigations in Central Italy, Magna Graecia, Sicily, and Sardinia.* Translated from the Italian by C. Densmore Curtis. Chicago, 1908.

_____ *Storia dell'Italia Antica e della Sicilia.* Vol. II, 2nd ed. Turin, 1933.

Pauly-Wissowa, *Real Encyclopädie der Classischen Altertumswissenschaft,* Vols. XLVII (1963) and II (R-Z), iv (Stoa-Tauris) (1932).

Perret, Jacques, *Les Origines de la Légende Troyenne de Rome* (281-31). Paris, 1942.

Piganiol, André. *La Conquête Romaine.* 4th ed. Paris, 1944.

*The Princeton Encylcopedia of Classical Sites.* Edited by Richard Stillwell et al. Princeton, New Jersey, 1976.

Randall-MacIver, David. *The Iron Age in Italy: A Study of Those Aspects of the Early Civilization Which Are Neither Villanovan nor Etrus can.* Oxford, 1927.

Robertson, Martin. *A History of Greek Art.* 2 vols. Cambridge, England, 1975.

Sachs, Kurt. *The Rise of Music in the Ancient World, East and West.* New York, 1943.

Santi, A. "L'Ultima Campagna di Pirro in Italia," *Neapolis,* vol. 2 (1914), 283-92.

Schubert, Rudolf. *Geschichte des Pyrrhus.* Koenigsberg, 1894.

Scullard, H. H. *The Elephant in the Greek and Roman World.* Ithaca, N.Y., 1974.

_____ *A History of the Roman World 753-146 B.C.* 4th ed., rev. from the 2nd ed. London and New York, 1980.

Smith, Arthur Hamilton. *Catalogue of the Sculptures in the Department of Greek and Roman Antiquities, British Museum.* London, 1954.

Stazio, Attilio. "L'Attività Archeologica in Puglia," in *Atti del sesto convegno di studi sulla Magna Grecia* (Naples, 1967), pp. 277-308.

Stebbins, Eunice Burr. *The Dolphin in the Literature and Art of Greece and Rome.* Menasha, Wisc., 1929.

Steinhauer, George. *Museum of Sparta.* Apollo Editions, No. 2. Vitoria, Spain, n.d.

Stipčević, Aleksander. *The Illyrians: History and Culture.* Translated by Stojana Čulić Burton. Park Ridge, N.J., 1977.

Strong, D. E. *Greek and Roman Gold and Silver Plate.* Ithaca, N.Y., 1966.

*Studi sulla Magna Grecia.* The following:
*Atti del secondo convegno: Vie di Magna Grecia.* Naples, 1963.
*Atti del terzo convegno: Metropoli e Colonie di Magna Grecia.* Naples, 1964.
*Atti del sesto convegno: Letteratura e Arte Figurate nella Magna Grecia.* Naples, 1967.
*Atti del decimo convegno: Taranto nella Civiltà della Magna Grecia.* Naples, 1971.

Tarn, William Woodthorpe. *Hellenistic Civilisation.* 3rd ed., rev. by the author and G. T. Griffith. London, 1952.

_____ "Macedonia and Greece," *Cambridge Ancient History,* Vol. VII. Cambridge, England, 1954; reprint ed., 1975.

_____ "The New Hellenistic Kingdoms," *Cambridge Ancient History*, Vol. VII. Cambridge, England, 1954; reprint ed., 1975.

Taylor, A. E. *Plato: The Man and His Work.* 6th ed., rev. and enl. London, 1949.

Toynbee, Arnold J. *Hannibal's Legacy: The Hannibalic War's Effects on Roman Life.* Vol. I: *Rome and Her Neighbours Before Hannibal's Entry.* London, 1965.

_____ *Some Problems of Greek History.* London, 1969.

Trendall, A. D. "La Ceramica," in *Atti del decimo convegno di studi sulla Magna Grecia* (Naples, 1971), pp. 249-65.

_____ *Early South Italian Vase-Painting.* Mainz, 1974.

_____ *Phlyax Vases.* 2nd ed., rev. and enl. University of London: Institute of Classical Studies, Bulletin Supplement no. 19, 1967.

_____ *South Italian Vase Painting.* London, 1966.

_____ *Vasi Antichi Dipinti del Vaticano. Vasi Italioti ed Etruschi e Figure Rosse.* 2 vols. Vatican, 1953-1955.

_____ and T. B. L. Webster. *Illustrations of Greek Drama.* London, 1971.

Turnbull, Herbert Westren. *The Great Mathematicians.* New York, 1962.

Ure, P. N. "The Outer Greek World in the Sixth Century," *Cambridge Ancient History*, Vol. IV. Cambridge, England, 1934; reprint ed., 1974.

Vallet, Georges. "Métropoles et Colonies: Leurs Rapports Jusque Vers la Fin du VIᵉ Siècle," in *Atti del terzo convegno di studi sulla Magna Grecia* (Naples, 1964), pp. 209-29.

_____ "Les Routes Maritimes de la Grande Grèce," in *Atti del secondo convegno di studi sulla Magna Grecia* (Naples, 1963), pp. 117-35.

Wade-Gery, H. T. "The Growth of the Dorian States," *Cambridge Ancient History*, Vol. III. Cambridge, England, 1929; reprint ed., 1970

Walters, H. B. *Catalogue of the Greek and Etruscan Vases in the British Museum.* Vol. IV: *Vases of the Latest Period.* London, 1896.

_____ *Catalogue of the Terracottas in the Department of Greek and Roman Antiquities, British Museum.* London, 1903.

Webster, T. B. L. *Greek Theatre Production.* London, 1956.

_____ *Hellenistic Poetry and Art.* New York, 1964.

Woodhead, A. G. *The Greeks in the West.* New York, 1962.

Wuilleumier, Pierre. "Les Disques de Tarente." *Revue Archéologique* (1932), pp. 26-64.

_____ "La Gloire de Tarente," in *Atti del decimo convegno di studi sulla Magna Grecia* (Naples, 1971), pp. 9-18.

_____ *Tarente des Origines à la Conquête Romaine.* Paris, 1939; reprint ed., 1968.

_____ *Le Trésor de Tarente (Collection Edmond de Rothschild).* Paris, 1930.

## III. Numismatics

American Numismatic Society, *Sylloge Nummorum Greacorum. The Collection of the American Numismatic Society.* Part I: *Etruria-Calabria.* New York, 1969.

Brett, Agnes Baldwin. *Catalogue of Greek Coins.* Boston: Museum of Fine Arts, 1955; reprint ed., New York, 1974.

Brunetti, L. "Sulla Frazioni dell'Argento Tarentino," *Numismatica* (1949), pp. 1-33.

Burnett, Andrew. "The Coinages of Rome and Magna Graecia in the Late Fourth and Third Centuries B.C.," *Schweizerische Numismatische Bundschau (Revue Suisse de Numismatique),* 56 (1977), 92-121.

Cahn, Herbert A. "Early Tarentine Chronology," in *Essays in Greek Coinage Presented to Stanley Robinson,* edited by C. M. Kraay and G. K. Jenkins. Oxford, 1968, pp. 59-74.

Côte, Claudius. Collection. See under Ratto.

Crawford, Michael H. *Roman Republican Coinage.* 2 vols. Cambridge, England, 1974.

Evans, Arthur J. *The "Horsemen" of Tarentum. A Contribution Towards the Numismatic History of Great Greece.* London, 1889.

———. "A Recent Find of Magna-Graecian Coins of Metapontum, Tarentum, and Heraclea," *Numismatic Chronicle,* 4th ser., vol. 18 (1918), 133-54.

Forrer, L. *Descriptive Catalogue of the Collection of Greek Coins Formed by Sir Hermann Weber.* Vol. I: *Italy and Sicily.* London, 1922; reprint New York, 1975.

Giesecke, W. *Italia Numismatica.* Leipzig, 1928.

Giubba, A. "Numismatica Tarentina," in *Studi di storia pugliese in onore di G. Chiarelli.* Vol. I (Galatina, 1972), pp. 61-86.

Gorelick, Leonard, and A. John Gwinnett. "Close Work Without Magnifying Lenses?" *Expedition,* vol. 23, no. 2 (Winter 1981), pp. 27-34, and no. 4 (Summer 1981), pp. 15-16.

Jenkins, G. K. *Ancient Greek Coins.* New York, 1972.

———. "A Tarentine Footnote," in *Greek Numismatics and Archaeology: Essays in Honor of Margaret Thompson.* Edited by Otto Mørkholm and Nancy M. Waggoner. Wetteren, Belgium, 1979.

Kraay, Colin M. *Archaic and Classical Greek Coins.* Berkeley and Los Angeles, 1976.

———. "Caulonia and South Italian Problems," *Numismatic Chronicle,* 20 (1960), pp. 53-82.

———. "The Coinage of Sybaris after 510 B.C.," *Numismatic Chronicle,* 18 (1958), 13-37.

———. "Hoards, Small Change and the Origin of Coinage," *Journal of Hellenic Studies,* vol. 84 (1964), pp. 76-91.

Lacroix, Léon. "Hyakinthos et les monnaies incuses de Tarente," in his *Études d'Archéologie Numismatique.* Université de Lyon II: Publications de la Bibliothèque Salomon Reinach III. Paris, 1974.

_____ *Monnaies et Colonisation dans l'Occident Grec.* Académie royale de Belgique: Classe de Lettres et des Sciences Morales et Politiques, 58, Fasc. 2. Brussels. 1965.

Luynes, Duc de. "Médailles de Tarente relatives à l'Apollon Hyacinthien," *Annales de l'Institut de correspondance archéologique,* vol. 2 (1830), 337-42.

_____ "Monnaies incuses de la Grande Grèce," *Annales de l'Institut de correspondance archéologique,* New Series, vol. 2 (1836), 372-83.

Noe, Sydney P. *A Bibliography of Greek Coin Hoards.* 2nd ed. *Numismatic Notes and Monographs,* no. 78. New York: American Numismatic Society, 1937.

_____ *The Coinage of Caulonia.* Numismatic Studies no. 9. New York: American Numismatic Society, 1958.

Parise, Nicola Franco. "Struttura e Funzione della Monetazioni Archaiche di Magna Grecia," in *Atti del dodicesimo convegno di studi sulla Magna Grecia* (Naples, 1975), pp. 87-124.

Poole, Reginald Stuart. *A Catalogue of the Greek Coins in the British Museum: Italy.* London, 1873; reprint ed., Bologna, 1963.

Raoul-Rochette, M. "Essai sur la Numismatique Tarantine," in *Mémoires de Numismatique et d'Antiquité (Mémoires de l'Académie des Inscriptions)* (Paris, 1840), pp. 167-256.

Ratto, Rodolfo. *Collection Claudius Côte, de Lyon: Monnaies de Tarente: la vente sous la direction de Rodolfo Ratto.* Lugano, 1929; reprint ed., New York, 1975.

Ravel, Oscar E. *Descriptive Catalogue of The Collection of Tarentine Coins formed by M. P. Vlasto.* London, 1947; reprint ed., Chicago, 1977.

Sambon, L. *Recherches sur les Anciennes Monnaies de l'Italie Méridionale.* Naples, 1863; reprint ed., Bologna, 1967.

Sear, David R. *Greek Coins and Their Values.* Vol. I: *Europe.* London, 1978.

Stazio, Attilio. "Aspetti e Momenti della Monetazione Tarantina," in *Atti del decimo convegno di studi sulla Magna Grecia* (Naples, 1971), pp. 147-81.

_____ "La Documentazione Numismatica," in *Atti del terzo convegno di studi sulla Magna Grecia* (Naples, 1964), pp. 113-32.

Thompson, Margaret. "Hoards and Overstrikes: The Numismatic Evidence," *Expedition,* vol. 21, no. 4 (Summer 1979), pp. 40-44.

_____, Otto Mørkholm and Colin M. Kraay, eds. *An Inventory of Greek Coin Hoards.* New York, 1973.

Vlasto, M. P. "Alexander, Son of Neoptolemos, of Epirus. His Gold, Silver, and Bronze Coinage," *Numismatic Chronicle,* 5th ser., vol. 6 (1926), pp. 154-231.

_____ "On a Recent Find of Coins Struck During the Hannibalic Occupation at Tarentum, *Numismatic Chronicle,* 4th ser., vol. 9 (1909), 253-63.

_____ *Taras Oikistes. A Contribution to Tarentine Numismatics. Numismatic Notes and Monographs* no. 15. New York: American Numismatic Society, 1922.

Weber Collection. See Forrer, L.

# Index

Acarnania, 128, 149
Accius, 207
Achaeans, 13-14, 18
Acheron River, 70-71, 116
Acheros River, 70-71
Achilles, 101, 129-30, 146
Acragas, 75, 152
Acrotatus, 75-77
Adriatic, 5-6, 43, 78, 88, 123, 178, 183, 207
Aegina, 28, 103
Aelian (Claudias Aelianus), 111, 209-210
Aelius, Caius, 122
*Aeneid,* 129
Aeschylus, 98-99
Aethra, 4-5
Aetolia, 127, 149, 193
Agamemnon, 92
Agathocles, 74-75, 77-79, 81-82, 128, 152
Ageladas, 27-29, 111
*Ager publicus,* 203
Agesilaus II, 62
Agis, 133
Agriculture, 104-105, 203, 206, 209
*Akrostolion,* on coins, 163, 195
Alcmene, 101
Alexander the Great, 62, 68-69, 89, 95, 102, 128-29, 131
Alexander the Molossian, 68-71, 73-74, 78-80, 89, 94, 122, 129; coinage during period of, 71-72, 79
Alexander, son of Cassander, 127
Alexandria, 117, 127, 130
Alexis of Thurii, 100
Amazons, 90, 94
Ambracia, 65, 126-27, 149
Amphitrite, 64
Amphorae: on coins, 160-62, 178
Amyclae, 4, 7, 19-20, 88
Anchor: on coins, 172
Andromache, 129
Andronicus, Livius, 170
Anochos, 111
Antigone, 101
Antigone of Egypt, 127-28
Antigonus Gonatas, 115, 128, 130, 132
Antiochus (historian), 3-4, 7, 13-14, 19
Antiochus I, 131
Antiochus III, 203

Antipater, 127
Antony, Mark 208
Aphrodite, 34, 64, 88, 115, 204
Apollo, 4, 8, 11, 18-20, 27-29, 62-63, 88, 101, 104, 114, 188; head of, as coin type, 82
Apollonia, 178
Appian, 123, 125, 135, 146, 152, 190
Appian Way, 171-72, 178
Appius Claudius, 147
Apulia/Apulians, 46, 50, 69-70, 73-75, 148, 150, 157, 183-84, 186, 191, 193, 204, 206
Archidamus, 62-63, 69-71, 78-79; coinage during period of, 63-68, 82, 89
Archilochus, 114
Archimedes, 48
Archytas: as strategus, 45-47; presumed beliefs and writings of, 47-49, 113; and Plato, 48-52; coinage under, 52-56; "Age of," 52-53, 175; mentioned, 61, 75, 80, 102, 104, 111-13, 195
Ares, 87-88, 195
Arethusa, 64
Argos, 28
Aristippus, 51
Aristophanes, 100
Aristophilides, 11, 25-27
Aristotle, 27-28, 45, 47, 102, 112-13
Aristoxenus, 112-13
Arrow: on coins, 144, 162
Artemis, 34, 87, 104
Aryballus and scraper: on coins, 34-36
Asclepius, 88
Atellan farce, 101
Athamanians, 149
Athena, 87, 115-16, 195; on coins, 160; head of, as coin type, 55-56, 72, 82-83, 87, 153, 195
Athenaeus, 88
Athens, 12, 15, 28-31 passim, 36-37, 45, 49-51, 61, 66, 90-91, 96, 100, 105, 112-14 passim
Athletes' Tombs, 25
Audoleon, 128
Augustus, 144, 148; 208 (Octavian)
Aulus Gellius, 68-69, 207
Ausculum, 148-51, 159
Avernus, Lake, 185-86